EURIPIDES, WOMEN, AND SEXUALITY

EURIPIDES, WOMEN, AND SEXUALITY

Edited by Anton Powell

ROUTLEDGE
London and New York

First published 1990
by Routledge
11 New Fetter Lane, London EC4P 4EE

Simultaneously published in the USA and Canada
by Routledge
a division of Routledge, Chapman and Hall, Inc.
29 West 35th Street, New York, NY 10001

Typeset by J&L Composition Ltd, Filey, North Yorkshire
Printed in Great Britain by
TJ Press (Padstow) Ltd, Padstow, Cornwall

British Library Cataloguing in Publication Data
Euripides, women and sexuality.
1. Drama in Greek. Euripides – Critical studies
I. Powell, Anton
882′. 01

Library of Congress Cataloging in Publication Data
Euripides, women, and sexuality / edited by Anton Powell.
p. cm.
1. Euripides – Political and social views. 2. Euripides –
Characters – Women. 3. Women in literature. 4. Sex in
literature.
I. Powell, Anton
PA3978. E89 1990
882′. 01 – dc20 89–10409

ISBN 0–415–01025–x

CONTENTS

LIST OF CONTRIBUTORS

Elizabeth Craik is Senior Lecturer in Greek at the University of St Andrews. In addition to many articles and reviews, she has published these books: *The Dorian Aegean, Marriage and Property,* Euripides' *Phoenician Women* (edition with translation and commentary), and *The Seven Deadly Sins,* selections from Stobaeus (limited fine art issue). Other professional interests are the Modern Greek novel and the application of computers to literary texts.

Christopher Gill is a Senior Lecturer in Classics at the University of Exeter. He has written extensively on Greek philosophy and literature; publications include (ed.) *Plato: The Atlantis Story* (Bristol, 1980), (ed.) *The Person and the Human Mind: Issues in Ancient and Modern Philosophy* (Oxford, 1989), and a translation of Longus, *Daphnis and Chloe* in *The Collected Greek Novels* (Berkeley, 1989).

Jennifer March is a British Academy Research Fellow at University College, London. Author of *The Creative Poet: Studies on the Treatment of Myths in Greek Poetry (BICS* Suppl. 49, London, 1987), she has a particular interest in the use of myths in Greek literature. Since 1987 she has been Deputy Editor at the Institute of Classical Studies.

William Poole graduated from Lincoln College, Oxford in 1958. He is at present an antiquarian bookseller specializing in Greek and Latin studies and the history of classical scholarship. He taught ancient drama and ancient history at the City Literary Institute, London. He is currently working on the fragmentary plays of Euripides.

Richard Seaford is a Senior Lecturer in Classics at the University of Exeter. He is the author of *Pompeii* (London, 1978), *Euripides' Cyclops* (Oxford, 1984), and numerous articles on Greek literature. His current project is a book on Greek literature, ritual, and the city-state.

John Wilkins is a Lecturer in Classics at Exeter University, working on tragedy and comedy, and the place of drama in Athenian society. He is currently completing a commentary on the *Heraclidae* of Euripides.

Margaret Williamson is Senior Lecturer in Classical Studies at St Mary's College, Strawberry Hill, Middlesex. Her research interests include contemporary literary theory and feminism as they relate to the study of Classics. She has written on various aspects of Greek literature including archaic lyric poetry, and is currently working on a book on Sappho.

EDITORIAL NOTE

Six of the seven papers in this volume were read to the second annual seminar of the reformed London Classical Society, in 1987. The paper by Margaret Williamson is reprinted by permission from the *JACT Review* (1985).

Anton Powell

ABBREVIATIONS

AJP	*American Journal of Philology*
ARV^2	J. D. Beazley, *Attic Red-Figure Vase-Painters,* 2nd edn (Oxford, 1963)
BICS	*Bulletin of the Institute of Classical Studies* (London)
CP(h)	*Classical Philology*
CQ	*Classical Quarterly*
G&R	*Greece and Rome*
GRBS	*Greek, Roman and Byzantine Studies*
HSCP	*Harvard Studies in Classical Philology*
JHS	*Journal of Hellenic Studies*
LCM	*Liverpool Classical Monthly*
LSJ	H. G. Liddell and R. Scott, *A Greek-English Lexicon,* revised by H. Stuart Jones and R. McKenzie
Nauck	A. Nauck, *Euripidis Tragoediae* (Leipzig, 1908–9)
N	A. Nauck, *Tragicorum Graecorum fragmenta,* 2nd edn (Lipsiae, 1889)
OCT	*Oxford Classical Texts*
PCP(h)S	*Proceedings of the Cambridge Philological Society*
P. Oxy.	*The Oxyrhynchus Papyri*
QUCC	*Quaderni Urbinati di Cultura Classica*
RE	Pauly-Wissowa-Kroll, *Real-Encyclopädie der classischen Altertumswissenschaft*
TAPA	*Transactions of the American Philological Association*
YCS	*Yale Classical Studies*
ZPE	*Zeitschrift für Papyrologie und Epigraphik*

1

SEXUAL IMAGERY AND INNUENDO IN *TROADES*[1]

Elizabeth Craik

SUMMARY

In *Troades*, produced 415 BC, Euripides depicts the horrors of war and the predicament of women caught up in war, spoils of war. The fall of Troy is seen through the eyes of a group of women: the sack of the city and the sack of the women go together. Euripides makes some use of this common, almost hackneyed, metaphor of sack, Hekabe lamenting that she is 'ravaged' (ἐκπορθηθεῖσ', 142; cf. usage, with reference to the city, in the prologue, 9, 72, 95). There is much overt allusion to the sexual aspect of the women's plight. Women of different ages, attitudes, and experience face together the harsh realities of the end of Troy. Hekabe the *mater dolorosa*, Andromache the widow, Kassandra the virgin, Helen the adventuress share with the chorus of ordinary wives and mothers a common fate in Greek beds. Collectively and individually, their perception of the future is a perception of the end of one era of marital or sexual experience and the start of another, for all of them grim or at best uncertain. Such is the literal content of the play. It is here argued that this explicit theme is implicitly reinforced by a strong underlying figurative content (sexual imagery of ships, especially their oars and prows); that this is allied with a further, more impressionistic, layer of suggestion (similar imagery of fire, smoke, firebrand);[2] also that these implications are boldly intensified by elements of innuendo and *double entendre* (especially with reference to gates and geographical terms) and by some visual symbolism.

PREAMBLE

Two interrelated difficulties arise. First, where there is a literal meaning on the surface, the presence of an additional non-literal dimension may be questioned: word association depends on the receptivity of an audience to nuances. Second, parallels for sexual imagery or symbolism and for *double entendre* come not primarily from serious poetry but from comedy, where they are perceived as humorous or obscene; and we do not expect humour or obscenity in tragedy.[3] Some preliminary general observations may be made to meet these difficulties.

1 Obscenity and humour are not necessarily elements in the portrayal of sex, which in life, literature, and art may have many facets (happy, sad; gentle, violent; caring, casual) and may be seen from many viewpoints (earnest, frivolous; sophisticated, naïve; deviant, straight).

2 To some extent, imagery and symbolism are not language-dependent but transcend language: the association of ideas is not word-dependent. The same metaphors occur in the poetry of different languages, and these coincide with the symbolism of the visual arts.

3 In Athens, the same audiences attended performances of tragedy and comedy, on the same days. Words which would be immediately associated with a particular idea in comedy can scarcely be completely dissociated from that idea in tragedy.

4 There was extensive interaction between Aristophanes and Euripides, especially in the last decade of Euripides' life. It is recognized that colloquialisms in Euripides can be isolated by reference to Aristophanic comedy; so too can other aspects of his diction.

5 Euripides' fondness for punning and word-play is well known; and he was notorious among his contemporaries for introducing realism into tragedy.

6 The argument is cumulative. While perhaps no one passage is conclusive in isolation, the evidence of the sum of passages is overwhelming.

7 The underlying content is highly germane to the overt theme. The dense occurrence of sexually suggestive words comes in a sexually significant context. The imagery is not irrelevant embroidery, but an integral part of the play's thematic texture.

GREEK SEXUAL IMAGERY

In Aristophanic usage, and in Greek literature generally, the main groups of words or ideas symbolizing sex are: agrarian, connected with the land; nautical, connected with the sea; burning, connected with fire; and equestrian or hunting terms. Taillardat (see n.3) lists 'métaphores agricoles', 'métaphores nautiques', 'métaphores sportives', and 'métaphores diverses' (pp. 100–4; cf. pp. 108–10) and discusses 'le feu du désir' (pp. 159–60). Henderson (see n. 3) has more bold, detailed, and extensive lists. On sexual congress (pp. 161–78) he includes nautical terminology, metaphors from sport, hitting and piercing, burning; on the male organs (pp. 120–4) he has phallic implements, among them spear and oar; and on the female organs (pp. 137–42) he has words for gates and passage-ways (e.g. θύρα, ἰσθμός), also for holes, pits, and hollows (e.g. κόλπος).[4]

The agrarian metaphor is a dead one, common to the point of the common-place. It occurs frequently in serious poetry (e.g. S. *Ant.* 569, *Tr.* 33), and also in legal terminology: the formula of betrothal refers to the 'sowing' (ἄροτος or σπορά) of legitimate children. This metaphor is used with especial reference to sex in marriage, the male agent being the farmer who ploughs, sows, and harvests the passive female earth, fertile or barren. By an extension of this usage, such substantives as 'plain' and 'meadow' (πεδίον and λείμων) are used for the female body as an object of sex.

Sea imagery too is common, and found in serious poetry (e.g. S. *OT* 420ff., 1207ff.; Theognis 457, cit. Ath. 13. 56a), but is rather more complex. The sea has contradictory aspects – harbour and anchorage spelling safety and shelter (often sex in marriage); storm and turbulence spelling danger and the risk of death. The motion of ships on the sea is evocative of the sexual act. Ships are ambiguous in that the image may suggest either a female or a male agent: they are hollow receptacles (decks and holds having female connotations) and also thrusting penetrators (oars, prows, and rudders having male connotations).

Like the sea, fire is ambivalent. It may be either a protective or a destructive force, expressed in the hearth, safety, and peace, or in the firebrand, danger, and war. Equestrian imagery has two main facets: the taming of the animal and subjection to the 'yoke' of marriage (a common metaphor, as *Tro.* 669–70, 676; cf.

the 'yoke' of slavery, 678); and the union of horse and rider which, like sailing, recalls the rhythmic motion of sex.

Let us turn now to *Troades*. There is throughout the play an almost schematic opposition between women with city (houses, gates, buildings of Troy) outraged on the one hand and men with ships (oars, spears, torches) attacking on the other. The men arrive at the city with their oars, penetrate it with the spear and devastate it with the firebrand. The women's fears for the future are expressed in terms of embarkation on Greek ships. The constant reference to ships and especially to oars (πλάται, κῶπαι, etc.) and prows (πρῷραι) goes far beyond the mere fact that to get from Troy to Greece one had to go by sea. The only Trojan male to survive is the child Astyanax – and he is killed. Talthybios, a sympathetic go-between, links the two groups and unifies the action.[5]

STAGING

The play is set against a double background, meshing with the double imagery: on the one hand Troy, with parts already smouldering in the prologue (8, 145) and all irrevocably ablaze in the exodos (1295 etc.), and on the other hand the ships of the Greeks. The *skene* rather loosely represents part of Agamemnon's encampment (32f., 37) or (later) the buildings of Troy.[6] In the prologue, Athena and Poseidon enter and leave by opposite parodoi, symbolizing their spheres, Athena to the 'city' and Poseidon to the 'ships'; then the chorus come on – in two groups at 153 and 176 – by a single parodos, that used by Athena. The *skene* door is used only for the entrances of Kassandra (308) and Helen (895); no one goes off by it. Hekabe, huddled in silent grief at the start (36ff.), remains present throughout the play. The static opening is offset by a series of grand entrances: Kassandra with her torch, Andromache in her chariot, Helen in her finery,[7] and Talthybios with the pathetic body of Astyanax outstretched on Hektor's shield. Andromache enters by the parodos (577); but from the ships, not from Troy, as she has seen the corpse of Polyxena by the tomb of Achilles (626–7). She must go off the way she came, back to the ships, while Talthybios takes off Astyanax by the opposite parodos to the city (789).[8] Afterwards, however, Talthybios must re-enter from the ships (1123), where he has reportedly seen and conversed with

Andromache (1130ff.). The parodoi, therefore, while notionally leading to different areas, become interchangeable, just as the *skene* itself shifts in focus. The increasing spatial fluidity complements the thematic coalescence of men and women, Greeks and Trojans, in a telling visual symbolism.

HEKABE

Euripides establishes his motifs early in the play with the extended use of the ship image in Hekabe's poignant monody. Hekabe's misfortunes are extreme: she has borne many children, only to lose them through war; her husband has been savagely murdered before her very eyes (481–3); and she now, in extreme old age (141, 191ff., 275ff., etc.), is to have one daughter forcibly wrested from her (616, Kassandra), to hear of the death – to her a meaningless slaughter – of another (624–5, Polyxena), to watch the brutal separation of Andromache from Astyanax and to sing the lament over her dead grandson. After a life of luxury, surrounded by the royal family of Troy, she finds herself utterly alone and destitute facing the privations of servitude in the house of Odysseus (489–97).

Lamenting her misfortunes, Hekabe sings first of her discomforts in a remarkable extended nautical metaphor (112–21); then in similar terms she visualizes the coming of the Greek ships to Troy, bringing destruction (122–37). In the earlier passage, Hekabe fancies herself supine (114), with limbs uncomfortably disposed (112–13), with aching head, temples, and sides (115–16), longing to twist and turn her back and spine (116–18).[9] Viewed in literal terms, with reference to ships, Hekabe's fears are bizarre and excessive; viewed metaphorically, with reference to rape, or to violent and unwelcome sex, they are understandable. And the details of her body's disposition – lying on her back, in acute discomfort, unable to move – are inappropriate to sailing, but precisely those of the woman helpless under sexual attack. The word κλίσις, used of the disposition of her limbs, a hapax in Euripides, recalls κλισία, used of a bed where sex takes place (*IT* 857, *Alc.* 994). And ἄρθρα is used specifically of the genitals (Hdt. 3.87 and 4.2 of mares; perhaps also in a phrase of the law of Solon on adultery, ἄρθρα ἐπ᾽ ἄρθροις). In the latter passage, the words are strongly suggestive of a secondary sexual connotation with the primary one of sailing:

the prows of the Greek ships, with thrusting oars, pass from the harbours of Greece through dark seas and moor, Τροίας ἐν κόλποις(130). With this phrase, the boldest of the song, Euripides makes his point forcefully clear, punning on the bays of Troy and the wombs of its women. (See LSJ s.v. for the original meaning 'bosom', 'vagina', 'womb'; then 'bay'.) In the exchange with the entering chorus, Hekabe continues to dwell on the imminent embarkation, with its implications expressed in the phrase κινεῖται κωπήρης χείρ – 'the hand with the oar advances' (159–60). The unexpected verb, κινεῖν (lit. 'move'), being the *mot juste* for initiating sex, openly brings out the secondary meaning. The women of the chorus take up the theme (162 ναυσθλώσουσιν, cf. 677 ναυσθλοῦμαι, 180–1 κινεῖν κώπας).

KASSANDRA

After the tableau effect of the opening comes the Kassandra scene, ablaze with action as the torch (both phallic and symbolic of destruction: the birth of Paris, the start of the troubles, was preceded by Hekabe's dream that she gave birth to a torch, 922) is held high, in a fantasy enactment of the marriage hymn. Even before Kassandra appears, Talthybios sees the blazing brand within (298) and fears the women intend to destroy themselves (301–3; cf. 1282, where Hekabe threatens to dash into the blazing ruins of Troy). The young Kassandra,[10] who earlier evaded Apollo's amorous advances (41–2, but the sexual character of this relationship is lightly glossed over in *Troades*), and who has been dedicated as a result to lifelong virginity (254) as his prophet-priestess (170ff., 307, 342, 408, 415, 500: 'possessed' by the god, 'Bacchic', 'mainas'), has been the victim of a sacrilegious attack by Ajax in Athena's temple and narrowly escaped rape (70, 618–19, cf. 172; that she did escape may be supposed from allusions to her 'purity', 453 and 501): she is now chosen by Agamemnon for the violent (44) and illicit (44, 251) consummation of his passions (255, cf. 414 Eros). But (69–70) Athena has identified with this virgin victim of sexual persecution, viewing her own person as ὑβρισθεῖσαν, using a term which in Attic law meant technically 'rape' (LSJ s.v. II.3); the verb used of Ajax's assault on Kassandra, εἷλκε, is similarly specific to sexual attack (LSJ s.v. II.3). It is as a direct result of Ajax's conduct, unpunished and uncensured by the Greeks (69, 71), that Athena has turned against them (73, 77ff.). After lyric evocation in the loftily emotional monody, Kassandra in rational rhesis is emphatic that she will destroy Agamemnon and extirpate his line (359, 405), then in the departing trochaic tetrameters she faces the reality of her present situation and immediate future in words which reintroduce the ship motif (455 ποῦ σκάφος τὸ τοῦ στρατηγοῦ; – 'where is the general's craft?').

ANDROMACHE

In the Andromache scene, Euripides employs the chariot as a variant on the idea of the ship. (For a double sexual metaphor, ship and chariot, see Ar. *Pax* 901–3, cited *MM* p. 151 with n. 3.) The thematic continuation is clear in the nautical metaphors used in the anapaests announcing the arrival of Andromache (568–71 ξενικοῖς ἐπ᾽ ὄχοις πορθμευομένην ... παρὰ δ᾽εἰρεσίᾳ μαστῶν ἕπεται φίλος ᾽Αστυάναξ – 'being ferried in a Greek chariot ... and her dear Astyanax follows the rowing of her breasts'). The rather odd phrase 'rowing of her breasts' probably implies no more than that Astyanax, held in his mother's arms, moves with the swaying of her bosom, as the body of the seated woman is jolted in the cart (LSJ s.v. ἕπω, I.5, 'follow the motions of another'): the metaphor relates to the motion acting on Andromache, who is 'being ferried', and, in turn, on the child.[11]

Andromache remains in the chariot throughout the scene, perhaps in a visual corroboration of what is verbally evident: that she contemplates her future sexual experience positively. The scene focuses first on Andromache's fate as wife, then on her fate as mother. Andromache, widow of Hektor, remembers her marriage with pride and affection, describing her virtuous conduct as a wife (645–56) and outlining Hektor's attributes as a husband (673–4). Chosen now by Neoptolemos, son of Achilles, as his share of the Trojan spoils (658ff.), she speculates to Hekabe with sombre resignation on her future, realistically outlining her dilemma: she must either be unfaithful to Hektor's memory or unpleasing to her new partner (661–4); will sex with Neoptolemos break down her present repugnance (665–6)? With answering frankness and great humanity, Hekabe recommends that Andromache put aside thoughts of the dead Hektor, respect Neoptolemos and please him (697–700). Attention is diverted to Astyanax as the child is taken off to his death; but Andromache's last words on stage refer to her coming union with Neoptolemos (779); and her later reported request that the boy be buried with Hektor's shield contains the wish that Hektor's arms should not be conveyed to her new bedroom (1139).

HELEN

Helen, unlike the other women, is in command of the present situation, as she was in command of the past. Helen is blamed by the Trojan women for the war (131ff., esp. 134, by Hekabe; 598ff. and 766ff. by Andromache; cf. 373, implied by Kassandra in the allegation that Helen was a willing party to abduction by Paris). The extent of her culpability and the degree of choice she exercised are debated in the *agon*, while Menelaos stands by.[12]

Speaking first, Helen anticipates (939) and rebuts (950) the charge that she left Menelaos of her own free will, implying that some force was used (cf. 998), stating that Menelaos went away while Paris was a guest (944 Σπάρτης ἀπῆρας νηί – 'having left Sparta in a ship': the word νηί is redundant), and alleging – her trump card – that anyway she was powerless under Aphrodite's will (940ff.); Hekabe powerfully contests this and we are left in no doubt of Helen's motivation.[13]

However, Hekabe does not directly counter Helen's assertion that after Paris' death, when she might have left Troy (954, 'go to the Greek ships'), she was taken by Deiphobos against her will (959, 962 βίᾳ– 'by force' – emphatically repeated; but 1016–17 may be an indirect reply). Despite Menelaos' initial bluster, it is clear that once he has ignored Hekabe's advice not to see Helen, in case she overwhelms him πόθῳ– 'by desire' (891), he is lost. Later, the chorus urge Hekabe to counteract Helen's πειθώ – 'persuasion' (967). There is surely a pun here: rhetorical persuasion and erotic inducement are equally appropriate in context. (Pothos and Peitho, personified, are associated in literary contexts as children or attendants of Aphrodite, e.g. A. *Su.* 1039.)[14] It may more tentatively be suggested that a punning *double entendre* is present when Helen says to Menelaos (899), 'I know I am *hated* by you, but ἐρέσθαι βούλομαι....' Here the meaning 'I want to ask a question' (aor. inf. ἐρωτάω) lies on the surface; but there is in context a hint of ἐρᾶσθαι βούλομαι, 'I

8

want to be *loved* (pres. inf. pass. ἐράω). Helen has prepared herself well for the reunion (1022–3) and the final manipulation comes when she clasps Menelaos' knees (1042): a conventional suppliant pose, but also a seductive one, calculated to arouse the susceptible male. The effect on Menelaos of Helen's décolletage was a stock element in portrayals of this scene (cf. *Andr.* 629, Ar. *Lys.* 156). The scene ends, as it began, with bluster from Menelaos; but it is evident that when Menelaos 'gets his hands on her', as he threatened, it will not be with violent intent (861; cf. *Cyc.* 177, with *MM* p. 27).

There is a clear innuendo in Hekabe's final plea that Menelaos will not take Helen on his own ship (1049). Menelaos' evasive reply betrays his awareness of the kneeling figure (1050, 'Is she heavier than before?'); clearly, he is still indeed infatuated (1051) and we place little credence in his belated promise that Helen will not travel in the same ship as he (1053–4). That the women of the chorus are sceptical is shown by their wish, expressed in the following lyric, that Menelaos' ship be struck by lightning 'through the middle of its oars' (1100–1); the gratuitous importation of the oar, here as elsewhere, gives point to the dual character of the ship motif.

CHORUS

Unlike Hekabe and Andromache, the women of the chorus have no luxurious royal past to mourn, but they too are wives (143, 1309) and mothers (201ff.), leaving happiness and security for uncertainty and misery. In the parodos exchange, they express anxiety to know the details of their fate, and that means to know what man will take them (185; cf. 292–3, the despairing question put to Talthybios). They recognize the rigours of the life facing them, and that means the horror of its sexual aspect (204ff.). In the ensuing choral lyric, the imagery of ships, introduced in Hekabe's monody, is intricately developed and the imagery of fire and flame, introduced in Kassandra's monody, is also sustained. It is in these terms that Troy's mythical past, recent past, and unpalatable present are reviewed.

In the first stasimon (511–67) the Trojan horse is likened to a dark ship (539), with weaponry (520), brought to breach the gates (521, 532) of Troy against a sinister background of smouldering fire and flashes of flame (548–9); immediately afterwards comes the entry of Andromache in her ship-like chariot. In the second stasimon (799–859) the first Greek expedition against Troy is recalled in terms reminiscent of Hekabe's monody: the ships thrust, like those of the present enemy, into the very heart of Trojan territory and 'relaxed their seafaring oar at fair-flowing Simoeis'. Rivers and channels commonly suggest the vagina. The verb σχάζειν, 'relax effort, cease an action, especially rowing' (LSJ 4), also has the meaning 'slit open' (LSJ 1, 2): thus, the penetration by oar of the Trojan river suggests the sexual penetration of Trojan women. The parallelism between the two expeditions is stressed (esp. 817–18); and flames again flicker in the background (815). Eros (840), the emphatic first word of the final antistrophe, serves to sum up the lyric themes of the relationships between Eos and Tithonos, Zeus and Ganymede, and to introduce the ensuing scene of piquant reunion between Helen and Menelaos.

The third stasimon (1060–1117) is a reprise of earlier themes: there is allusion in the strophe to the fire of destruction (1080) and the fire and smoke at the altars of Troy, now deserted by the gods; then in the antistrophe the women lament their husbands and reflect on their plight. They allude to the 'seafaring ship speeding with wings' (1085–6) and the 'dark ship with seagoing oars' (1094–5), now waiting to take them to Greece. The phrase ἀίσσον πτεροῖσι – 'speeding with wings' – is particularly suggestive, as there is some evidence that πτερόν – 'wing' – could have a phallic sense.[15] The chorus speculate on the locality in Greece to which they will be taken:

ἢ Σαλαμῖν' ἱεράν
ἢ δίπορον κορυφάν
Ἴσθμιον, ἔνθα πύλας
Πέλοπος ἔχουσιν ἕδραι

(1096ff.)

'... holy Salamis or the peak of the Isthmos with its two channels, where the seat of Pelops has its gates.'

The geographical allusions are not randomly chosen, but are pointed, with strong sexual implications. In comedy, Salamis is synonymous with sex (*Lys.* 39).[16] '... the peak of the Isthmos with its two channels, where the seat of Pelops has its gates' is the boldest *double entendre* of the play. πύλη – 'gate' – is slang for the vagina (*Lys.* 250; cf. *MM* p. 137) and ἕδρα – 'seat' – is occasionally used of the buttocks (*Nu.* 1507, *Thesmo.* 133; cf. *MM* p. 199). Euripides indicates the genital area with some precision: the 'peak' is the perineum and the 'channels' anus and vagina. Isthmos is a common comic pun for this region and there was a hetaira name Isthmias (*Thesmo.* 647, *Pax* 879f.; cf. *MM* pp. 137–8); the seat of Pelops, whom Poseidon pursued, was mythologically renowned. The chorus seem to be speculating about regions of Greece; but in reality are brooding on the sexual fate they will meet there.

In the kommos which ends the play, the expression φλογέας δαλοῖσι χέρας διερέσσοντας – 'rowing their hands, blazing with firebrands' (1257–8), as the chorus catch sight of their captors brandishing blazing torches in a rowing motion, arrestingly combines the two pervasive symbolic motifs of the play. The metaphor of the plume of smoke may have phallic overtones (1298, 1320). Certainly, when Talthybios orders the firing of the city and the taking of the women to the ships (1260ff.), literal reference to these acts (1279) coincides with hints at their implications. With the last line of the play, the chorus proceed finally ἐπὶ πλάτας Ἀχαιῶν. It is tempting to find here and elsewhere in the play a punning association between πλάτη – 'oar' – and πελάτης – 'bedfellow'; the words have the same endings in all cases except nominative and genitive singular. The feminine form πλᾶτις occurs in verse as an abbreviated form of πελάτις (Ar. *Ach.* 132; cf. πελάτης, LSJ II, and the verb πελάζω).

TROADES AND LYSISTRATA

The effect of the punning and *double entendre* in *Troades* must have been electrifying; it is a striking example of interaction between tragedy and comedy in the late fifth century BC. This was a two-way process. Aristophanes presents in *Lysistrata*, produced 411 BC, a dramatic situation broadly analogous to that of *Troades*. During the Peloponnesian War (often presented in contemporary literature as a simulacrum of the heroic Trojan War), a group of female characters (one of them, like Helen, a Spartan), backed by a chorus who share their aims and aspirations, occupy an acropolis of which the 'gates' are attacked by 'crowbars' and other weapons with the threat of fire, in a confrontation between men eager for sex and women holding them off; the play ends with the sexual union of the two groups. Both plays, on their different planes, show the effects of war on women. There are some striking verbal similarities as well as these thematic parallelisms. In addition to the pervasive idea of gates being breached, geographical punning is present in both plays. In *Lysistrata* the key place names are τὰν Πύλον ... τὸν Ἐχινοῦντα καὶ τὸν Μηλιᾶ κόλπον τὸν ὄπισθεν καὶ τὰ Μεγαρικὰ σκέλη – Pylos, Echinous, Melos, and Megara; all given anatomical reference (1162–70).[17] One further small but suggestive correspondence between the plays is the mention in both (and in both cases in the last lyrics of the chorus) of a peculiar cult of Athena, in a temple surrounded by bronze plates, at Sparta (*Tro.* 1113f., *Lys.* 1320ff.). It seems possible that *Lysistrata* was conceived as an extended parody of *Troades*.

Erotic motion, approaching the simulation of sex, was clearly part of the stage action of *Lysistrata* (most evidently in the Kinesias scene). It is probable that in *Troades* too the suggestive words in the lyrics were accompanied by a sinuous swaying motion, with visual and verbal presentation combined for maximum impact. There is good evidence for the existence of a rowing schema in the dance of tragedy,[18] and it may be conjectured that this was the basis of the choreography. While rowing is a symbol for the forced sex of the future, dance itself symbolizes, in word and probably also in action, the happy sex of the past (555), when main characters and chorus were protected by Trojan sceptre (150), not threatened by Greek spear and oar. (Cf. *El.* 432–41, *Hel.* 1451–6 for association in Euripidean lyric between rowing and dancing.)

EURIPIDEAN PARALLELS

There is some evidence in other Euripidean plays of súggestive punning with sexual overtones. In *Medea*, the oracle given to Aigeus is quoted as ἀσκοῦ με τὸν προύχοντα μὴ λῦσαι πόδα – 'not to loose the projecting foot of the wine-skin' (*Med.* 679), and this is glossed by Plutarch (*Thes.* 3) μηδεμιᾷ γυναικὶ συγγένεσθαι – 'not to sleep with any woman'. This is a one-liner and, as a riddling oracular utterance, perhaps not truly parallel. In *Hippolytos* the usage is more pervasive. Certain aspects of it have already been noticed. One critic comments on Phaidra that 'Her yearning for the poplar and the grassy meadow, for the chase and the taming of colts on the sand, is a hysterical expression of her desire for Hippolytus', and explains, 'Both λειμών and κομήτης have sexual associations; see E. *Cyc.* 171 for λειμών and Ar. *Lys.* 827 for κομήτης. The taming of πῶλοι (231) is a common sexual metaphor (cf. Anacreon 75).'[19] It may be added that κλιθεῖσα (211) implies a female body reclining in readiness for sex, as S. *Tr.* 1226.[20] It has been tentatively suggested too that in the much discussed *aidos* passage (385ff.) the 'bad' *aidos* disparaged by Phaidra is sex.[21] In the case of Hippolytos, the relationship of devotee and goddess is tinged with erotic adoration, lightly adumbrated in Euripides' choice of terminology (especially 17 and 1441). Euripides returns to the theme of sexual assault in *Helen*. Here, the imagery is less open than in *Hippolytos*, less sustained than in *Troades*.

CONCLUSION

In conclusion, we may reiterate that *Troades* is about sex and war: great and perennial, perhaps the greatest and most perennial of all, literary themes. The case of the Trojan War and the Trojan women is universalized by wide-ranging reminiscence of earlier wars (the first Trojan expedition) and more remote affairs (Zeus and Ganymede; Eos and Tithonos); sexual motivation is a factor in historical causation (cf. Hdt. 1. 1ff. and Ar. *Ach.* 527). War, conducted by men on a battlefield reached by the oar, with sword and spear which breach gates and with fire which destroys houses, is seen in the play from the point of view of the women whose persons – identified with country, city, and buildings – are attacked. Imagery flows into punning and innuendo, notably πλάτη – πελάτης, κόλπος, πύλαι (of a piece with the play on πειθώ and the ἐρᾶσθαι – ἐρέσθαι ambiguity). The visual symbolism of the staging (use of parodoi, Kassandra's torch, Andromache's chariot) reinforces its literal and metaphorical content.

NOTES

1 On Greek attitudes to sex and marriage generally, see Elizabeth M. Craik (ed.), *Marriage and Property* (Aberdeen, 1984), ch. II.
2 The lyrics are skilfully analysed by Shirley A. Barlow, *The Imagery of Euripides* (London, 1971), esp. pp. 114–19; without, however,

any suggestion that ships and fire symbolize sex. See also Anne Burnett, 'Trojan women and the Ganymede ode', *YCS* 25 (1977), pp. 291–316.

3   The evidence for Aristophanes is collected by Jeffrey Henderson, *The Maculate Muse* (New Haven and London, 1975) – hereafter *MM* – subtitled 'Obscene language in Attic comedy'. The word 'obscene' is unfortunate, implying pornography, and does not do justice even to Aristophanes, who is capable of introducing sex in a subtle and oblique way as well as bluntly and directly. See also J. Taillardat, *Les Images d'Aristophane* (Paris, 1962).

4   In his enthusiasm, Henderson overstates his case, and many of his categories and supposedly illustrative examples are dubious. One recalls the story of Freud's patient who indignantly repudiated the interpretation in sexual terms of a particular dream with the retort that when he had a sexual dream he dreamt about sex.

5   On the role of Talthybios, see K. Gilmartin, 'Talthybios in the Trojan Women', *AJP* 91 (1970), pp. 213–22.

6   It is not necessary to postulate a change of scene. The difficulties are discussed by N. C. Hourmouziades, *Production and Imagination in Euripides* (Athens, 1965), pp. 24–5, 69, 122, 133.

7   M. Lloyd, 'The Helen scene in Euripides' Troades', *CQ* 34 (1984), pp. 303–13, rightly stresses the parallelism of these scenes (but mistakenly states, pp. 303 and 313, that Andromache emerges from the tent).

8   On this double exit, see O. Taplin, *The Stagecraft of Aeschylus* (Oxford, 1977), p. 91 n. 2.

9   The precise meaning of 116–18 is uncertain. It is not clear whether Hekabe imagines her body is a tossing ship (with her back its keel and her sides its sides), or whether she envisages herself on shipboard. The latter is the more natural interpretation (literally translated: 'longing to twist and give alternately back and spine to one side or the other, to the accompaniment of laments and piteous tears'). See K. H. Lee (ed.), *Euripides Troades* (London, 1976) ad loc.; also Barlow (n. 2).

10 See P. G. Mason, 'Kassandra', *JHS* 79 (1959), pp. 80–93, for the treatment of Kassandra in Greek literature and art.

11 K. H. Lee, 'Observations on ἐρέσσειν, μαστός and E. *Tro.* 570–571', *Philologus* 117 (1973), pp. 264–6, makes rather heavy weather of the passage, preferring, of the different translations offered in LSJ and LSJ Suppl. the former, 'heaving breasts' (indicative of nervous excitement), to the latter, 'rhythmic beating of her breast'.

12 The scene is treated by E. M. Blaiklock, *The Male Characters of Euripides* (Wellington, NZ, 1952), pp. 80–4; and by M. Lloyd (n. 7). In my view, Lloyd is mistaken in supposing that Menelaos still intends to kill Helen at the end of the scene.

13 In *Troades*, Euripides simplifies human motivation to terms of subjective internal emotion, without objective external impetus; contrast the complexities of *Hippolytos*. Similarly, he simplifies Apollo's conduct to Kassandra; contrast the critical standpoint of

Ion. On Gorgias' *Helen* as a Euripidean source, see Ruth Scodel, 'The Trojan trilogy of Euripides', *Hypomnemata* 60 (1980), p. 144.

14 For the various aspects of Peitho, see R. G. A. Buxton, *Persuasion in Greek Tragedy* (Cambridge, 1982).

15 Pl. *Phdr.* 252b4ff. See *MM* p. 128 and (esp.) W. Arrowsmith, *Arion* ns 1/1 (1973), pp. 164ff.

16 Cf. Taillardat (n. 3), pp. 101, 180.

17 On punning in *Lysistrata*, see *MM* and also J. Henderson, 'Lysistrate: the play and its themes', *YCS* 26 (1980), pp. 153–218.

18 Lillian B. Lawler, *The Dance of the Ancient Greek Theatre* (Iowa, 1964), p. 45.

19 B. Knox, 'The Hippolytus of Euripides', *YCS* 13 (1952) pp. 3–31, repr. in B. Knox, *Word and Action* (Baltimore, Md, 1979), 205–30; p. 208 with p. 229 n. 8.

20 On the interpretation of this scene, see R. P. Winnington-Ingram, *Sophocles. An Interpretation* (Cambridge, 1980), p. 81 n. 28.

21 D. J. Conacher, *Euripidean Drama* (Toronto and London, 1967), pp. 54–5. Το τὰ αἰδοῖα in the explicit anatomical sense may be added the similar use of αἰδώς, Hom. *Il.* 22. 74–5, πολιόν τε κάρη πολιόν τε γένειον αἰδῶ τ'... κταμένοιο γέροντος and perhaps also *Il.* 2. 262 (*MM* p. 4).

2

A WOMAN'S PLACE IN EURIPIDES' *MEDEA*

Margaret Williamson

The main stimulus for this treatment of the *Medea* was a distinction which has recently been gaining currency in the study of the Athens of the fifth century BC – namely that between public and private spheres. The recent growth of interest in this dichotomy has many sources, among them the concern of structuralist anthropology with the social categories constructed by different cultures. Another more specific one is the discussion within modern feminism of the long-standing association of women with the private sphere[1] – an association which was challenged by the 'private is political' slogan of the early 1970s.

Fifth-century Athens was clearly a crucial period in the construction of the idea of the private, and tragedy is an important source for our understanding of it. Two writers who have recently dealt with the public–private split in a way which opens up many possibilities for the interpretation of the plays are Sally Humphreys and John Gould. In the opening chapters of *The Family, Women and Death*[2] Humphreys sketches the way in which the private world of the *oikos* and the public one of the *polis* became more sharply differentiated, and she points to tragedy as one index of the conflicts caused by this polarization. The distinction is invoked from a different angle by Gould in his essay on dramatic character, and again in considering our evidence about the position of women in classical Athens.[3] These two writers concur in relating the prominence of female characters in tragedy to the primary association of women with the *oikos*, in contrast to the public, male world of the *polis*. Thus, in Humphreys' view, the peculiarly active and larger-than-life women in tragedy 'belong to a discourse on the relation between

16

public and private life rather than to a discourse on the relations between the sexes'.[4]

The Greek stage was, of course, rich in semantic possibilities when it came to exploring this relationship. Most of the action in a play takes place in an open, public space, the *orchestra*, which is partially surrounded by the audience; this space is also defined as public by the presence in it of the chorus for most of the play. Behind the *orchestra*, however, is the *skene*, the stage-building, and behind that a more remote space which the audience normally cannot see. In this and many other plays this unseen space represents the interior of a house: it is, in a phrase adapted by Gould from Wilamowitz, an 'offstage indoors',[5] and the tragedy takes place at the intersection between inside and outside, private and public. When Medea, in this play, emerges with the words 'I have come out of the house' (ἐξῆλθον δόμων, 214), her statement can be read symbolically as well as literally, as a movement from the private sphere of the house into the public one – normally associated with men – of the city.[6] An important corollary of this transition is the corresponding change in the language she uses. From within the house we hear her expressing extremes of rage, misery, and hatred in lyrical anapaests; as soon as she steps outside it her language becomes controlled, abstract, intellectualizing and indistinguishable from that of any of the male characters she confronts in the early scenes of the play – including Jason. It is the gap – never to be bridged – between these two modes which chiefly concerns me, and I shall suggest that it is intimately linked with the violence which the play portrays.

In what follows I shall do three things. First I want to consider some of the manifestations and implications of Medea's transition into the public sphere. Then I shall look at some of the registers in which she speaks in the early scenes of the play, and the language which she shares with the male characters; and finally I shall consider what the play seems to be implying about that language.

To dwell a little longer on the spatial semantics of the play: comparison with some of the plays which preceded this one suggests how problematic the relationship between public and private spaces will be here. In both Aeschylus' *Oresteia* and Sophocles' *Antigone* (both obvious comparisons because of the dominant female characters in them) the sphere represented by the 'off-stage indoors' is the house of the ruling family, which is thus also the centre of the city: the spheres of *oikos* and *polis* are concentric. Despite disorder within both spheres (in the *Oresteia*) or conflict between them (in the *Antigone*), the possibility of a restoration of harmony is always there. In this play, however, the off-stage space has been displaced.[7] The centre of Corinth is not Medea's house but Creon's; Medea's house is in a kind of no-man's-land, and would be so even without Jason's desertion. The other thing which gives her household its problematic quality is the fact that she is barbarian, so that the space from which she emerges is not only inner, but also outer and alien. This troubling paradox makes the 'off-stage indoors' even more remote and inaccessible to the audience.[8]

In addition, of course, as the prologue makes clear, the *oikos* for Medea is fractured by betrayals, and has been so ever since her marriage to Jason. Even before telling us of Medea's present situation, the Nurse recounts her destruction of Pelias through his daughters (9); and shortly afterwards we hear that Medea has also betrayed her own father and home (31–2). It is these events, no less than Jason's desertion, which are responsible for her present plight: she has, unlike a divorced Athenian woman, no home to return to, and so she is precipitated perforce into the public domain.

This movement occurs, I think, on many levels, one of which is also indicated in the prologue. The Nurse tells us that Medea's marriage to Jason was guaranteed by ὅρκοι – oaths – and δεξιαί – pledges; it is these, and the gods who witnessed them, which the betrayed Medea invokes (21). The significance of this is two-fold. First, oaths did not normally form part of either the betrothal or the actual giving-away stages of a marriage ceremony;[9] they are usually associated with public life and especially, as Humphreys points out, with entry into it.[10] Second, any contract involved in a marriage would normally be between the husband and the wife's father or guardian. Medea, however, represents Jason's oaths and pledges as having been given to herself. In contracting a marriage on this basis she has already translated herself into the role of a male citizen, operating in the public sphere as Jason's equal.

There is a similar bias in her celebrated speech to the Corinthian chorus about their common lot as women. Medea's account of the giving of dowries contains a subtle distortion: she

again represents the woman as an active partner in the transaction when she says that women must 'buy a husband for an
extravagant sum' (χρημάτων ὑπερβολῇ πόσιν πρίασθαι, 232–3).
In fact, once again, it would be a woman's father who engaged in
the transaction, not the woman herself; and her dowry, rather
than being exchanged for a husband, would both accompany
her and, if she was divorced, return with her. Medea is here
representing all women as practitioners of exchange, just as she
herself contracted her own marriage; rather than, in Levi-
Strauss's phrase, the exchange of women, she talks here of
exchange by women.[11]

In the speech in which she first attempts to dissuade Creon
from banishing her (292ff.), the extent to which she speaks like a
male citizen is again remarkable. To his order to leave she
replies with a sententious speech about the dangers of having a
reputation for *sophia*. No *man* (ἀνήρ), she says, with any sense
would have his children brought up to be very clever (σοφοί):
because the ignorant will not understand you if you are clever,
whereas those with aspirations will be made envious by your pre-
eminence. She goes on to apply this to her own situation; but up
to the point at which she makes explicit reference to herself, her
words describe a community of male citizens and are scarcely
applicable to the situation of a woman – much less of a foreigner
in fifth-century Athens.[12]

The most remarkable manifestation of her entry into the
public sphere is, however, her transaction with Aegeus. She and
Aegeus meet as equals, and form a contract based on exchange;
and in Medea's case what she both offers and receives is a
version of what a woman would give and receive in marriage.
She offers Aegeus fertility – the power to beget children; he
gives her in return, not the safety of an *oikos*, but that of the
Athenian *polis*. The equivalence between this exchange and the
contract of marriage is confirmed by the account Medea later
gives of it to Jason: she tells him that she is going to 'live with
Aegeus' (Αἰγεῖ συνοικήσουσα, 1385). This relationship too,
like Medea's with Jason, is sealed by oaths, and the transaction
can be seen as completing the translation from private to public
of the marriage bond which her relationship with Jason had
already initiated.

Medea's move out of the house, then, is paralleled by other
moves into the sphere and the discourse of male citizens, and its

most remarkable effect is this version of the marriage relationship. Instead of a relationship based on an absolute and irrevocable difference of status, and a change in status which is usually also permanent, marriage has become a contract based on exchange and reciprocity between equals.

One of the reasons why this transmutation is interesting is that these two types of relationship are themselves the subject of discussion within the play, and Medea is an active participant in the discussion. They are particularly at issue in the scenes between her and Creon, and then between her and Jason. The degree to which, in these scenes, Medea commands the same range of arguments and analyses as her interlocutors is another indication of her transition into the world which they inhabit. However, the manner in which these arguments are wielded casts considerable doubt on their validity; and in addition, the very fact that Medea's exit from the house has involved the kind of transmutation and distortion which I have mentioned puts in doubt any claim she may have had to speak for the *oikos*. We would expect her, as a woman, to be closely associated with the sphere from which, symbolically, she emerged at line 214; but the early scenes of the play suggest that her emergence has fatally weakened her association with the *oikos* – and also that it is irreversible. This is of crucial importance when – as in her debate with Jason – the topic at issue is the relationship which is at the heart of the *oikos* – marriage.

It is possible to sketch in the early scenes with Creon and Jason a spectrum of types of relationship. At one extreme are close blood-relationships – primarily those between parents and children – which are asymmetrical, fixed and irrevocable, and based on an absolute distinction of status between the people involved. At the other are relationships involving exchange between equals, which are fluid and subject to alteration. The first extreme is characteristic of relationships within the private sphere, and the second of relationships between male citizens in the public sphere of the *polis*.[13] Between these two poles are other kinds of relationship, most notably that between suppliant and supplicated, and that of ξενία (guest-friendship), which are based on differentiation and inequality in status but involve a change in status, effected by ritual and witnessed by the gods.

The scene between Medea and Creon alludes to the full range of these types of relationship, and juxtaposes them so sharply as to emphasize their discontinuity and set them against, as much as alongside, each other. Medea's attempt to persuade Creon to allow her to stay opens with the account of the dangers of being considered clever to which I have already referred. She continues with another highly abstract argument against his fear of her, this time framed in judicial terms. Creon has not, she says, wronged her in marrying his daughter to whomever he chose, and therefore should expect no retribution from her (307–10). This is an argument about the relationship between two equals whose exchange with each other is defined in terms of an abstract concept of justice. It is also partial in that it takes no account of personal feeling, and indeed runs counter to her inclusion of Creon in the category of enemies earlier in the scene (278); and he rejects it as mere words (321).

The next tactic which Medea employs is more successful. She becomes a suppliant, adopting a posture in which she has a tangible, and not merely theoretical, claim on Creon. The suggestion made by Gould about this episode seems to me right: that she begins by beseeching Creon only verbally, but becomes effective at the point when she adopts the physical posture of a suppliant and clings to him (335, 339, and later 370).[14] She has thus moved to what I have defined as the middle ground, and appealed to a relationship based on a sharp differentiation in status whose obligations are guaranteed by ritual. The success initiated by this move is consolidated by an appeal to Creon as being, like Jason, a father (344–5). She does not, obviously, appeal to an actual blood-relationship between Creon and her own children, but to Creon's feeling within a parallel relationship; and in so doing she has now moved to the other end of the spectrum.

Medea employs, then, in her persuasive assault on Creon three approaches which are sharply differentiated in every possible way. The first begins with a generalization which is elaborated at length before being applied to her own situation, and which entirely excludes personal feeling. The second, her supplication, is stichomythic; the third, which is based on personal feeling alone, is made in a speech of eight heavily alliterative lines. The discontinuity which is thus formally highlighted reflects particularly harshly, I think, on the abstract and judicial language of the first appeal. Besides being, in itself, an improbably sententious response to a sudden personal disaster, it is also the least successful of her ploys. All three approaches, however, are overshadowed by a mode of persuasion – Medea's supplicatory pose – which, if Gould is right, is effective by means of gesture rather than of words, and which thus casts doubt on the efficacy of any of Medea's arguments if taken alone.

The linguistic discontinuities which are thrown into relief in this scene do not end here. Medea's rationalistic arguments to Creon, and her adoption of the perspective of a male citizen in 292ff., can only heighten our sense of the gulf separating this from the voice we first heard from within the house. As if to widen this gulf Euripides now, on Creon's departure, gives to the chorus a lament which echoes the first cry we heard from Medea:

δύστανε γύναι,
φεῦ φεῦ, μελέα τῶν σῶν ἀχέων

(357–8)

'Oh unhappy woman, alas, wretched in your pain', they sing, echoing Medea's

ἰώ,
δύστανος ἐγὼ μελέα τε πόνων

'Oh, unhappy that I am, wretched in my troubles' at 96. The mode of Medea's earlier expression of suffering is, it seems, no longer available to her, but only to the chorus: their evocation of it here, set beside the abstract and rhetorical way in which she is now using language, points to what has been lost in her exit from the house. The suffering she expressed from within the house is now issuing, in characteristic Euripidean sequence, in action outside it; but the sense of dislocation which this linguistic gap produces already – before we know what Medea's plans are – casts a shadow over that action. It is becoming clear that her emergence from the house involved both distortion and loss, and the eventual outcome of her plans is marked in advance by that distortion too.

The *agon* between Medea and Jason begins with another verbal echo hardly less significant than that of the chorus. Jason's first speech opens with a line which differs by only two words from that with which Medea began her attempt to sway Creon: compare her οὐ νῦν με πρῶτον, ἀλλὰ πολλάκις, Κρέον ...

'This is not the first time, Creon; [I have] often [had the same experience] ...' at 292 with his first words in this scene:

οὐ νῦν κατεῖδον πρῶτον ἀλλὰ πολλάκις ...

(446)

'This is not the first time: I have often seen...' The association not only marks him as what he will indeed turn out to be – the arch-rationalizer and theoretician of the play – but also locates the debate, for Medea and Jason equally, at that level of persuasive rhetoric which emerged from the Creon scene as least successful.[15] In this scene what is at issue between Medea and Jason is principally the nature of their relationship. In this context, more than any other, we might expect Medea to associate herself with the relationships most characteristic of the *oikos*, and particularly with blood-relationships. However, the range which she commanded in the Creon scene, as well as the parallel already allusively suggested between her and Jason, should warn us that this will not be so; and indeed the case turns out to be more complex.

Both she and Jason have a range of ways of conceptualizing their relationship. Each at some point refers to it as one of exchange. Medea cites the fact that she saved him, and details the way in which she did so; it was, she says, after receiving this treatment from her that he betrayed her (488–9). We recall the Nurse in the prologue quoting Medea's cry to the gods to witness what kind of recompense – οἵας ἀμοιβῆς (23) – she has received from Jason: there the vocabulary of exchange was quite clear. Jason in turn invokes the same concept when he tells her that she has received more than she gave in saving him (534–5), and proceeds to list the benefits to her.

At the other extreme, Medea invokes blood-relationships when, after listing her benefits to Jason, she charges him with contracting a new marriage even though children have been born, saying that if he were childless his desire for a new marriage would be pardonable (490–1). The existence of children, according to her, creates a bond between husband and wife which, though it is not a blood-relationship, derives an inalienable quality from the relation of each to their children.

23

In this scene too, then, there are appeals made to ways of thinking about relationships which are fundamentally different; and once again the effect of their juxtaposition is to put them all in question. Although Medea invokes blood-relationships, she has no stable association with this as a way of thinking about marriage: she is equally capable of regarding exchange between equals as the basis of her link with Jason. In this scene even more than the previous one, each protagonist uses language to assault the other, and the scene abounds in allusions to language as instrument and even as weapon.[16] Here, however, the relationship which is at issue is of central importance to the continuation of the *oikos*; and the fact that Medea's and Jason's heterogeneous and colliding arguments have no purchase on it is the more damaging for this reason.

It is not, however, from either of the two extremes which I have mentioned that the motive force of Medea's revenge – which takes the action forward from this point – comes. The argument which she consistently offers, from now until her famous monologue at 1021ff., is that Jason's crime was to harm his *philoi*. This is the first charge she makes against him in the *agon* (470), and the chorus seem to confirm her definition of their relationship as one of *philia* in the two-line interjection (520–1) in which they say that anger is particularly implacable when it is between *philoi*. It was also stressed in the prologue that Jason had offended against the principle of doing good to one's friends and harm to one's enemies (84).

But the speech in which Medea pleads this principle before Jason also shows how problematic is its application here. Although a relationship of *philia* can arise in other ways, the sphere in which it can normally be assumed is with regard to relatives: the range of an individual's *philoi* would begin with his kin and spread outwards.[17] But in Medea's case Euripides makes it very clear that this central point does not exist. In her catalogue of benefits to Jason (476ff.), it is explicitly mentioned that saving Jason involved, twice over, the destruction of the bond between parent and child – first when she betrayed her own father, and again when she destroyed Pelias and his *oikos* by means of his daughters. She reiterates her account of both these crimes later in the speech, again stressing the damage to the two *oikoi* which was involved, and this time she makes it clear that she too, like Jason, has inverted the treatment due to friends and enemies:

τοῖς μὲν οἴκοθεν φίλοις
ἐχθρὰ καθέστηχ', οὓς δέ μ' οὐκ ἐχρῆν κακῶς
δρᾶν, σοὶ χάριν φέρουσα πολεμίους ἔχω.

(506–8)

'To my friends [*philoi*] at home I have become hateful; and in helping you I have made enemies of others I had no cause to harm'. When she speaks to Jason, then, of the duty to do good to one's *philoi*, her words are – almost literally – hollow. The relationship which she claims Jason has violated was itself based on a similar violation. She cannot, therefore, invoke the kind of relationship in which the claims of *philia* are clearest; the only place where she can take her stand is in an area where the relations involved are more fluid and ambiguous. Besides referring to close kinship the word can also cover less permanent associations between male citizens, including members of the same drinking group and those who, somewhat as Jason aspires to do, have formed a tie with another *genos* through marriage.[18] Logically, in view of her own actions, Medea can only be defending this much less clear-cut and less stable category of *philia*: the central area, and the one with which we would expect her, as a woman, to be associated, is absent.

This makes it all the more remarkable that the spur to action which she constantly places before herself and the chorus is the duty to do good to one's *philoi* and harm to one's enemies. In her monologue at the end of the Creon scene she refers twice to her enemies (374, 383), and she takes up the same theme again after her exchange with Aegeus. There she not only refers to her enemies four times, but also ends with an explicit statement of the old heroic ethic: she wants, she says, to be thought 'hard on her enemies and good to her friends' (βαρεῖαν ἐχθροῖς καὶ φίλοισιν εὐμενῆ, 809) because it is this kind of behaviour that wins renown.

Both these speeches, as Bernard Knox and others have pointed out, are framed in the language and style of a Sophoclean hero.[19] Medea's implacable anger against her enemies, and her definition of them as such, are equally uncompromising. Both the grief which she expressed earlier from inside the house and the range of arguments she deployed against Jason are absent from these two speeches. Instead, Jason, Creon, and his daughter are all defined in absolute terms as

25

enemies, and her revenge on them as a matter of heroic daring, expressed in such lines as

ἕρπ' ἐς τὸ δεινόν· νῦν ἀγὼν εὐψυχίας

(403)

'On to the terrible deed; this is the test of my spirit' and

νῦν καλλίνικοι τῶν ἐμῶν ἐχθρῶν...
γενησόμεσθα

(765–6)

'Now I shall win a glorious victory over my enemies'.

Medea thus adds another vocabulary, another kind of discourse, to those over which she has already shown such mastery. One reading of this new style is that it gives Medea heroic dignity, and adds weight to her as a spokesman for the rights of women.[20] But the shift to a heroic, Sophoclean, and once again masculine style has another function too: it heightens even further our sense of the gaps and dislocations not only between her voice from within the house and that with which she speaks after emerging into the open, but also within her public voice. Her heroic stance is paradoxical and contradictory not only in its central formulation but also in its consequences: the distinction on which it rests has already been subverted by Medea herself, and it leads yet again to the destruction of the most intimate bond of *philia*, that between parents and children. It reappears twice in her crucial and apparently wavering monologue, each time as an argument in favour of the children's death, and each time with an uncompromising reference to her enemies (1049–50, 1059–61).

When Medea subsequently goes inside to carry out the murder, she is both re-entering the *oikos* and entering it for the first time. The transmutations and distortions which we have seen to be involved in her exit at line 214 mean that – to use the terms with which I began – it is partly as a representative of the public, male sphere that she now crosses the threshold. She now shares with Creon and Jason a vocabulary which has been discredited as a means of understanding the relationship central to the *oikos*, and her heroic language is equally inappropriate to it. It is inevitable, therefore, that the consequence of her entry into the house should be wordless violence – the murder of the children who are the most stable measure of its central relationship.

26

The violence can, indeed, be traced further back than this. Medea's relationship to the *oikos* has always been marked by violence: her emergence at line 214 represented in spatial terms a movement which in fact began long before the action of the play, and which was initiated by destruction within her own *oikos* and then Pelias'. It is this destruction which is the condition of her presence on stage: violence to the *oikos* is both cause and consequence of her emergence into view at line 214. In marking that emergence so sharply by means of the linguistic and conceptual discontinuities and distortions which I have discussed, the play seems to me to be pointing, among other things, to the inadequacy of the language available for thinking about the *oikos*. The private, it suggests by analogy, cannot be spoken in the language of the public except on condition of its destruction; and Medea's status as representative of the private was compromised as soon as she emerged into public view.

I began by relating the two juxtaposed theatrical spaces in this play to the division between public and private; but it would be misleading to suggest that this is the only meaning which they have. Some of their other resonances are suggested by the work of Ruth Padel, who argues that women's possession of an inner space makes them particularly suited to the representation of inner experience in general: the inner space of the *oikos* would be an extension of the same metaphor.[21] This can be related to another opposition which is important in the play but which I have not mentioned – between *eros* and the rationality exemplified in its purest form by Jason (though also, of course, shared by Medea) – as well as between the languages of passion and of action. The discrepancies I have mentioned between different ways of defining relationships can be related to conflicts existing within public life as well as between public and private life; so that the *oikos* may stand both for itself and for a type of relationship within the public sphere.[22]

I would not want, however, to lose sight entirely of the fact that, whatever else it may represent, the *oikos* is the province of women, so that the linguistic inadequacies to which the play points are in part inadequacies in the representation of women. The opposition between male and female may be articulated with that between public and private; but this does not mean that the former opposition need be completely displaced by the latter in the interpretation of the plays. This may seem like a move back towards a simplistic and over-literal kind of reading. I find support for it, though, in the ode which the chorus sing immediately after Medea's first monologue, and which is directly about the representation of women.

In this monologue (364–409) Medea has for the first time revealed a plan to kill Creon, his daughter, and (at this point) Jason, using the heroic language to which I have referred. This heroic mode is, however, undercut even here, most obviously at the end of the speech. After asserting her determination not to be her enemies' laughing-stock, Medea closes the speech by saying that women are, after all

ἐς μὲν ἐσθλ' ἀμηχανώταται,
κακῶν δὲ πάντων τέκτονες σοφώταται.

(408–9)

'incapable of doing good, but the cleverest contrivers of all evil'. Immediately after this comes an ode in which the chorus seem, at first sight, to be singing the praises of women. They begin with a reference to general moral and religious disorder, which they appear, in the following line, to attribute to the faithlessness of, above all, men:

ἀνδράσι μὲν δόλιαι βουλαί ...

(412)

'It is men who make deceitful plans. ...' They conclude the strophe by saying that women's reputation and honour will now be enhanced.

As a response to Medea's speech, this is strange; and the ode is in fact in a deeply paradoxical relationship with what went before it. It is Medea who has just exposed her 'deceitful plans', and whose mastery of strategy has been revealed in the exchange with Creon. In view of this, and of her own closing comment, the improvement in women's standing which the chorus are projecting seems a dubious honour: it is based on a judgement which Medea has shown to apply at least equally to herself, and at best it can only consist of women not being as bad as men.

The antistrophe builds on the paradoxical nature of this praise by pointing to the inadequacy of the terms being used, even by the chorus themselves – and they are, we remember, a chorus of women played by male actors and orchestrated by a male poet. Essentially the chorus say that the true history of women is as yet unspoken. If women had been granted the power of divine song, they could have countered that of men, and the story would be a different one:

μακρὸς δ᾽αἰὼν ἔχει
πολλὰ μὲν ἁμετέραν ἀνδρῶν τε μοῖραν εἰπεῖν

(429–30)

'The passing of time has much to tell of our lot and of men's.' Knox, writing about this ode, declares that it is unnecessary for the chorus to use the future tense in predicting a change of direction in legends about women; because, he says, 'Euripides' play itself is the change of direction'.[23] I should prefer to see this change as dependent on a more complex syntactical alteration. The appropriate mode both for this ode and for the play is that of an unfulfilled condition – in which one does not use the future, or even the present, tense. The possibility of true speech by and about women remains, like the domain from which Medea emerged, off-stage.

NOTES

1   See, for example, Michelle Rosaldo, 'A theoretical overview', in M. Z. Rosaldo and L. Lamphere (eds), *Woman, Culture and Society* (Stanford, 1974) pp. 17–42.
2   S. C. Humphreys, *The Family, Women and Death* (London, 1983).
3   J. Gould, 'Dramatic character and "human intelligibility" in Greek tragedy', *PCPhS* ns 24 (1978) pp. 43–67, and 'Law, custom and myth: aspects of the social position of women in classical Athens', *JHS* 100 (1980) pp. 38–59. There is also an interesting section on the private-public dichotomy in Helene Foley's essay 'The conception of women in Athenian drama', in H. Foley (ed.), *Reflections of Women in Antiquity* (New York, London, and Paris, 1981).
4   Humphreys (n. 2), p. 72.
5   Gould, 'Dramatic character' (n. 3), p. 64 n. 21.
6   The importance of this moment is also stressed in a suggestive essay by K. Reckford, 'Medea's first exit', *TAPA* 99 (1968) pp. 329–59.
7   This point is made by A. P. Burnett, who refers to other 'centrifugal' plays – *Ajax, Hecuba, Trojan Women* – but points out that Medea's household is in an even more unstable position (A. P. Burnett, *'Medea* and the tragedy of revenge', *CPh* 68 (1973), pp. 1–24). It was also nicely made in a recent adaptation by Barney Simon

of *Medea* at the Riverside Studios, London, in which Medea's 'home' was a makeshift canvas tent.

8   Vernant's discussions of the organization of space in ancient Greece are relevant here: see particularly 'Hestia-Hermes', in which he explores the paradoxes inherent in the position of a wife, who comes into the *oikos* from outside but is also at its centre (ch. 5 in J.-P. Vernant, *Myth and Thought among the Greeks*, London, 1983), and 'Space and political organisation in ancient Greece' (ch. 8 in the same volume).

9   A brief account of both stages of a marriage is given in R. Flacelière, *Daily Life in Greece at the Time of Pericles* (London, 1965), pp. 60–6.

10 Humphreys (n. 2), p. 1.

11 Humphreys comments on this speech as a whole that it represents a man's view of 'what it would feel like ... to be the kind of wife Athenian men wanted' (73), and she regards this as symptomatic of the limitations of 'even the most strenuous attempt ... to see life from a woman's point of view' on the part of the dramatists. Sophocles, however, puts into the mouth of Procne, in his *Tereus*, a far more orthodox version of this transaction: 'When we are girls, our life in our father's house is sweetest.... But when we come to years of discretion, we are thrust out and sold in marriage (διεμπολώμεθα) far away from our ancestral gods and from our parents. ...' (Radt 583, tr. Jebb). This suggests that more is involved in Euripides' account than a simple failure of imagination.

12 Line 300 – τῶν δ'αὖ δοκούντων εἰδέναι τι ποικίλον ('Those who have a reputation for subtlety ...') – bears some resemblance – perhaps fortuitous – to parts of the passage in which Plato, fifty years later, represents Socrates as describing the dangers which arose from his reputation: see *Apology* 20d–23c, esp. 21b–22.

13 This association is most clearly described by Michael Shaw, 'The female intruder: women in fifth-century drama', *CPh* 70 (1975), pp. 255–66. On the different types of relationship in general, and contemporary thinking about them, see Reckford (n. 6), pp. 340–2, Humphreys (n. 2), p. 74 and *passim*, Vernant (n. 8), p. 227 and *passim*.

14 J. Gould, 'Hiketeia', *JHS* 93 (1973) pp. 74–103, esp. 85–6.

15 Another striking echo occurs at l. 583: compare Medea's description of Jason as οὐκ ἄγαν σοφός ('not so very clever') with her earlier εἰμὶ δ' οὐκ ἄγαν σοφή (305) ('I am not so very clever').

16 See, for example, 523–5, 546, 585.

17 'The Greek is surrounded, as it were, by a series of concentric fortifications against the outside world ... the innermost fortress includes his nearest kin and friends, the outermost wall embraces all Hellenes': F.R. Earp, *The Way of the Greeks* (London, 1929), p. 32. See also K. J. Dover, *Greek Popular Morality in the Time of Plato and Aristotle* (Oxford, 1974), esp. pp. 273ff.

18 W. R. Connor, *The New Politicians of Fifth Century Athens* (Princeton, NJ, 1971), esp. pp. 30ff.

19 B. M. W. Knox, 'The *Medea* of Euripides', *YCS* 25 (1977), pp. 193–225.
20 See esp. Knox (n. 19), p. 211.
21 R. Padel, 'Women: model for possession by Greek demons', in A. Cameron and A. Kuhrt (eds), *Images of Women in Antiquity* (London, 1983), pp. 3–19.
22 See the works cited in notes 13 and 18, and esp. Connor, p. 53.
23 Knox (n. 19), p. 224. On the place of the idealizing odes in the play, see Reckford (n. 6), pp. 342–6, and P. Pucci, *The Violence of Pity in Euripides' 'Medea'* (Ithaca, NY, and London, 1980), esp. pp. 116ff. The influence of Pucci's reading of the play on my argument will be apparent.

3

EURIPIDES
THE MISOGYNIST?[1]

Jennifer March

We begin by going back in time almost two and a half thousand
years: to 411 BC, and the first performance of Aristophanes'
Thesmophoriazusai. The scene: a street in Athens. The characters:
the poet Euripides is speaking to an elderly male relative. 'I
fear', says Euripides, 'that this day will be my last. The women
have been plotting against me. And today, at the Thesmophoria,
they're going to discuss my liquidation.'

'But why on earth ...?' responds the relative.

'They say I slander them in my tragedies.'

'Well, so you do. Serve you right if they did get you!'[2]

And so the Athenian women's supposed desire for revenge on
Euripides, for all his slanders of them, sets in motion the events
of one of Aristophanes' funniest comedies. But this play was to
become, of course, one of the pieces of contemporary 'evidence'
that led to Euripides' later reputation for misogyny.[3]

But can we in fact say, on the evidence of his extant plays, that
Euripides really was a misogynist? The purpose of this chapter is
to answer that question, and let me say at once that my final
answer will be a decided negative: Euripides was certainly not a
misogynist. But that is to anticipate the end before time.

There are, of course, various ways in which one might tackle
this question, so first let me mention three possible approaches
which I have chosen not to make. One could simply pick out
passages which demonstrate Euripides' extreme sympathy with
women's lot in life, and let them speak for themselves; passages
like the famous speech by Medea that begins, 'Of all the
creatures that have breath and intelligence, we women are the
most wretched', and ends, 'Men talk of how our life is passed
indoors, far from all dangers, while they go out and fight. Fools!

I would rather stand in the ranks of battle three times than bear a child once';[4] or indeed a whole play – the *Trojan Women* – which shows an intense sympathy for the fate of women in a war-torn, defeated city.[5] Or one could pick out some of Euripides' fine women, his noble, courageous, self-sacrificing women, and say that no man who puts such women on the stage could possibly be a misogynist: women like Alkestis, Makaria in the *Herakleidai*, Iphigeneia in the *Iphigeneia at Aulis*.[6] Or one could stress Euripides' acute knowledge and understanding of female psychology.[7] Each of these direct approaches could without doubt give a certain insight into Euripides' attitude to women. But I have chosen to take a rather less obvious approach: one that centres on Euripides' manipulation of myth and on the innovations that he makes in translating a traditional story into acted drama; one that investigates what these innovations mean for his play as a whole and for his women characters in particular. We shall concentrate on plays where Euripides puts bad women on the stage; women who do wicked deeds; the kind of females who actually earned him his reputation for woman-slander and misogyny; and try to demonstrate that here we have no misogyny at all, but in fact quite the opposite, with Euripides, by the very manner in which he portrays their 'wickedness', teaching compassion and an ultimate forgiveness for these women, and showing an intense pity for the ways in which mankind all too often is brought to grief.[8]

So let us begin by looking briefly at another scene from Aristophanes, this time from the *Frogs*, where we hear more about Euripides and his habit of putting bad women on the stage. This is part of the *agon* between Aischylos and Euripides in Hades, where another important theme is raised, the theme of the poet as teacher. Aischylos accuses Euripides not only of putting wicked women on the stage, but also of utterly failing in the poet's crucial duty of being a teacher to his audience. Aischylos is speaking:

> From the very earliest times the really great poet has been the one who had a useful lesson to teach ... I depicted men of valour, lion-hearted characters like Patroklos and Teukros, encouraging the audience to identify with these heroes when the call to battle came. *I* didn't clutter up *my* stage with harlots like Phaidra or Stheneboia. No-one can say I have ever put an erotic female into any play of mine.

'How could you?' responds Euripides, 'You've never even met one'; and then, later, 'And did I invent the story of Phaidra?'

'No', says Aischylos, 'No, such things do happen. But the poet should keep quiet about them, not put them on the stage for everyone to copy. Schoolboys have a master to teach them, grown-ups have the poets. We have a duty to see that we teach them what is right and proper.'[9]

Now sadly Euripides' *Stheneboia* and first *Hippolytos*[10] are lost to us except for a few fragments, just about enough for us to work out their plots.[11] Other plays with so-called wicked women are also lost, plays like the *Cretan Women* with Aerope, whom, Apollonios tells us, 'Euripides introduced prostituting herself'.[12] So we cannot use these plays as evidence one way or the other. The plays that I intend to use are three extant tragedies, where Euripides puts on the stage three women who cause great harm: Medea, who murders her children (431 BC); Phaidra, in the second *Hippolytos* (428 BC), who is in love with her stepson, and brings him to his death with her false accusations against him; and Agaue, in the *Bakchai*, written just before Euripides' death in 406, who tears her own son Pentheus to pieces. All of these are women whom the Aischylos of the *Frogs* would certainly have condemned, and ones who would have outraged the Athenian women in *Thesmophoriazusai*.[13]

Now, these three plays deal with stories taken from the traditional body of myth that had been passed down the generations; and in their *general* outline (I stress the *general*) would have been familiar to Euripides' audience: Medea, who has helped Jason to win the Golden Fleece, and then later avenges herself on him when he turns away from her to another woman;[14] Phaidra, who loves her stepson Hippolytos, and, when he will have nothing to do with her, makes lying accusations against him to Theseus which bring him to his death;[15] Pentheus, who refuses to accept the worship of Dionysos in Thebes, and is torn to pieces by the maenads.[16] But in each case Euripides adapts his traditional material so as to achieve the dramatic effect that he wants to create: he makes changes to the myths; he adds or subtracts elements for his own particular dramatic purposes. And it is, I suggest, these innovations to what we might call the 'given' myth, the places where he deliberately steps aside from the usual version and creates his own, which can throw most light on Euripides' unique tragic vision in any given play, and therefore on his own attitudes – attitudes to many things, including, of course, women. So we shall look at each of these three plays with three questions in mind. What actually were Euripides' innovations here? What do they mean for the play as a whole? And what do they specifically tell us about his women characters? Let us start with the *Medea*.

First of all, Euripides has chosen a novel subject for a play. Other excerpts from the legend of Jason and Medea were familiar subjects for tragedies. Jason, with the help of Medea, wins the Golden Fleece at Kolchis – Sophokles wrote the *Women of Kolchis* on this theme.[17] They flee back to Iolchos, Jason's home, and there Medea kills old king Pelias with her deceitful promise to rejuvenate him that results in his death – Euripides produced the *Peliades* (one of his first plays, of 455) which contained this theme, and probably Sophokles' *Rhizotomoi*, the *Rootcutters*, also told this story.[18] The events at Athens, where Medea was living with king Aigeus and tried unsuccessfully to engineer the death of his son Theseus, were dramatized in plays by both Sophokles and Euripides, both called the *Aigeus*.[19] But only Euripides, it seems, produced a play with the particular events at Corinth detailed in his *Medea*.[20]

Here Medea and Jason have fled to Corinth after the murder of old Pelias. But, as the Nurse says in the prologue, νῦν δ' ἐχθρὰ πάντα, καὶ νοσεῖ τὰ φίλτατα (16), 'now all is hostility, and love has turned sick'; now Jason has deserted Medea and has married the daughter of Kreon, king of Corinth. The play centres on Medea's revenge: savage with jealousy and rage she at first plans to murder all three people who have wronged her – Jason, Kreon and the new bride (366–94). But the final revenge is more horrible: she certainly kills Kreon and his daughter, but also her own children by Jason, and she leaves Jason himself alive, to grow old, childless, and thus to suffer for ever the grievous results of his betrayal of her. Now, Euripides' innovation here was Medea's deliberate murder of her children. In earlier versions of the legend, the children had died, but for other reasons. In one version by Eumelos, Medea unintentionally killed them while trying to make them immortal.[21] In another, by Kreophilos, Medea killed Kreon, then left her children in the temple of Hera, where the Corinthians killed them and then spread the rumour that Medea was the murderer.[22] But Euripides made Medea herself choose to murder them as part – indeed the most hurtful part – of her revenge against Jason. This is new;[23] and it perhaps sounds at first as if this might tell in favour of the idea that Euripides was hostile to women. But in fact it turns out to have quite the opposite result, because of the way in which Euripides treats his material.

This innovation has two very powerful dramatic effects: first, on the structure of the play, which is built around the one dominant theme of parent/child relationships; and, second, on Euripides' portrayal of his principal character, Medea. I shall deal with the more formal point first, that of the play's structure.

Children, and parents' love of children, lie at the heart of the whole dramatic action, and therefore also behind all that Medea feels and does in this play. The tragic action itself is first set in motion by Jason's desire to marry again, to have a Greek wife and to father legitimate children (547–67). Then, because of Medea's jealous and angry response to his new marriage, Kreon puts on her and her sons a sentence of exile: because he fears her, for his daughter's sake (282–3):

δέδοικά σ'–οὐδὲν δεῖ παραμπίσχειν λόγους–
μή μοί τι δράσῃς παῖδ' ἀνήκεστον κακόν.

Kreon says to Medea, 'I fear you – there's no need to wrap up what I say – I fear you may do my child some incurable harm.' This turns out to be, of course, a very justified fear. He tries to stand resolute against Medea's pleas to stay, but in so doing shows her the exact policy needed to get her own way (326–9):

Μη. ἀλλ' ἐξελᾷς με κοὐδὲν αἰδέσῃ λιτάς;
Κρ. φιλῶ γὰρ οὐ σὲ μᾶλλον ἢ δόμους ἐμούς.
Μη. ὦ πατρίς, ὥς σου καρτα νῦν μνείαν ἔχω.
Κρ. πλὴν γὰρ τέκνων ἔμοιγε φίλτατον πολύ.

'Then will you drive me out and have no heed of my prayers?' cries Medea.

'Yes, for I love my family more than you.'

'My country', she responds, 'How my thoughts turn to you now.'

And 'Yes', says Kreon, 'That is much the dearest thing to me – except for my children.'

So he shows Medea his one weak spot, his love for his children, and Medea attacks it, and appeals to him as a father. 'Pity my sons', she begs (I paraphrase); 'Let me stay one more day to give thought to their future. You're a father; you know what it's like.' And Kreon gives in, of course, and grants her just one more day. But this one day will be enough to kill the daughter he loves so much, and Kreon himself too, because he loves her. His daughter dies in agony in the poisoned robe and crown that Medea sends her (and notice that here again is the child motif: it is the children who carry the gifts to the princess, the children who are the instruments of vengeance here too). And Kreon himself dies when he holds his dead daughter in his arms and grieves over her. 'Alas, let me die with you, child', he cries (1210); and die he does, because the poison from the robe has now contaminated him too. In fact it is possible that Euripides himself invented the robe as a tool of death, since there is evidence only of the crown in earlier tradition.[24] Perhaps he particularly wanted the daughter to be the means of death for the father, again to stress his dominant theme.

Even after these deaths, there still remains the climax of the revenge action: Medea's murder of the children themselves. I shall return to this when I consider Euripides' portrayal of Medea. But another occurrence of the child motif has given Medea the idea for their deaths. In the central scene of the play, king Aigeus of Athens calls at Corinth on his way back from the Delphic oracle, where he was looking for advice: on childlessness. He explains this to Medea (669–70):

Αι. παίδων ἐρευνῶν σπέρμ' ὅπως γένοιτό μοι.
Μη. πρὸς θεῶν ἄπαις γὰρ δεῦρ' ἀεὶ τείνεις βίον;

'I went to enquire how children might be born to me', says Aigeus; and Medea's surprised retort is: 'Ah god, all these years and still childless!'[25] This, reminding her of what childlessness means to a man, not only gives her an added motive for murdering the new bride, but also the idea of killing her own sons by Jason, as we see from her change of plan once she is alone (803–6): Jason's bride will die, as planned earlier, but now Jason's sons also, and Jason, instead of being killed (42, 163f., 374f.), will be left alive to suffer their loss. Thus her revenge will mean that Jason neither will see his sons by Medea alive for the future, nor will he father more children on his new bride, and thus will pass childless to a lonely and sorrowful old age.[26]

Two final points tie in with this theme of parent/child relationships. Medea promises to cure Aigeus of his childlessness if only he will give her a home in Athens, and he agrees (709ff.). So because of his desire for children she gains a safe refuge after her murders. And at the end of the play she escapes to Athens on the chariot of the Sun, the chariot of Helios, her father's father (1320–2).[27]

This, then, is the effect that Euripides' innovative infanticide has on the structure of his play, with all the forward movement of the drama and the motives for Medea's subsequent actions being provided by different aspects of the parent/child theme;[28] and we now move to its effect on the character of Medea herself, in Euripides' new interpretation of the myth. He has changed Jason too, of course. In earlier legend Jason was the great hero who won the Golden Fleece;[29] here he is an ordinary middle-aged man, with ambitions for respectability and a concern for civilized values. And this reduction of a hero to ordinary human size is, of course, typical of Euripides. He does it with other great figures from legend: for instance with Oidipous in the *Phoinissai*, with Klytaimnestra in the *Elektra*, with Elektra and Orestes themselves. In Aischylos and Sophokles these all have great heroic stature. But in Euripides they are very ordinary human beings; and Jason too.

Now Medea also has been made intensely human (though far from ordinary), but in a quite different way. In legend she was a barbarian witch. But here Euripides has been at pains to omit any hint of magical powers in his Medea. In the usual legend she killed old Pelias using some kind of magic; in this play there is no reference to that. In lines 9–11 we hear that she 'persuaded the daughters of Pelias to kill their father', κτανεῖν πείσασα Πελιάδας κορας πατέρα, before she came to live in Corinth with her husband and children; and in lines 486–7 that 'she killed Pelias, the most painful of deaths, at the hands of his own children, and ruined his whole house' (which is, incidentally, another occurrence of the child theme):

Πελίαν τ' ἀπέκτειν', ὥσπερ ἄλγιστον θανεῖν,
παίδων ὑπ' αὐτοῦ, πάντα τ' ἐξεῖλον δόμον.

This is all, with no mention of magic. Medea is clever, certainly, as she herself admits – σοφή – a woman of great intellectual capacity (294ff., 539). And she has φάρμακα, drugs or poisons; so she has destructive powers with these φάρμακα, as any woman might have. But she seems to have no powers of creative magic,

38

else she would not be in the state she is, with a husband lost and a sentence of exile on her head. However, these destructive powers are not witchcraft.[30] Consider Kreousa's poison in the *Ion*, or Deianeira's poisoned robe in the *Trachiniai*: neither of these women is ever thought of as a witch, and neither is Medea a witch in Euripides, in this play at least – just very human.[31]

So, to recap briefly: we have seen how Euripides chooses a novel setting and a novel subject for his play, in Corinth, with Jason's betrayal and Medea's revenge. We have seen how his invention of Medea's deliberate infanticide as the crux of that revenge has had its effect on the dramatic structure, with the whole dramatic action revolving around children and child/parent relationships. The climax of this dramatic action must be the innovative infanticide itself; and this new murder is committed by a new and very human Medea. Thus we would expect a consideration of this new Medea, in relation to the child-killing, to throw most light on Euripides' intentions and attitudes in this play; and this we shall find, if we look at the infanticide from conception to completion, and beyond.

As we have seen, the idea for Medea's final revenge comes to her in her scene with Aigeus. She will pretend complete reconciliation with Jason, a complete change of heart; 'I shall speak soft words to him', she says (776). She, after all, will be content to go into exile. But she would like her sons to take gifts to the princess, to beg that they, at least, may stay in Corinth (780ff.). Then, having made sure by means of the poisoned robe and crown that the bride will bear no children to Jason, she will kill her own sons (791–6):

ᾤμωξα δ' οἷον ἔργον ἔστ' ἐργαστέον
τοὐντεῦθεν ἡμῖν· τέκνα γὰρ κατακτενῶ
τἄμ'· οὔτις ἔστιν ὅστις ἐξαιρήσεται·
δόμον τε πάντα συγχέασ' Ἰάσονος
ἔξειμι γαίας, φιλτάτων παίδων φόνον
φεύγουσα καὶ τλᾶσ' ἔργον ἀνοσιώτατον.

'I grieve at the deed I must do next. I shall kill my children. No one will take them from me. When I have brought down Jason's whole house I shall leave the country, flying from my dearest children's blood and burdened with this foulest sin.'

However painful this will be to Medea, the children must be

killed, because only by their deaths can she hurt Jason to the utmost (817):

οὕτω γὰρ ἂν μάλιστα δηχθείη πόσις.

'This is the way to deal my husband the deepest wound.'[32]

Jason is completely taken in by her pretences. He praises Medea for her change of heart, greets his sons, prays for their future lives, and speaks with pride of their growing into fine young men (916ff.). At this Medea weeps, and the audience understands her sorrow and the irony of her reply when Jason asks why and she answers, 'When you prayed that they might live, sorrow came over me in case this might not happen' (930–1). Nevertheless, despite these regrets, she persuades Jason to agree that the gifts be taken to his bride, and she sends her children off with them with no more apparent qualms: the qualms come later, when the Paidagogos returns with the children, saying that the princess has taken the gifts with delight. Now there is no going back, for the gifts must kill her. But must the children after all be killed as well?

At first it would seem so. Medea weeps at the Paidagogos' news, and he tries to comfort her: 'Take heart', he urges, 'Some day your children will bring you home.' 'Before then I shall bring others home', she grieves; and then, pathetically, 'Go indoors and get ready for the children their everyday needs.'

But then, with Medea alone on the stage with her sons, there follows her great monologue, with her anger at Jason, her hurt pride, her longing for a revenge as extreme as possible, her fear of being laughed at by her enemies, all battling with her love for her children and her rational knowledge that by killing them will come the greatest possible unhappiness for herself too. Consider what effect this speech, with all Medea's anguished indecision, would have had on that very first audience, who would not have known whether or not the children were to be killed at the end of it: they would have been on the edge of their seats.

Medea begins by grieving that now she must be parted from her sons: she must go into exile, while they, unknowing, are to die. All for nothing she bore them and brought them up, and they will never now look after her when she is old. These are the kind of things so often said in tragedy by a mother over a dead child.[33] 'What shall I do?' she cries. And then (I paraphrase), 'No, I can't do it; goodbye to my plans, χαιρέτω βουλεύματα. I shall go, and take my children with me. Why should I hurt their father by hurting myself twice as much – δὶς τόσα κακά?' And again, 'χαιρέτω βουλεύματα'.

But then – 'What am I saying? Do I want to be laughed at by my enemies? I have to do it! How could I even entertain such soft thoughts!

'But no, my θυμός, don't do it, spare their lives.[34] Only if they live will they bring me happiness ...

'And yet I have no choice. Now the princess is already dying by her gifts. I *must* kill my sons before my enemies do so. I have to travel the cruellest of roads, and send these children on a crueller road still.'

Then we have the tearing anguish of her farewell to her children (1071–5);[35] and then, 'Go away, go away, I can't bear it any more'; and finally (1078–80):

καὶ μανθάνω μὲν οἷα δρᾶν μέλλω κακά,
θυμὸς δὲ κρείσσων τῶν ἐμῶν βουλευμάτων,
ὅσπερ μεγίστων αἴτιος κακῶν βροτοῖς.

'I know the horror of what I am going to do, but my passion, my θυμός, is too strong for my reason; and this is to blame for man's worst evils.'

This, as well as being surely one of the most moving speeches in Greek tragedy, is also essential both to the characterization of Medea, and to the meaning of the play. Here we have the two sides of Medea's nature battling with one another: her all-consuming desire for revenge in conflict with the clear knowledge that by killing her children she will hurt herself the most; her passionate, emotional side at war with her rational, logical intelligence.[36] In a sense, of course, the infanticide will come about because of the coupling, the uniting, of these two divided aspects of her nature: the infanticide is really her *passionate* desire for revenge carried to its *logical* conclusion, that which will hurt Jason most. The two aspects come together. But here Euripides draws with intense compassion the agonized conflict within this human being who, faced with this tragic choice, suffers such tortured self-division, such mortal tearing-apart. Without this insight into Medea's nature, without this genuine conflict, the play would become not tragedy but simply melodrama; and in fact the meaning of the play will lie in the results of Medea's final tragic choice.

41

The children go indoors, and the messenger brings the news of the horrible deaths of the princess and Kreon; the point of no return has been reached, and so Medea must kill her sons, and put her terrible decision into practice. These are her last words before she goes in to carry out her dreadful deed, and I quote them in full, since they paint so movingly Medea's resignation and grief at her own choice of action (1236–50):

φίλαι, δέδοκται τοὔργον ὡς τάχιστά μοι
παῖδας κτανούσῃ τῆσδ' ἀφορμᾶσθαι χθονὸς
καὶ μὴ σχολὴν ἄγουσαν ἐκδοῦναι τέκνα
ἄλλῃ φονεῦσαι δυσμενεστέρᾳ χερί.
πάντως σφ' ἀνάγκη κατθανεῖν· ἐπεὶ δὲ χρή,
ἡμεῖς κτενοῦμεν, οἵπερ ἐξεφύσαμεν.
ἀλλ' εἶ' ὁπλίζου, καρδία. τί μέλλομεν
τὰ δεινὰ κἀναγκαῖα μὴ πράσσειν κακά;
ἄγ', ὦ τάλαινα χεὶρ ἐμή, λαβὲ ξίφος,
λάβ', ἕρπε πρὸς βαλβῖδα λυπηρὰν βίου,
καὶ μὴ κακισθῇς μηδ' ἀναμνησθῇς τέκνων,
ὡς φίλταθ', ὡς ἔτικτες· ἀλλὰ τήνδε γε
λαθοῦ βραχεῖαν ἡμέραν παίδων σέθεν,
κἄπειτα θρήνει· καὶ γὰρ εἰ κτενεῖς σφ', ὅμως
φίλοι γ' ἔφυσαν—δυστυχὴς δ' ἐγὼ γυνή.

'Friends, my course of action is clear: as quickly as possible to kill the children and then leave this land, not delay and give my children over to be killed by another and less loving hand. They are bound to die in any case, and since they must, then I shall kill them, I who bore them.[37] Come, my heart, steel yourself. Why do I hesitate before this fearful yet necessary evil? Come, wretched hand, take the sword, take it; go forward to the point where life turns into grief.[38] No cowardice, no memories of your children, how dear they were, how your body gave them birth. For one short day forget your children – and then weep. For though you kill them, yet they were dear – and I wretched.'

There is no need to doubt Medea's sincerity here, her genuine grief. But in fact after committing this murder she becomes so changed, so hardened, that one doubts if she will ever weep again. For these are her last words in the play spoken on the human plane: the next time we see her, in her final bitter scene with Jason, she is in the chariot sent by Helios, her grandfather, high up in the air, on the divine plane where only the gods

42

appear. And in fact she has become something more than human. She appears where the gods appear; she speaks with a god's tone; she acts as the gods act, giving judgement, prophesying the future, announcing the foundation of a religious ritual.[39] It seems as if this act of infanticide itself has transformed her, translated her; she has forfeited her humanity by her tragic choice. In fact she has become utterly inhuman in her gloating over Jason's loss ('You don't know yet what grief is: wait until you're *old*' (1396)), and for the first time there is pity for him as well, who in his human grief and powerlessness acquires a certain stature, a tragic dignity which he did not have before.

Euripides has created this new Medea who chooses to kill her own children. He shows us with painful insight and utterly without condemnation the mind of the woman who has the ability to do such a murderous deed: the torment before the final decision, the ultimate grief, and, here in the final scene, the inevitable results. Medea is now finally untouched, untouchable by human hands (1320) and by human emotions; she has by her tragic decision destroyed herself, and has truly become as inhuman as the rock or the wave of the sea to which the Nurse likened her in the prologue (28–9).

Jean Anouilh, in his 1946 version of the *Medea*, has Medea commit suicide in the flames of her children's funeral pyre after she has murdered them. Perhaps after such an act as this deliberate killing of her own children, which is the culmination of a mortal battle within Medea herself between passion and reason, the only two possible results can be death, as in Anouilh, or the kind of translation that Euripides gives us, with Medea transformed into something other than human. Or perhaps these two possible ends are in fact one and the same. As Schlesinger puts it: 'The granddaughter of Helios may stand in triumph on her dragon chariot, but Medea the woman is dead.'[40]

We now move to Phaidra in the *Hippolytos*. The essentials of this legend are always the same: Phaidra, wife of Theseus, falls in love with her stepson, Hippolytos; when he rebuffs her she accuses him to Theseus of rape or attempted rape; Theseus prays to Poseidon to kill him, and he is killed; Phaidra herself commits suicide.[41]

This is a common theme in legend: the married woman who

falls in love with a young man, tries to seduce him, and accuses him to her husband when he rejects her advances. We find it in the stories of Peleus and the wife of Akastos,[42] Bellerophon and Stheneboia,[43] and, in the Old Testament, of Joseph and the wife of Potiphar;[44] and there is no doubt that originally the legend of Hippolytos was in the same simple form.[45]

But around this traditional framework the playwrights of the fifth century BC made three very different tragedies. Euripides' second *Hippolytos*, produced in 428 BC and the only one of the three extant, was probably the last to be written, and certainly the most novel of the three in its treatment of the legend. In his first *Hippolytos* he apparently adopted the usual legend without change: Phaidra made a deliberate attempt to seduce Hippolytos, which he rebuffed, and she, in anger and self-defence, accused him to Theseus; Theseus cursed him, Poseidon sent the bull and he was killed; Phaidra's treachery was exposed, and she killed herself.[46] The play was a failure, and it may well be that Sophokles produced his *Phaidra* sometime later, had better success with it, and it was this that moved Euripides to write his second *Hippolytos*.[47]

Sophokles, in his *Phaidra*, kept to the basic lines of the story too, but made Phaidra less overtly shameless: 'We may assume that Phaidra had the virtue necessary for tragic stature', says Barrett (p. 12). Certainly it seems that Phaidra had some justification for her love, since Theseus had been gone some years and was believed dead, so her love was not in theory adulterous; and at the end of the play she apparently committed suicide not on discovery, but after confession and remorse.[48] So here there was the same story, but with a different slant on Phaidra.

Euripides' second *Hippolytos* is quite different; and he won one of his rare first prizes with it,[49] so the Athenians must have appreciated his changes. The fundamental change lies in Phaidra's character. She is now a virtuous woman, compelled into love by a powerful and pitiless Aphrodite to avenge Hippolytos' rejection of all this goddess stands for,[50] who strives to the utmost to conquer her love in silence. Aphrodite tells us in the prologue of her divinely inspired passion for Hippolytos (26–8):

... πατρὸς [sc. Theseus] εὐγενὴς δάμαρ
ἰδοῦσα Φαίδρα καρδίαν κατέσχετο
ἔρωτι δεινῷ τοῖς ἐμοῖς βουλεύμασιν.

'His father's noble [51] wife, Phaidra, saw him and was seized in her heart by a terrible love at my instigation.'[52] But Phaidra is now nobly and silently resisting the goddess's onslaught (38–40):

ἐνταῦθα δὴ στένουσα κἀκπεπληγμένη
κέντροις ἔρωτος ἡ τάλαιν᾽ ἀπόλλυται
σιγῇ, ξύνοιδε δ᾽ οὔτις οἰκετῶν νόσον.

'Now, groaning and driven to frenzy by the goads of love, the poor woman is dying, and in silence. None of the household knows the secret of her disease.' And Phaidra will indeed die of it (47–8):

ἡ δ᾽ εὐκλεὴς μὲν ἀλλ᾽ ὅμως ἀπόλλυται
Φαίδρα.

'Phaidra, although she is honourable, nevertheless will die.'

Moreover Aphrodite as prologue speaker is quite possibly an innovation too, since the audience needs to know of Phaidra's love, and no one knows but Phaidra herself, and she cannot and will not tell them; so it must be a god who speaks. Notice that to Aphrodite Phaidra is 'poor woman' – ἡ τάλαινα (39) – but she will use Phaidra without compunction as the tool for her revenge on Hippolytos.

Phaidra too explains why she is striving to keep silence, when the Nurse tries to worm the secret out of her (331):

ἐκ τῶν γὰρ αἰσχρῶν ἐσθλὰ μηχανώμεθα.

'I am contriving good out of my shameful plight.' So although she cannot overcome her passion, she will not speak of it.

Eventually she is too weak to keep it to herself; her resolution fails,[53] and the Nurse finds out what her sickness really is. Now, with the truth known, Phaidra is free to speak of what she has suffered, and we hear of the measures she has taken to deal with her plight. First of all she resolved to keep silence (393–4), hoping, presumably, that her passion would simply die down. When this did not work, she tried to overcome it with self-control (398–9). This too failed, so she has now decided that the best, the only, way out is to die (400–2). She could never put a bold face on adultery (413–14):

μισῶ δὲ καὶ τὰς σώφρονας μὲν ἐν λόγοις
λάθρᾳ δὲ τόλμας οὐ καλὰς κεκτημένας.

'I hate those women who are chaste in word, but who have secretly acquired dishonourable ideas of daring', she says, perhaps referring to her *alter ego*, Phaidra the willing adulteress of the first *Hippolytos*.[54] No, she must die; and again we see her concern for honour and her care for her family (419–21):

ἡμᾶς γὰρ αὐτὸ τοῦτ' ἀποκτείνει, φίλαι,
ὡς μήποτ' ἄνδρα τὸν ἐμὸν αἰσχύνασ' ἁλῶ,
μὴ παῖδας οὓς ἔτικτον.

'This very thing is killing me, friends, since I will never bring dishonour on my husband, nor on the children whom I bore.'

But she is not allowed to die by fading away nobly and in silence, since (and here is another innovation) the Nurse, seeking to save the life of the mistress she loves, approaches Hippolytos on Phaidra's behalf, despite Phaidra's pleas for her to do nothing of the sort.[55] Hippolytos responds to the Nurse's well-meant overtures with extreme and bitter rage against women in general and Phaidra in particular; and now Phaidra knows that her death must come about even more swiftly than she had planned (599–600):

οὐκ οἶδα πλὴν ἕν, κατθανεῖν ὅσον τάχος,
τῶν νῦν παρόντων πημάτων ἄκος μόνον.

'I know nothing except that a death as quick as possible is the only cure for what I'm suffering now.' But she can no longer die with honour as she had sought to do (687–8), since she believes that Hippolytos will speak of what has happened, so now a new plan is called for; and thus (yet another change) Euripides has his Phaidra commit suicide immediately after Hippolytos' bitter and unjust (again, unjust for the first time) accusations of her, and with the new motive of keeping herself and her children free from dishonour (716–18):

εὕρημα δή τι τῆσδε συμφορᾶς ἔχω
ὥστ' εὐκλεᾶ μὲν παισὶ προσθεῖναι βίον
αὐτή τ' ὄνασθαι πρὸς τὰ νῦν πεπτωκότα.

'I have thought of something for this trouble of mine', says Phaidra, 'so as to provide an honourable life for my sons, and myself gain some benefit now that things have fallen out as they have.' So in a letter to Theseus, out of anger and shame, she accuses Hippolytos of rape as her one means of defending her children against a disgrace which they do not deserve, and in so doing salvages what she can of her marriage.[56] Then she hangs herself from the rafters, despite the fact that they have witnessed no guilt of hers (cf. 415–18). Theseus will in due course learn of the falsity of her letter and the truth of what has happened, but Artemis will make clear to him that Phaidra was in fact honourable and that it was the Nurse who acted on her behalf (1298–1301, 1304–5):

ἀλλ' εἰς τόδ' ἦλθον, παιδὸς ἐκδεῖξαι φρένα
τοῦ σοῦ δικαίαν, ὡς ὑπ' εὐκλείας θάνῃ,
καὶ σῆς γυναικὸς οἶστρον ἢ τρόπον τινὰ
γενναιότητα ...
γνώμῃ δὲ νικᾶν τὴν Κύπριν πειρωμένη
τροφοῦ διώλετ' οὐχ ἑκοῦσα μηχαναῖς.

'I came here for this purpose, to reveal both your son's righteous heart, so that he may die in honour, and your wife's wild passion – or in a way nobility .... . She strove to overcome Kypris with her reason, but schemes plotted against her will by her Nurse destroyed her.' As Barrett notes: 'Those who believe that Phaidra consented in the end to the Nurse's scheme are doing so in the face of the poet's own denial: Artemis has no axe to grind for Phaidra, and her judgement here is certainly the poet's own.'[57]

Thus Euripides has once again made fundamental changes to the legend. We have seen that, in the case of Medea, Euripides has made innovations to the myth which mean that she kills her own children, but has drawn his new Medea in such a way that even this dreadful deed must be viewed with compassion, not condemnation. In the case of Phaidra, Euripides has given us a woman of great moral integrity, and he takes all guilt from her by means of Aphrodite on the mythological level, and by the Nurse on the human level. He clearly means his audience to feel nothing but compassion for this new Phaidra, torn apart by the love imposed on her by a merciless goddess, fighting against it, failing and dying.[58] She is Aphrodite's victim, whatever we make of Aphrodite herself, whether she is, at one extreme of interpretation, simply a vengeful goddess whose worship has been neglected, or, at the other, a symbol of the force of physical love working within Phaidra herself.[59] Either way, Phaidra is her victim, as she herself says (725–7):

47

ἐγὼ δὲ Κύπριν, ἥπερ ἐξόλλυσί με,
ψυχῆς ἀπαλλαχθεῖσα τῇδε ἐν ἡμέρᾳ
τέρψω· πικροῦ δ' ἔρωτος ἡσσηθήσομαι.

'Today I shall be rid of life, and so shall give pleasure to
Aphrodite, who is my destroyer. Bitter the love whose victim I
shall be.'[60] Either way, Phaidra, like Medea, is victim of a force
against which all reason, all rational behaviour, is powerless.

This similarity to Medea is emphasized particularly when
Phaidra says (380–1):

τὰ χρήστ' ἐπιστάμεσθα καὶ γιγνώσκομεν,
οὐκ ἐκπονοῦμεν δ' ...

'We understand what is right and recognize it, but we fail to
carry it out.' She is talking generally, but also of herself, of her
own principles and her own weakness. Here is once again reason
defeated by passion, as with Medea. This similarity has often
been noted.[61] But in the words with which she faces that defeat
there is another reminiscence of Medea, and of Medea's words
as she goes in to kill her children. 'I go forward to the point
where life turns into grief', says Medea; and then, 'I am an
unhappy woman – δυστυχὴς δ' ἐγὼ γυνή.' Phaidra says (677–9):

... τὸ γὰρ παρ' ἡμῖν πάθος
πέραν δυσεκπέρατον ἔρχεται βίου.
κακοτυχεστάτα γυναικῶν ἐγώ.

'My suffering reaches the boundary of life, and the passing is
cruel. Of all women I am the most unfortunate.' Euripides has
refashioned the legends of both women: both approach a
watershed in their lives that must lead to grief; they see it clearly
ahead of them, but cannot avoid it. Medea in some sense dies of
it; Phaidra dies in actuality. For both women, reason failing in
the face of passion leads to their tragedy. This is what it means to
be human; and let me quote here Reckford on Phaidra (1974,
p. 328):

In tragedy, it is no simple matter to escape from Crete. ..[62]
Theseus, grown old, rages like the evil Minos; he invokes
his father's promise, to destroy his son; and Poseidon once
more sends a bull from the sea, like the one Pasiphae loved,
as if to round off the tragic cycle of action and reaction.

The monster is not just in faraway Crete. It is in Theseus' domain, and within our several hearts. We cannot escape evil by sailing into a safe harbor of Athenian reason and control: hence Phaedra's tragedy evokes terror as well as pity. We all have our appointment in Crete, unless a god's grace cancels it; replay and re-enactment of evil mock our every effort of intelligence and will to escape that fatal pull backward: yet we would be less than human, and much less than noble, if we did not (like Phaedra) try.

Finally we come to the *Bakchai*, to another play about a god, a cosmic force, avenging himself on mortals who fail to honour him: Dionysos, who comes to Thebes, his birthplace, to manifest himself as a god. He drives the townswomen mad into the mountains, on to Kithairon, as maenads; and when their young king Pentheus persists in opposing him, he bewitches him on to Kithairon too, disguised as a maenad, and here Pentheus is torn to pieces by the women there, with his mother, Agaue, leading them. It is she who is the first to rend him. And this, I suggest, is what is new here: Agaue as the killer of her own son. (This again, as in the case of Medea, appears to be a factor in favour of Euripides' being a misogynist, but again turns out to be quite the opposite.) I take the evidence for this statement from two sources: from vase-paintings,[63] and from the text of the *Bakchai* itself.[64] I shall deal with vase-paintings first.

The death of Pentheus was a popular subject; but nowhere is Agaue identified on the vases. Indeed, on a red-figure psykter in Boston of about 520,[65] the maenad rending Pentheus' torso is named Galene; and the same name appears on a red-figure bell-krater of about 430, showing Dionysos with his maenads. Furthermore, on other vases from the latter part of the fifth century, we see Pentheus in armed combat with the maenads; or, in one case, an armed Pentheus hiding between two trees; or in another case, Pentheus setting out from his palace with net and hunting spears to hunt the maenads. So it does seem as if the vase-painters saw Pentheus as going armed against the maenads before being torn to pieces by them: no woman's dress, no madness, no Agaue.

Now, to turn to the literary evidence, this seems to have been the version of the legend which Aischlos also knew. He wrote a trilogy on Dionysos at Thebes, the plays being probably the

Semele, the *Xantriai*, and finally the *Pentheus*.[66] Only one fragment is left of the *Pentheus*, of no help in telling how Pentheus died. But Aischylos does refer to his death in a later play, the *Eumenides* of 458 (25–6):

... Βάκχαις ἐστρατήγησεν ϑεός,
λαγὼ δίκην Πενϑεῖ καταρράψας μόρον.

'The god led out his army of Bakchai, contriving for Pentheus a just fate, the death of a hare.' The god was at the head of his maenadic army, and Pentheus was torn to pieces by them, as a hare is by hounds, we must assume. The most natural image conjured up by these words is one of armed conflict. There is no hint of Agaue's presence (though of course there need not be in so short a reference). But in Euripides' own *Medea* of 431 BC the chorus sing (1282ff.) of Ino as 'one woman, the only one, who in time past raised her hand against her own children'. Page notes that they might have added Agaue[67] – but not, of course, if this child-murder was a later innovation by Euripides.

Now, to turn to the text of the *Bakchai* itself: we have here references to a similar kind of outcome to that discussed above – Pentheus killed when he went into battle against the maenads with Dionysos leading them – but unfulfilled, because the end of Euripides' play was to be quite different in kind from this.

In the prologue, Dionysos outlines his plans (47–52):

ὧν οὕνεκ' αὐτῷ ϑεὸς γεγὼς ἐνδείξομαι
πᾶσίν τε Θηβαίοισιν. ἐς δ' ἄλλην χϑόνα,
τἀνϑένδε ϑέμενος εὖ, μεταστήσω πόδα,
δεικνὺς ἐμαυτόν· ἢν δὲ Θηβαίων πόλις
ὀργῇ σὺν ὅπλοις ἐξ ὄρους βάκχας ἄγειν
ζητῇ, ξυνάψω μαινάσι στρατηλατῶν.

'Because of this [Pentheus refusing to honour Dionysos] I shall prove to him that I am a god, and to all the Thebans. When I have set all in order here, I shall go to another land and manifest myself. But if this town of Thebes in anger seeks to drive the Bakchai by force of arms from the mountain, then I shall lead out my army of maenads and engage them in battle [μάχην understood].' Now, this is not what happens, of course. Dionysos is opposed, Pentheus does decide in anger to take his citizens armed to Kithairon – ὀργῇ σὺν ὅπλοις. But in fact Dionysos' revenge is subtler and more ghastly than his first plan, and it falls on Pentheus alone – μόνος, twice repeated just before he goes to his death (961–4):

Πε. κόμιζε διὰ μέσης με Θηβαίας χϑονός·
μόνος γὰρ αὐτῶν εἰμ' ἀνὴρ τολμῶν τόδε.
Δι. μόνος σὺ πόλεως τῆσδ' ὑπερκάμνεις, μόνος·
τοιγάρ σ' ἀγῶνες ἀναμένουσιν οὓς ἐχρῆν.

'Lead me through the midst of this land of the Thebans; alone of them I am the man who dares this', says Pentheus; to which Dionysos replies, 'Alone you suffer for this city, alone. Therefore your destined ordeal is awaiting you.' And it is a mad, degraded and pitiful Pentheus who alone dies, not the body of men implied in line 50, Θηβαίων πόλις. This is very odd, for we expect a god's predictions to be carried out – or, at the least, some reason to be given for a change of plan.[68] But Dionysos gives no hint of it, and the change of direction comes suddenly at line 810, out of the blue, and – significantly, I think – just after Pentheus has finally decided to go out and fight.

I suggest that the most satisfactory explanation of this strange discrepancy is that in the prologue Euripides was referring to the familiar version of the legend, and was leading his audience on to expect that as his conclusion too, so that his new version of Pentheus' death would have an even stronger effect. He continues to lead them on in this expectation in the following scenes as well. Pentheus, in his scene with Kadmos and Teiresias, threatens to hunt the maenads from the mountain and chain them up (228, 231–2):

ὅσαι δ' ἄπεισιν, ἐξ ὄρους ϑηράσομαι ...
καὶ σφᾶς σιδηραῖς ἁρμόσας ἐν ἄρκυσιν
παύσω κακούργου τῆσδε βακχείας τάχα.

'Those who are at large I shall hunt from the mountain ... and soon put a stop to this Bacchic villainy by fitting them with iron fetters.' We must be meant to assume force of arms in the hunt. Then the chorus, singing of Dionysos' powers, says that he sends φόβος among an army (302–4):

Ἄρεώς τε μοῖραν μεταλαβὼν ἔχει τινά·
στρατὸν γὰρ ἐν ὅπλοις ὄντα κἀπὶ τάξεσιν
φόβος διεπτόησε πρὶν λόγχης ϑιγεῖν.

'And he shares a certain portion of Ares' province, for sometimes fear strikes an army under arms and in its ranks with panic, before the men have touched a spear.' This, on the surface, is very odd too, since this kind of terror was usually attributed to Pan, as our term 'panic' testifies.[69] Any connection between Dionysos and war was very tenuous, even paradoxical (consider the chorus at *Phoinissai* 784ff., where Dionysos and Ares are elaborately contrasted). But again this is easily explained if it is another reminder from Euripides to his audience of the kind of end they are expecting, with Dionysos intervening, and Pentheus and his army routed by the maenads.

In his long second scene with Dionysos, Pentheus finally decides to go and fight. But first he hears the messenger's story of the events on Kithairon, which should act as a warning to him if only he would listen. This tale is clearly meant as a doublet of later events, a foreshadowing of what will happen to Pentheus himself,[70] playing on the audience's expectations and full of ominous hints for the future. Here we have peace, rapidly turning to horror, flesh is torn and tossed, here that of cattle, later to be that of Pentheus. And what else do we find? The herdsmen on the mountain hide in ambush until they leap out at the maenads, and then are put to flight by the maddened women. This too, I suggest, is what the audience were expecting Pentheus to do: to hide in ambush, as on the vases, then to leap out, be pursued and (a direr fate than that of the herdsmen) finally to be killed.

Pentheus' immediate reaction to the messenger's story is decisive (778–85):

ἤδη τόδ' ἐγγὺς ὥστε πῦρ ὑφάπτεται
ὕβρισμα βακχῶν, ψόγος ἐς Ἕλληνας μέγας.
ἀλλ' οὐκ ὀκνεῖν δεῖ· στεῖχ' ἐπ' Ἠλέκτρας ἰὼν
πύλας· κέλευε πάντας ἀσπιδηφόρους
ἵππων τ' ἀπαντᾶν ταχυπόδων ἐπεμβάτας
πέλτας θ' ὅσοι πάλλουσι καὶ τόξων χερὶ
ψάλλουσι νευράς, ὡς ἐπιστρατεύσομεν
βάκχαισιν.

'Now close at hand blazes up like fire this outrage of the Bakchai, a great reproach to Greece. But we mustn't hesitate. Go to the Elektran Gate; bid all the shieldbearers and riders of swift-footed horses to muster, and all the peltasts and all who pluck the bowstring, and we shall march against the Bakchai.' (Such grandiloquent phrases, and so pathetic in their uselessness.)

Dionysos responds, 'Don't take arms against a god; Bromios will not tolerate your driving his Bakchai from the holy hills.' But again Pentheus cries (796–7):

θύσω, φόνον γε θῆλυν, ὥσπερ ἄξιαι,
πολὺν ταράξας ἐν Κιθαιρῶνος πτυχαῖς.

'I'll sacrifice woman's blood as they deserve; much of it I'll scatter in Kithairon's glens'; and Dionysos replies (798–9):

φεύξεσθε πάντες· καὶ τόδ' αἰσχρόν, ἀσπίδας
θύρσοισι βακχῶν ἐκτρέπειν χαλκηλάτους.

'You will all be put to flight. And it would be shameful, to have your shields of beaten bronze turned aside by the thyrsoi of the Bakchai.' Again: a reminder of what the audience are expecting to happen. All this is working up to Pentheus' final decision to march. The audience are waiting for it. And at line 809 it comes:

ἐκφέρετέ μοι δεῦρ' ὅπλα, σὺ δὲ παῦσαι λέγων.

'Bring out my armour', cries Pentheus; and, to the god, 'And *you* stop talking.'

Here, at this significant point, there comes a dramatic break in the action, emphasized by a break in the metre with the single response of Dionysos: 'ἆ', he cries, the sign of readjustment; and makes a complete change of direction to a quite different and unexpected revenge, on a Pentheus suddenly transformed from military strength to womanish weakness.[71] He begins to take possession of Pentheus' mind.[72] This point marks the division between what had been familiar to the audience, and what was to be new and shocking; though they are still kept guessing just a little as to the final outcome when Pentheus seems to hesitate (836–8):

Πε. οὐκ ἂν δυναίμην θῆλυν ἐνδῦναι στολήν.
Δι. ἀλλ' αἷμα θήσεις συμβαλὼν βάκχαις μάχην.
Πε. ὀρθῶς· μολεῖν χρὴ πρῶτον εἰς κατασκοπήν.

'I couldn't put on woman's dress', protests Pentheus.

'But you will cause bloodshed if you join battle with the Bakchai.'

'You're right. First I must go and reconnoitre.' And at the end of the scene Pentheus says (845–6):

53

στείχοιμ' ἄν· ἢ γὰρ ὅπλ' ἔχων πορεύσομαι
ἢ τοῖσι σοῖσι πείσομαι βουλεύμασιν.

'I shall go in. Either I shall come out under arms – or I shall
take your advice.' So the outcome still seems a little open. But
Dionysos is to invade Pentheus, just as he did Agaue his mother
(850–3):

... πρῶτα δ' ἔκστησον φρενῶν,
ἐνεὶς ἐλαφρὰν λύσσαν· ὡς φρονῶν μὲν εὖ
οὐ μὴ θελήσῃ θῆλυν ἐνδῦναι στολήν,
ἔξω δ' ἐλαύνων τοῦ φρονεῖν ἐνδύσεται.

'First drive him out of his mind', he says, 'and put him in an
inconstant frenzy. For never in his senses will he be willing to put
on woman's dress, but driven out of his wits he will put it on.'
And Pentheus comes on-stage after the next choral ode in
woman's dress, now completely possessed by Dionysos' madness,
'dedicated', as he says himself (ἀνακείμεσθα, 934), to the god.[73]

Now he is ready for his venture into the mountains; ready,
though he does not know it, for his final, fatal confrontation
with his mother. The second messenger describes it. When,
finally, the maenads have uprooted the tree in which Pentheus
had been seated by Dionysos, and he is hurled to the ground
with screams of terror, Agaue, 'priestess of slaughter' (1114),
falls on him (1115–21):

... ὁ δὲ μίτραν κόμης ἄπο
ἔρριψεν, ὥς νιν γνωρίσασα μὴ κτάνοι
τλήμων 'Αγαύη, καὶ λέγει, παρηίδος
ψαύων· 'Εγώ τοι, μῆτερ, εἰμί, παῖς σέθεν
Πενθεύς, ὃν ἔτεκες ἐν δόμοις 'Εχίονος·
οἴκτιρε δ' ὦ μῆτέρ με, μηδὲ ταῖς ἐμαῖς
ἁμαρτίαισι παῖδα σὸν κατακτάνῃς .

'He tore the headband from his hair, so that wretched Agaue
might recognize him and not kill him, and said, touching her
cheek, "Mother, it is I, your son Pentheus, whom you bore in the
house of Echion. Pity me, mother, do not, for my offences, kill
your own son."'
So twice he calls Agaue 'mother', touching her cheek, but to
no avail.[74] Foaming at the mouth, and with rolling eyes, she
tears his arm out from the shoulder. The other Bakchai follow

on. Then, with Pentheus finally dead, Agaue fixes his dismembered head to the top of her thyrsus and carries it home in triumph, thinking it to be that of a lion killed in the hunt. Here, for the moment, we shall leave her.

The pre-Euripidean version of the legend perhaps also provides the reason why Euripides uses military imagery so frequently in his description of Pentheus' venture into the mountains as a maenad: for instance Pentheus is called κατάσκοπος, scout, three times (916, 956, 981), and we have κατασκοπή in line 838, both military terms.[75] In line 819 we have ἐπιχειρεῖν ὁδῷ, 'attempt a journey', as in Herodotos of a military campaign;[76] in 1159 Dionysos is called a commander, προηγητήρ;[77] the maenads attack Pentheus with spears and epic missiles χερμάδας κραταιβόλους;[78] and κόρυς, helmet, is the term used of Pentheus' hair by Agaue when she carries his head home in triumph (1186). Dodds translates this as 'crest', and says, 'κόρυς does not occur elsewhere in this sense.'[79] Pentheus' robing of himself, too, can be seen as a fantastic inversion of an arming scene so familiar from Homer. Perhaps these are all reminders of the old version of the legend, which are meant to set Euripides' innovations in deliberate contrast, to emphasize them, and – in the case of Agaue stroking her son's hair and calling it κόρυς, with a blend of the old and the new – to stress their horror and poignancy.

That, then, is an all too brief summary of the evidence which suggests that Euripides may well have innovated the death of Pentheus, mad and in woman's dress, at his mother's hands. Now, it might be objected that Agaue as killer of her son was a traditional part of the legend, because other myths of opposition to Dionysos have the same motif: Minyad mothers, for instance, kill their own children. But this is not always the case: take another Dionysos legend, that of Lykourgos. In an early version of this legend, in Homer (Il. 6.130ff.), Lykourgos hunted Dionysos and his 'nurses' into the sea, and was blinded as a punishment. In later legend this punishment changed: he was driven mad, and while mad killed his own son. Apollodoros (3.5.1) gives us the details. But this version was much earlier than Apollodoros, since the episode also occurs on vase-paintings, the earliest evidence being a hydria of about 440.[80] So it was current well before the *Bakchai* (it may be that Aischylos used it in his Lykourgos trilogy), and in fact it could have given Euripides the idea of making Agaue also the killer of her own son. Or the idea may even have come directly from such Dionysiac myths as those of the Minyads, where mothers rend their children.[81]

So these are possible influences on Euripides' choice of material. But what was his motive in having Agaue kill her own son? Most of the work done in the past on the *Bakchai* has concentrated on the god, and asked: what is Euripides saying about Dionysos and his worship? Is it praise or is it condemnation? – and suchlike questions. But I suggest that this is not where Euripides' own concentration lay. If he did for the first time have Agaue kill Pentheus, then perhaps in fact his concentration was not so much on the god, but rather on his human figures – on Pentheus, and the fall of the house of Kadmos, and most of all on Agaue. So let us first of all move on to discuss what kind of characters Euripides has created in Agaue and Pentheus.

Both are inevitably drawn in very human terms. In the prologue we hear of Agaue's reason for doubting that Semele was mother to a god, which turns out to be a quite different reason from that given by Aischylos of divine intervention: in the *Xantriai* Hera enters Thebes disguised as a begging priestess with the express aim of stirring up opposition against Semele and her son.[82] But in Euripides, as Dionysos tells us in the prologue, Agaue and her sisters say that Semele became pregnant by a man, and tried to palm it off on Zeus – a very natural, rational reaction, one feels (26–31):

... μ' ἀδελφαὶ μητρός, ἃς ἥκιστα χρῆν,
Διόνυσον οὐκ ἔφασκον ἐκφῦναι Διός,
Σεμέλην δὲ νυμφευθεῖσαν ἐκ θνητοῦ τινος
ἐς Ζῆν' ἀναφέρειν τὴν ἁμαρτίαν λέχους,
Κάδμου σοφίσμαθ', ὧν νιν οὕνεκα κτανεῖν
Ζῆν' ἐξεκαυχῶνθ', ὅτι γάμους ἐψεύσατο.

'My mother's sisters, who least of all should have done so, said that I, Dionysos, was not the son of Zeus, but that Semele had been seduced by some mortal and then – a subtle wile of Kadmos, this – ascribed to Zeus her loss of virginity; and they loudly claimed that this was why Zeus had killed her, because she lied about her marriage.' (Theirs is a commonsense interpretation of the facts: Semele said that Zeus had fathered her child, and then was struck by lightning – which must have seemed to prove that she had lied sacrilegiously.) It is for this reason that Agaue and her sisters, together with the rest of the women of Thebes, have been driven mad by Dionysos on to the mountains (32–3):

τοιγάρ νιν αὐτὰς ἐκ δόμων ᾤστρησ' ἐγὼ
μανίαις, ὄρος δ' οἰκοῦσι παράκοποι φρενῶν.

'Therefore I have goaded those same sisters mad from their homes, and they are living on the mountain, their wits gone.'

We shall return to Agaue when the final scene of the play is discussed. But what about Pentheus? Primarily he is very young; young like the young god, his opponent; hardly more than a boy, as Dodds notes on 974, where Dionysos calls him νεανίας (974–6):

... τὸν νεανίαν ἄγω
τόνδ' εἰς ἀγῶνα μέγαν, ὁ νικήσων δ' ἐγὼ
καὶ Βρόμιος ἔσται. τἄλλα δ' αὐτὸ σημανεῖ.

'I bring this young man to a great contest, and the victory will be with me and Bromios.'

We find νεανίας again in 274 and 1254; τέκνον, child, three times in Kadmos' speech of grief over Pentheus' corpse (1308, 1317, 1319); παῖς, boy, in 330 and 1226. And Agaue, when she carries Pentheus' head triumphantly in her arms, says over it (1185–7):

νέος ὁ μόσχος ἄρ–
τι γένυν ὑπὸ κόρυθ' ἁπαλότριχα
κατάκομον θάλλει.

'The bull is young; his cheek is just growing downy under its crest of delicate hair.'[83] As Dodds says, he is hardly more than a boy. But he adds, on νεανίας in 974, that here is 'the first preparation for a shift of sympathy which the next two scenes will bring about'. This is not entirely true; this is very much the reaction of a man reading the play quietly in his study. True, Pentheus' youth is here made explicitly clear in the text. But we have to remember the performance: Euripides' audience had the mask to judge by, and it would obviously have been the mask of a very young man throughout. From Pentheus' first entry they would have been basing all their reactions to him on the fact that he was so young.[84] We ought to do this too. But instead of this, Pentheus is all too often damned; judged as a mature man is judged and found wanting. Dodds calls him 'the dark puritan whose passion is compounded of horror and unconscious desire'; he accuses him of the 'sexual curiosity of a Peeping Tom', and of the 'traits of a typical tragedy tyrant'.[85] But this will not do. He is instead this very young king, very much aware of his responsibilities, taking his duties as a ruler very seriously. He comes home to hear that all the women of his city have deserted their homes (216–23):

> I hear of strange evils abroad in the city: that our women have left their homes on the pretence of Bacchic rites, and are gadding about in the dark mountain woods, honouring with dances this upstart god Dionysos, whoever he is; that full mixing bowls stand in the middle of their thiasoi; and that they creep, one here, one there, to solitude, to serve the lusts of men.

He has *heard* that these things are so – line 216, κλύω – just as he has been *told* about the actions of the dangerously seductive stranger: λέγουσι δ' ὥς τις εἰσελήλυθε ξένος ..., 'They say a stranger has arrived, a wizard enchanter from Lydia, with scented golden curls and the charms of Aphrodite wine-dark in his eyes, who day and night consorts with young girls, dangling before them his mysteries of joy' (233–8). He reacts accordingly, just as a prudent, rational and caring ruler would act: the women must be brought home, and his city saved from chaos.[86] He sees Teiresias as standing in his way with his sophistic arguments, and Kadmos as well, with his willingness to lie about the god out of false family pride (333–6), Kadmos whom he loves (250–4, cf. 1308–22), and who he feels should know better. He sees Dionysos too – or, rather, the Lydian Stranger who was, after all, in Pentheus' opinion simply trying impiously to introduce a new god (cf. 467)[87] – as doing the same with what are to Pentheus clever and bewildering quibbles (cf. 475, 479, 491, 650, 655, 800–1, 805). This is especially clear in the first scene between Pentheus and Dionysos, where they are speaking on two entirely different levels, Pentheus on the literal, Dionysos on the allegorical. Lines 506–7 in particular emphasize this contrast: 'You do not know what your life is, nor what you are doing, nor who you are', says Dionysos; and Pentheus, blind to any deeper meaning, answers prosaically, 'Pentheus, son of Agaue, and my father was Echion'.

Then the first messenger, who tells of the peaceful maenads, goes on to tell of that peace wiped out by horror. It is small wonder that Pentheus tries to cling to rationality, confused as he is by Dionysos' verbal juggling; tries to be firm when he is uncertain and out of his depth, and calls for his arms: he must take practical action, in the only way he believes possible, against this new threat. And he is not a puritan, I think, not prurient, as so many say – simply a young boy with no sexual knowledge. Certainly the fact that he is so young and therefore has no sexual partner helps to emphasize his tragic loneliness throughout, which culminates in the μόνος – μόνος – μόνος of lines 962–3. His uncertain visualizing of the women on the mountain can also surely be explained as the product of his extreme youth and inexperience, and his anxieties about what they are doing up there become prurient fantasy only under the persuasion of Dionysos' madness (957–8). This is something altogether different in kind from what it would be in a full-grown man; and Euripides must have meant his youth to be continually borne in mind.

Moreover, as to Pentheus' purpose in actually going on to Kithairon: this is summed up by Kadmos, who, asked about it by Agaue, says that 'he went to mock Dionysos and your Bacchic rites' – ἐκερτόμει θεὸν σάς τε βακχείας μολών (1293) – and there is no reason to believe that his judgement is not Euripides' own. So his desire to see the women on the mountain (812) and convict them of debauchery can be put down to his wish to expose his hated enemy;[88] as indeed can his desire to hear the worst about their doings from the first messenger, as he himself specifically explains (674–6): 'The more terrible the things you tell me about the Bakchai, the sterner the punishment I shall inflict on the man who taught our women their wickedness.' The Pentheus in Euripides' text is in fact a rather different Pentheus from the one who is all too easily assumed if one comes to that text with modern psychological assumptions in mind.[89]

I have laboured this point in some detail, because our view of Pentheus' character must affect our response to his death; and a more sympathetic Pentheus than is normally acknowledged does, of course, make Agaue's killing of him even more repulsive and pitiful. So, of course, does the fact that he is so young, so close to the age when her attitude to him would have been all protective love and care.[90]

And so to Agaue in the final scene: a mother has killed her son, and she comes on-stage in triumph, with his head in her arms, believing it to be that of a lion which she has killed in the hunt, and boasting of her prowess. This, we see, is what Dionysos can do to mortals who deny him. Agaue had rationalized Semele's pregnancy. Pentheus had tried to cling to rational solutions when bemused by Dionysos and his miracles.[91] But the rational world of Agaue and Pentheus was not enough. For both of them Kithairon was waiting, Kithairon which becomes in the play the symbol for the kingdom of Dionysos.[92] Here on Kithairon the maenads worship their god; here, though they do not know it, they wait for Pentheus. As Segal says, 'One does not return from that mountain quite the same person as one was in setting out.'[93] Moreover Kithairon and Thebes represent the two polarities of φύσις and νόμος, familiar from the debates of the sophists. Thebes, the city, stands for νόμος, the civilized life, with law and order, and personal responsibilities; Kithairon, the wild, for φύσις, the free life of nature, with no personal ties. The women have been forced to leave Thebes – their homes, their looms, their babies – to go as maenads into the wild (ἣ τὰς παρ' ἱστοῖς ἐκλιποῦσα κερκίδας / ἐς μεῖζον' ἥκω, θῆρας ἀγρεύειν χεροῖν (1236–7), boasts Agaue: 'I have left weaving at the loom and have risen to higher things, to hunting wild beasts with my bare hands'); having deserted their human babies, they suckle wild animals; they scratch springs of milk from the ground, and later kill the milk-giving cows made tame and useful for civilization. All this is by the power of Dionysos. Pentheus had tried to oppose that power, had tried to assert νόμος in the face of this φύσις; had failed, and was killed. Human rationality in the face of cosmic irrational powers; human desire for order; the power of λόγος; all, it seems, are futile. And this dramatized defeat of νόμος by φύσις culminates, and is embodied, in the killing of a son by a mother.[94] This, I think, is why Euripides gave Pentheus this new way of death.

And so in the final scene the mad Agaue comes on-stage with her son's head in her arms. φύσις, it would seem, has triumphed. But no: φύσις may have taken over temporarily, a mother may have killed her son in madness; but in this final scene there is a reassertion of human values, personal affections, personal responsibilities, and all centred on the figure of Agaue herself. It is interesting that Pentheus has no *kommos*, no lyric song with the chorus, which all major characters normally have (and which Agaue, of course, does have). Perhaps this is because the chorus are hostile to him, so such a *kommos* did not seem dramatically feasible to Euripides. But it may also be because the greater concentration was always meant to be on Agaue, despite the fact that we are aware of her only 'in the wings', as it were, for the greater part of the play.[95]

In this final scene Kadmos gently, and with a quite amazing forbearance, brings Agaue back to sanity, to recognize whose head she holds in her arms – perhaps the most moving ἀναγνώρισις in Greek tragedy. ὁρῶ μέγιστον ἄλγος (1282), she cries, 'I see the greatest anguish.' But there is worse to come. 'Who killed him?' she asks; and she has to hear 'σύ νιν κατέκτας', '*You* killed him' (1289). And then, I think, she achieves a real victory, a genuine triumph in contrast to her earlier mad imaginings, because she now accepts fully her own responsibility for what she has done (1301):

Πενθεῖ δὲ τί μέρος ἀφροσύνης προσῆκ' ἐμῆς;

'What part did my madness have in Pentheus' fate?' she asks; and she uses the term ἀφροσύνη – not μανία, which could be sent by a god, but ἀφροσύνη, with all its implications of her own responsibility. Sadly her speech over the corpse of Pentheus has been lost, though we know that she grieves over his fate, blaming herself for his death, and reassembles his broken body.[96] But it would have reinforced even more her grief and self-reproach for her child-murder, and would have been a kind of reintegration, a reassertion of the essential human values in the face of suffering and death.

The play ends with an anguished farewell between Agaue and Kadmos before they go off into separate exile, each in their mutual embrace both giving and seeking comfort (1363–7), which gives an assertion of human concern and love in contrast to the attitude of the pitiless god.[97] As in the *Hippolytos*, the stage is left to the human sufferers, and the god, having done his worst, no longer seems important. Agaue's last words are a rejection of Kithairon and all it stood for, the beauty and the horror, which voices the similar rejection that Euripides

must have meant his audience to be feeling, and which finally
reasserts human values (1383–7):

> ἔλθοιμι δ' ὅπου
> μήτε Κιθαιρὼν <ἔμ' ἴδοι> μιαρὸς
> μήτε Κιθαιρῶν' ὄσσοισιν ἐγώ,
> μήθ' ὅθι θύρσου μνῆμ' ἀνάκειται·
> Βάκχαις δ' ἄλλαισι μέλοιεν.

'May I come where neither unclean Kithairon may see me,
nor I see Kithairon, and where there is no dedicated thyrsos to
remind. Let other Bakchai care about them.' So although νομός
would seem to have been defeated by φύσις when a mother,
blinded and maddened by the god, turns on her own son and rips
him to pieces, although the rational world of Pentheus and Agaue
was not enough to allow them to escape catastrophe, nevertheless
that world, with its human ties and affections and responsibilities,
does in the end survive, and even win a kind of triumph.

So, to sum up all of these three plays, Euripides seems to have
taken a traditional myth, and has asked himself what that myth
means in human terms, what it says about the human predicament. The answer is always, it seems, suffering; and he gives
that answer by the changes that he makes to the given legend,
changes which are centred on his female characters. Certainly in
the *Medea*, there is at the end pity for Jason in his sorrow. But
tragic concentration is on the Medea who has destroyed herself,
through the way in which Euripides has drawn the conflict of
passion and reason in the human heart which leads to such
terrible results. 'I know the horror of what I am going to do, but
my θυμός is too strong for me', says Medea; and, as she goes in to
kill her children, 'I go forward to the point where life turns into
grief.' Hippolytos' fate wins pity; but Phaidra, as the instrument
of that fate, is the well-intentioned, innocent victim of his
rejection of Aphrodite, fighting a futile battle with her god-
driven love for him: 'I understand and recognize what is right,
but don't carry it through'; and later, 'My suffering reaches the
boundary of life, and the passing is cruel.' In the *Bakchai* there
must be great pity for Pentheus' terrible death. But he knew
only briefly the tragedy that was coming to him. Agaue learnt of
it, accepted fully the blame for it, and had to bear the knowledge
of what she had done, the truth of those terrible words σύ νιν
κατέκτας, for ever.

Euripides has drawn three women, three 'wicked' women, who cause great harm. But he has drawn them without blame or condemnation, and instead with clear insight and an intense compassion for their predicament, as they are brought to tragedy against all reason. We have looked at only three plays, but I am willing to wager that if we possessed Euripides' lost plays – even his *Stheneboia*[98] and his first *Hippolytos*[99] – we should find there this same understanding of what it means to be human, this same plea for compassion, when he dramatizes the stories of other abandoned women, other so-called wicked women.

And so I should like to reconsider the passage from the *Frogs* that I quoted near the beginning of this chapter. 'A poet should teach', says Aischylos; '*I* taught courage with *my* characters'; and to Euripides, by implication, he says, '*You* didn't teach anything worth anything.' Wrong: Euripides felt, and for any thinking member of his audience he taught, a supreme compassion for the painful precariousness of the human condition; and he taught it most of all through his women characters. In no way can he be called a misogynist.

NOTES

1   This chapter, despite its general title, in fact treats only three of Euripides' plays in detail: the *Medea*, the *Hippolytos* and the *Bakchai*. Nevertheless, this seems to be an appropriate place to include a general bibliography of contemporary work on women in Greek tragedy in general and on Euripides and his female characters in particular (especially works referring to the plays with which I am most concerned), which together offer a variety of approaches to the subject (see pp. 74–5). Some of this literature I shall refer to, but not all, since in this chapter my own approach to the question of Euripides' views on women is, as will become clear, from an angle quite unrelated to most current work in this field; and here I must extend my warmest thanks to Mr Richard Hawley, of St John's College, Oxford, who is working specifically on women in Greek drama, and who supplied me with many useful references for the bibliography.

2   Ar. *Thesm.* 100ff. Penguin translation: Aristophanes, *The Frogs and Other Plays*, translated with an introduction by David Barrett (Harmondsworth, 1984).

3   And quite wrongly, of course, since in fact the laughter is directed quite as much against the women themselves as it is against Euripides, who through the whole play is treated with sympathetic

affection (as are his works). Aristophanes suggests that the women deserve Euripides' slanders, that they are in fact angry simply because he has exposed truths that they would rather have kept concealed. See also n. 13 below.

4   *Med.* 230–51. This is perhaps the passage most quoted as evidence for Euripides' sympathy with women, which it certainly seems to show. But, in general, single passages should not be taken out of context and judged as *necessarily* representing Euripides' own views, neither Medea's words here, on the one hand, nor, on the other, such passages as Jason's condemnation of women generally in lines 573–5, nor (perhaps the most misogynistic passage in the whole of Greek tragedy) Hippolytos' bitter rage against women in *Hipp.* 616–48. Furthermore, I suspect that lines 248–51 here are meant to be saying quite as much about Medea herself, ready and able to act like the traditional male hero – Knox 1979b (see Bibliography which follows these notes), pp. 296–302 – as they are about Euripides' sympathy for women in general (and far more, incidentally, than they are about what women in general would themselves have felt).

5   See Elizabeth Craik's chapter in this volume.

6   This is too simple an approach, since all these characters can be balanced by others less sympathetic, like Elektra in the *Elektra*, or Hermione in the *Andromache*. What these fine women do perhaps show is that Euripides could not have been an out-and-out misogynist.

7   This is demonstrated throughout the whole corpus of Euripides' works, and it does, of course, suggest (though not prove) that Euripides had a strong sympathy with the female sex. It is also, perhaps, significant that, as Dodds points out, 'it is a peculiarity of Euripides that his thinkers are nearly always women' (E. R. Dodds, 'Euripides the irrationalist', in *The Ancient Concept of Progress* (Oxford, 1973), p. 80). For a particularly sympathetic investigation into Euripides' attitude to women, see Vellacott, 1975, ch. 4, *passim*. I do not always agree with him when he detects irony in any particular context in the plays. Nevertheless, he makes some good and sensitive points generally about Euripides' depiction of women; for instance, '. . . much of what Euripides had to say about women is directed not to peculiarities of his own society and age but to those features of it which are hardly less familiar to us today – to the almost (though not quite) universal and timeless elements in the relative situation of men and women' (p. 82).

8   Perhaps this is the place to mention how unsure I am that Euripides (or any other ancient tragedian) saw women as the race apart which so much work on women in antiquity seems to assume. This clear-cut dichotomy of male/female, active/passive, etc., is a modern concept, and its application too often results in a simplistic and even false analysis. Let me take two examples from Lefkowitz 1981. It is unjust to speak of the *Iliad* as showing an 'essentially female' pattern of acquiring knowledge passively 'through

observation and through loss' (p. 4). Yes, women do watch their young men die in battle, they do mourn, showing what Lefkowitz calls a 'passive heroism'; but so do men: the figure of the mourning father (who is not necessarily an *old* man) is quite as frequent as that of the mourning woman. There are many examples throughout the whole work (e.g. 5.152–8; 11.328–34; 13.643–59; cf. 23.222–3), which culminate in old Priam of Book 24, who has lost sons and grieved, but is also heroic in his venture into the Greek camp to win back Hektor's body. Nor in tragedy does Hippolytos show 'a heroine's capability to understand and forgive' (p. 10), since understanding and forgiveness should not be thought of as simply female prerogatives (consider also, for instance, Kadmos in the *Bakchai*). These kinds of fashionable polarities often prove to be very unilluminating tools of analysis (see the careful discussion in Foley 1981, pp. 140–63), and it should certainly not be assumed that Euripides viewed the world in this way, nor that he saw the human race as being divided into two separated halves. (See also my comments on Shaw in n. 36.) Rather, I think, Kitto's judgement was nearer the mark, although made nearly fifty years ago: 'In the last analysis Euripides' tragic hero is mankind' (H. D. F. Kitto, *Greek Tragedy* (London, 1939), p. 195).

9   Ar. *Frogs* 1030ff. Penguin translation. On the poet as teacher, see now Malcolm Heath in 'Political Comedy in Aristophanes', *Hypomnemata* 87 (1987), pp. 18ff.

10   It must be the first *Hippolytos* referred to here: see W. S. Barrett, *Euripides: Hippolytos* (Oxford, 1964), pp. 30–1; T. B. L. Webster, *The Tragedies of Euripides* (London, 1967), p. 65.

11   For these reconstructed plots, see Barrett (n. 10), pp. 11–12, 18–45; Webster (n. 10), pp. 64–71 (*Hipp.*), 80–4 (*Sthen.*).

12   Schol. Ar. *Frogs* 849; see Webster (n. 10), p. 38, Vellacott 1975, p. 95.

13   But we must remember that these are *comedies*, and not take them as serious statements of how Aristophanes himself, and Aischylos, had he been able to, would, as artists, have reacted to Euripides' plays. Euripides' choice of plots (*not* his treatment of women in them) would have been quite enough to raise in Aristophanes' mind the comic idea of Aischylos' condemnation in the *Frogs* and of the women's rage in *Thesmophoriazusai*.

14   For earlier versions of the legend, see D. L Page, *Euripides: Medea* (Oxford, 1952), pp. xxi ff.

15   For the legend before Attic tragedy, see Barrett (n. 10), pp. 6–10.

16   For earlier versions of the Pentheus legend, see E. R. Dodds, *Euripides: Bacchae* (Oxford, 1960), pp. xxv ff.

17   For a discussion of the fragments, see A. C. Pearson, *The Fragments of Sophocles* (Cambridge, 1917), vol. II, pp. 15–23; D. F. Sutton, *The Lost Sophocles* (Lanham, New York, London, 1984), pp. 32–3.

18   See Pearson (n. 17), pp. 172–7; Sutton (n. 17), pp. 117–18 (Soph.); Webster (n. 10), pp. 32ff. (Eur.).

19 See Pearson (n. 17), vol. I, pp. 15-21; Sutton (n. 17), pp. 5–6 (Soph.); Webster (n. 10), pp. 77ff. (Eur.).

20 For Neophron's later *Medea*, see below, n. 23.

21 Paus. ii. 3. 10: Eumelos fr. 3 Kinkel; and see the discussion in Page (n. 14), pp. xxii ff.

22 See the discussion in Page (n. 14), pp. xxiii ff.

23 For an analysis of the fragments of Neophron's *Medea*, where again Medea intentionally murders her children, see Page (n. 14), pp. xxx ff. His arguments for dating this play after 431 BC are convincing. Lesky agrees with Page, and summarizes the debate over the dating (A. Lesky, *Greek Tragic Poetry*, 3rd edn (New Haven, Conn., and London, 1972), p. 220). On the infanticide generally, see P. E. Easterling, 'The infanticide in Euripides' *Medea*', *YCS* 25 (1977), pp. 177–91. S. P. Mills ('The sorrows of Medea', *CP* 75 (1980), pp. 289–96) shows how the story of Jason and Medea in this play follows the pattern of the Ino/Prokne myth: was this myth, perhaps, Euripides' inspiration? For a good discussion of the audience's expectations in the play, see T. V. Buttrey, 'Accident and design in Euripides' *Medea*', *AJP* 79 (1958), pp. 1–17.

24 For details of this part of the legend, see Page (n. 14), p. xxvi. See also Mills (n. 23), p. 291 esp. n. 12.

25 See Page (n. 14), ad loc., and pp. xxix f.; also Schlesinger 1968, p. 88.

26 The implication is that Jason will never marry again and acquire more children in that way. Indeed, what woman, knowing his history, would be willing to take him on as husband, particularly with Medea still in the background?

27 The sudden arrival of this chariot, in every sense out of the blue, must have been deliberately meant to shock. The audience, at lines 1313–16, would have been expecting the doors to open and the corpses to be displayed, as usual, on the ekkyklema; instead, in comes Medea on this completely unanticipated chariot. The intense drama of this moment was splendidly emphasized in the excellent production of the *Medea* by University College, London, in March 1988: for a few seconds the lights were shone dazzlingly at the audience, so that all stage business was effectively blacked out. When the lights were once more aimed at the stage, there was Medea, high above the palace in her dragon-chariot, set magnificently godlike against a background of streaming clouds. Euripides, I felt quite convinced, would have applauded. (And how dearly we would love to know how he achieved his own *coup de théâtre* in 431 BC!)

See also N. E. Collinge, 'Medea *ex machina*', *CP* 57 (1962), pp. 170–2.

28 This theme is emphasized also in the choral ode at 1081ff., at the key point in the play when Medea, after agonized debate, has decided finally to kill her children.

29 See, for instance, the heroic depiction of Jason in Pindar, *Pyth*. 4.

30 On this, see Reckford 1968, *passim*; Knox 1979b, pp. 306–9.

31 Many of the audience would, of course, have been aware of Medea's reputation in traditional myth. But that does not alter the fact that Euripides has chosen not to mention it, let alone stress it, in this play.

32 There is, I think, no need to doubt the sincerity of Medea's love for her children. But her need for revenge is stronger. See also n. 37 below.

33 As, for instance, by Andromache over Astyanax: Eur. *Tro.* 740ff., esp. 758–60.

34 Medea addresses her *thumos* as though it were something quite outside herself. See Dodds (n. 7), p. 81: 'It is the traditional appeal of the victim to the tyrant: only here victim and tyrant are bound together in one personality – which is, nevertheless, in some dreadful way not one but two. Jason, like the conventional Greek he is, would fain put the blame on an ἀλάστωρ (1333), but Medea is *her own* ἀλάστωρ.'

35 I do not quote these lines here, since any translation of them must fail, I think. In the Greek they are simple and moving (how like Euripides to bring in the detail that little children smell so sweet), in English sadly maudlin.

36 I do not find Shaw's discussion (1975, pp. 258–64) of the aspects of male/female within Medea very convincing. He claims that 'the pure female [Medea] meets the pure male [Jason], and there is an impasse. Next, the female intrudes into the male domain, and the male image is reformed. ... When Medea begins to avenge herself on Jason, she becomes a man'. He adds that Medea's monologue is a 'war of male [who has decided on murder] and female [who pleads for the children's lives] within the heart of Medea'. But Medea is what she is, this combination of passion and reason, from the very beginning: contrast her shrieks of rage and grief from within the house at the start of the play with the calm reasoned intelligence of her first speech outside the house, where she seeks to win the female chorus over to her side so that they back her revenge. See also my more general comments on this type of approach in n. 8 above.

37 This, to me, is one of Euripides' most moving insights into female reactions: he means there to be, I think, truly no choice about the children's fate at this point – because of the now certain royal murder they have to die one way or the other – and so the mother, out of love, takes on herself the task of killing them. (This is in a sense quite independent of the fact that it is Medea herself, by her decisions and actions, who has brought them all to this point of crisis.)

38 See Page (n. 14) ad loc. on πρὸς βαλβῖδα λυπηρὰν βίου.

39 See Knox 1979b, pp. 303–6; also p. 316: 'The energy she had wasted on Jason became a *theos*, relentless, merciless force, the unspeakable violence of the oppressed and betrayed, which, because it has been so long pent up, carries everything before it to

destruction, even if it destroys also what it loves most.' See also n. 27 above on the drama of Medea's appearance here in the chariot.

40 Schlesinger 1968, p. 89. And see M. P. Cunningham, 'Medea ἀπὸ μηχανῆς', *CP* 49 (1954), pp. 151–60: 'The final scene of the play presents visually and strikingly the dehumanising effect upon Medea of what she has done' (p. 159).

41 On the general legend, see Barrett (n. 10), pp. 6–7.

42 See, for instance, the *Catalogue of Women*, frr.208 and 209; Apollodoros, 3.13.3ff.

43 See, for instance, *Il.* 6.155–70. For Euripides' own *Stheneboia*, see Webster (n. 10), pp. 80–4.

44 Genesis 39.

45 See Barrett (n. 10), pp. 30–1.

46 For this probable plot, see Barrett (n. 10), pp. 11–12, 18–45; Webster (n. 10), pp. 64–71; Reckford 1974, pp. 309–13. On the character of this early Phaidra, see also n. 99 below.

47 As Barrett (n. 10) suggests, pp. 12–13; see also Webster (n. 10), p. 75.

48 For the arguments behind this reconstruction, see Barrett (n. 10), pp. 12–13, 22–45.

49 Ar. Byz., in *arg. Hipp.* 25. See on this Barrett (n. 10), p. 29.

50 A punishment by a god or goddess for a neglected honour of some kind is a very frequent theme in myth: see, for instance, the myths of Meleagros (*Il.* 9.529–49), punishment by Artemis, and of Helen and her sisters (Stesichoros, fr.223 (*Poetae Melici Graeci*, ed. D. L. Page, Oxford, 1962), cf. *Catalogue of Women*, fr.176 MW), punishment by Aphrodite. It seems likely that Euripides was the first to apply this theme to the Hippolytos myth.

51 See on this, Barrett (n. 10), p. 159: 'εὐγενής is not mere padding: ... the feeling that she must not let herself or her family down is a leading trait in Phaidra's character and a prime motive of her actions in the play.'

52 See D. J. Conacher, *Euripidean Drama* (London, 1967), p. 27: 'Phaedra's passion, ... and her own reflections on it, are treated in terms so realistic and rational that we seem justified in viewing her part in the action in natural, as opposed to supernatural, terms. Nevertheless, if we ask why Phaedra has fallen helplessly and hopelessly in love with Hippolytus, we must accept the only answer which is given to us in the play: the mythical answer of the prologue, that Aphrodite has caused this as a means of vengeance on Hippolytus. ... Nevertheless, it may be possible to restrict the helplessness of Phaedra to the simple fact that she is incurably in love with Hippolytus. In what she elects to do about it, she seems to show her own moral personality.'

53 See R. P. Winnington-Ingram, *Hippolytus: A Study in Causation*, Fondation Hardt, Entretiens, vol. vi (1960, pp. 172–97); p. 181: 'At 335 she responds simultaneously to the appeal of the suppliant, to the desire for outward recognition, and to the deepest cravings of her love-stricken heart.'

54 See Reckford 1974, *passim*, for other echoes of the first *Hippolytos*.
I cannot agree with him in seeing the second Phaidra as coming to
a moral ruin that in fact equates her with the first Phaidra (see also
Barrett's comment on 1305, p. 47). But I feel that he makes many
fine and sensitive points in his reading of the play. On the second
play's functioning as a mirror reversal of the first, see Zeitlin 1985,
pp. 102–6, esp. n. 107.

55 Phaidra 'has gone through the cycle of conscious choice, first
silence, then speech, and come at last to abandon choice all together,
and entrust her destiny to another. And the result will be, as she
said herself, destruction' (Knox 1979a, p. 212). This perhaps
reverses the set-up of the first *Hippolytos*, where it was quite possibly
the Nurse who tried to dissuade Phaidra from her decision to
approach Hippolytos herself (see Reckford 1974, pp. 310–11).

56 On Phaidra's death as the conclusion of her wedding journey, see
Burnett 1986, pp. 175–6.

57 Barrett (n. 10), ad loc. See also Segal 1965, pp. 180–2.

58 Whether in fact he completely succeeded is perhaps uncertain: see
Vellacott's (1975) comments, pp. 234–6; for instance, '[In the
Frogs] it is demonstrated that the Athenian public knew Phaedra
was a whore and would never have any other opinion, however
often they listened to the first episode of the *Hippolytus*' (p. 235).
But see also n. 99 below.

59 On the nature of Aphrodite in this play, see, for instance, Dodds
(n. 7), p. 87, Conacher (n. 52), pp. 50–3, Segal 1965, pp. 165–70.

60 As Conacher (n. 52) comments, p. 341: 'In the *Hippolytus*, the
whole logic of theme and action alike is predicated on the idea of
Hippolytus as tragic hero; yet who has "taught" the play on this
premise without having to explain too insistently for comfort how
the more interesting, more moving, but non-tragic,
characterisation of Phaedra is really ancillary to the tragedy of
Hippolytus?' He makes the point earlier (p. 30) that it is
Hippolytos' relation to Phaidra, in his reaction to the suggestions
made by the Nurse, which is crucial to Euripides' characterization
of Hippolytos himself: 'It is for this reason that the dramatist takes
such pains with the Queen's character and situation; while the
nature and fate of Hippolytus form the central issue of the
tragedy, it is only by an intimate and sympathetic understanding of
Phaedra and her plight that we can see the culpable and fatal
aspect of Hippolytus.'

Rabinowitz' (1987) conclusion that 'the ending of the play . . . by
founding its resolution on the basis of the father/son reunion'
indicates 'that Phaedra is merely important in relation to the men'
(p. 136), and the inferences on male/female attitudes that she
draws, all combine, I feel, to give a distorted reading of the play.
For instance it is, I suggest, not true that in Phaedra's noble attempt
to reject her love 'she accepts what her culture and its misogynistic
representative Hippolytus says is appropriate for a woman and
seeks to repress her desire without speaking', that she accepts 'the

values of the patriarchy and her place in it' (p. 130). Phaidra has been compelled by Aphrodite into an illicit love – physical lust – for her *stepson*, and there is no reason to believe that Euripides would have portrayed a man, similarly smitten with lust for a stepdaughter, as *necessarily* with different reactions to his feelings, different attitudes as to what was right.

61 See, for instance, B. Snell, 'Passion and reason: Medea and Phaedra in *Hippolytos* II', in *Scenes from Greek Drama* (Berkeley and Los Angeles, Calif., 1964), pp. 47–69.

62 '"Crete" ... comes to stand metaphorically for evil itself, for the pull backward into the subhuman past that contradicts, as it frustrates, all the designs of mind and spirit.'

63 Webster (n. 10), pp. 268–9, suggests on the evidence of vase-paintings that perhaps it was Euripides who first had Agaue kill Pentheus, but he does not develop the idea further.

64 This evidence, and the conclusions that I draw, are presented fairly briefly here. See, for much more detail, my article 'Euripides' *Bakchai*: a reconsideration in the light of vase-paintings', *BICS* 36 (1989). I thank the Editor for his permission to reprint certain parts of that article here.

65 For details of this and the other vases mentioned here, see my article (n. 64) in *BICS*.

66 For these earlier Dionysiac plays, see Dodds (n. 16), pp. xxviii–xxxiii.

67 Page (n. 14), p. xx n. 8.

68 The only other extant play where a god's predictions in the prologue do not come true is the *Ion*, but here reasons are given (see 1563ff.).

69 See Dodds (n. 16), ad loc.

70 Cf. 737, 740, and 747, with its suggestion of the closing of the eyes in death. 'The first messenger speech gives Pentheus the precise scenario for his own death and a chance, by learning through presentation, to avoid it': Foley 1985, p. 244.

71 See on this Anne Pippin Burnett, 'Pentheus and Dionysus: host and guest' (*CP* 65 (1970), pp. 15–29), pp. 23–4: 'Quite suddenly a prophet who has been kind, effeminate, languid, weak, scorned and threatened with death, imaged as a hunted animal, becomes hard, bull-like, energetic and powerful, one who controls the lives of others and is described as a hunter is. In exactly the same moment a ruling prince undergoes the reverse transformation; forgetting his cruel, masculine strength, his contempt, and his public role, he becomes a creature who is pliable, womanish and weak, who is scorned, disguised and hunted like a beast. All this happens in a swift and magical pause that is marked by a break in the stichomythia. ...'

72 Winnington-Ingram describes this as 'a process comparable to hypnotism': *Euripides and Dionysus* (Cambridge, 1948, repr. Amsterdam, 1969), p. 160. Rosenmeyer argues convincingly that this point marks a kind of death: 'The truth is that the change is

not a transition from one phase of life to another, much less a lapse into sickness or perversion, but quite simply death. When a tragic hero in the great tradition is made to reverse his former confident choice, especially if this happens at the instigation of the archenemy, the role of the hero has come to an end. We remember Agamemnon stepping on the crimson carpet, after Clytemnestra has broken down his reluctance. The blood-colored tapestry is a visual anticipation of the murder. Instead of the corporeal death which will be set offstage, the audience watch the death of the soul. With Agamemnon slowly moving through the sea of red the contours are blurred and the king of all the Greeks is annihilated before our eyes. Aeschylus uses a splash; Euripides, less concretely but no less effectively, uses a change of personality.' (T. G. Rosenmeyer, 'Tragedy and religion: the *Bacchae*', in *Oxford Readings in Greek Tragedy*, ed. E. Segal (Oxford, 1983, pp. 370–89), p. 387.)

73   And it must follow that if the usual version until Euripides had been Pentheus in armed combat with the maenads, then this Pentheus in woman's dress must be new too (see further on this in my article (n. 64) in *BICS*). So perhaps Ovid was drawing directly on the pre-Euripidean version of the legend for his account in *Met.* 3 of the military Pentheus going to his death on the mountain.

　　If Euripides meant the costuming of Pentheus by Dionysos to be part of a 'play within a play' as Foley, for instance, argues (1985, pp. 205–58), then this would suggest a theatrical self-consciousness appropriate to the later fifth century (p. 206), and thus too an innovation by Euripides himself (possibly inspired by the toilet scene in Aristophanes' *Thesmophoriazusai*, suggests Foley: see p. 228).

74   See Gould 1987, p. 37: 'There is a terrifying emptiness as the god vanishes and mother and son are left to come face to come face, watched by the horrified messenger, and through his eyes by us: whatever else was hallucination in this play, this is not.'

75   Richard Hamilton ('*Bacchae* 47–52: Dionysus' plan', *TAPA* 104 (1974), pp. 139–49), p. 144, points out that Euripides uses this terminology only in the *Bakchai*, the *Rhesus* (nine times!), and once in the *Hecuba*, and that it is always clearly military. (Hamilton in fact sees Pentheus' foray into the mountains as the engagement which Dionysos predicted in the prologue.)

76   Hdt. 7.43.

77   See Xen. *Cyr*. 2.1.1, 4.2.27.

78   On this see Hamilton (n. 75), p. 144.

79   Dodds (n. 16), ad loc.

80   Cracow 1225; *ARV²* 1121.17; *CV* pl. 12, 1.

81   Other possible influences on Euripides are from religion and ritual. Richard Seaford has argued that many details in the *Bakchai* derive from the ritual of mystic initiation: see 'Dionysiac drama and the Dionysiac mysteries', *CQ* 31 (1981), pp. 252–75, and 'Pentheus' vision: *Bacchae* 918–22', *CQ* 37 (1987), pp. 76–8. He notes that in the myth of the death and rebirth of the child

Dionysos, the god's torn limbs are reassembled by his mother (*CQ* 31, p. 267): perhaps this suggested the moving recomposition onstage of the limbs of Pentheus, Dionysos' victim, by Agaue, and thus the actual *sparagmos* of the son by the mother herself. This would have perhaps seemed especially suitable for performance at a festival expressly designed to honour Dionysos (see on this Seaford, pp. 266ff., and P. E. Easterling, 'Putting together the pieces: a passage in the *Bacchae*', *Omnibus* 14 (1987), pp. 14–16).

82   See Dodds (n. 16), p. xxx.

83   Dodds' translation.

84   And, as Dodds (n. 16) says (p. 197, with references): 'That is the one plea which a Greek audience would accept in extenuation of his conduct. The Greeks were very susceptible to the pathos inherent in the rashness of inexperienced youth.'

85   Dodds (n. 16), pp. 97–8. Others who take similar lines are, for instance, Charles Segal, *Dionysiac Poetics and Euripides' Bacchae* (Princeton, 1982), pp. 204–5; W. Sale, 'The psychoanalysis of Pentheus in the *Bacchae* of Euripides', *YCS* 22 (1972), pp. 63–82. For a more sympathetic view of Pentheus, see E. M. Blaiklock, 'The Natural Man', *G&R* 16 (1947), pp. 49–66; Rosenmeyer (n. 72), esp. p. 385; H. D. Rankin, 'Pentheus and Plato: a study in social disintegration', Inaugural Lecture at Southampton University (1975); Justina Gregory, 'Some aspects of seeing in Euripides' *Bacchae*', *G&R* 32 (1985), pp. 23–31; and, most of all, H. Oranje's careful discussion in *Euripides'* Bacchae: *The Play and its Audience* (Leiden, 1984), pp. 34–98. Seaford (*CQ* 31 (1981), p. 268) notes that Pentheus' youth is untypical of the tyrant of tragedy.

86   Gregory (n. 85) is right to warn that we must 'recognise that what strikes us as sexual pathology in Pentheus, for example, might not have appeared in that light to an audience with different cultural references. It is salutary to recall that to the late Victorian J. E. Sandys Pentheus' concern for the virtue of the Theban women – in the view of modern critics a symptom of neurosis – was [and to Euripides' audience also, I suggest] "a redeeming part of his character".' This same careful attitude towards women can be seen also in such a passage as *Andr.* 590ff., where Menelaos is condemned by Peleus for taking no precautions (bolts and slaves) to see that Helen was suitably guarded and watched over.

87   Pentheus is certainly not a *theomachos*, he is not against gods as gods, for Dionysos himself mentions his worship of others (45–6): he is just against *one* god, one new god, whom he has not recognized as a god.

88   See also Hans Diller, 'Euripides' final phase: the *Bacchae*', in *Oxford Readings in Greek Tragedy*, ed. E. Segal (Oxford, 1983, pp. 357–69), p. 365.

89   I realize that in this modern era it can be difficult to take a character in Greek tragedy at face value, without taking current psychological assumptions into account. Nevertheless, if we mean to seek out what the dramatist consciously intended, it should be

done – if at all possible. Sometimes it is almost impossible: consider Iokaste's statement at *O.T.* 981–2 – 'Many a man before this has in dreams lain with his own mother.' How can we ever forget what we know of Freud and persuade ourselves back two and a half thousand years to imagine either the state of mind that wrote those lines or the way in which the audience responded?

90   And he does of course have other sympathetic characteristics, such as his conspicuous loyalty to his grandfather (see Kadmos' lament, 1302ff., and Dodds' comments, on 251, on Pentheus' affection for Kadmos).

91   'Miracles cannot happen in Pentheus' ordered world': Blaiklock (n. 85), p. 56. As Gregory (n. 85) comments, p. 29, 'Both his perceptions and his responses are drawn from the realm of the secular and of the everyday'.

92   Lines 62, 797, 1142, 1177–8, 1219, 1292, 1384–5, 726–7, 1084–5, and ὄρος throughout.

93   Segal (n. 85), p. 304. To digress: those words always put me in mind of Lob's wood in J. M. Barrie's *Dear Brutus*.

94   On the emphasis on mothers in the play, see Gould 1987, *passim*. He notes that the day of the first performance of the *Bakchai* was also the day of the first performance of the *Iphigeneia at Aulis*, where again there is dramatic importance laid on the mother's relationship with her child.

95   And the play is called the *Bakchai* – of whom Agaue is one.

96   For its known contents, see Dodds (n. 16), pp. 234–5. On Agaue's self-accusations and the reassembling of Pentheus' body, and what they mean for the play, see Pat Easterling (n. 81), *passim*.

97   Dionysos' revenge may have been 'just', but on this 'justice' see Dodds (n. 7), p. 89: 'It is the justice of Kypris, the justice of Dionysus, an unpitying, unreasoning justice that pauses for no nice assessment of deserts, but sweeps away the innocent with the guilty, Phaedra with Hippolytus, Cadmus with Pentheus.'

98   See Vellacott 1975, pp. 93–4 ('... I do not believe ... that the creator of Phaedra had no profound moral concept underlying his depiction of Stheneboea ...').

99   Perhaps, as Conacher (n. 52) suggests, p. 342, Phaidra was here a full-scale tragic figure, no longer 'pegged' by Aphrodite, but a woman who freely, if inevitably, chose her own passion and her own destruction.

    The impropriety of Phaidra's *actions* was clearly condemned by Euripides' audience. But the very strength of their reaction suggests that Phaidra as a *character* was drawn with sympathy (an utterly immoral and unsympathetic character would not, one feels, have had anything like the same effect). Certainly it seems that sympathy can be detected in the few fragments of the play that we possess: from what are probably Phaidra's first words (Barrett fr. A, p. 18), when she numbers herself among the ill-starred (τοῖσι δυστυχοῦσιν), and from what is perhaps a final judgement on

Phaidra and her god-driven ills (Barrett fr. S, p. 22, θεηλάτων κακῶν). It seems too that Theseus was drawn in an unfavourable light (Barrett fr. B, p. 18, τὰς ἐκείνου παρανομίας), which would therefore have increased sympathy for Phaidra.

BIBLIOGRAPHY

Assael, Jacqueline (1985) 'Misogynie et féminisme chez Aristophane et chez Euripide', *Pallas* 32, pp. 91–103.

Burnett, Anne Pippin (1965) 'The virtues of Admetus', *CP* 60, pp. 240–55; repr. *Oxford Readings in Greek Tragedy*, ed. E. Segal (Oxford, 1983), pp. 254–71.

Burnett, Anne Pippin (1986) 'Hunt and hearth in Hippolytus', *Greek Tragedy and its Legacy* (essays presented to D. J. Conacher), ed. M. Cropp, E. Fantham, and S. E. Scully (Calgary), pp. 167–85.

Cantarella, Eva (1987) *Pandora's Daughters* (Baltimore, Md. and London), ch. 5, esp. pp. 63–9.

Foley, Helene P. (1981) 'The concept of woman in Athenian drama', *Reflections of Women in Antiquity* (New York), pp. 127–68.

Foley, Helene P. (1982) 'The female intruder reconsidered: women in Aristophanes' *Lysistrata* and *Ecclesiazusae*', *CP* 77, pp. 1–21 (a reply to Shaw, see below).

Foley, Helene P. (1985) *Ritual Irony: Poetry and Sacrifice in Euripides* – see index under 'Women in Euripides' – Ithaca, NY, and London.

Gallo, Luigi (1984) 'La Donna Greca e la Marginalità', *QUCC* 18, pp. 7–51.

Goldhill, Simon (1986) *Reading Greek Tragedy* (Cambridge), ch. 5.

Gould, J. P. (1978) 'Dramatic character and human intelligibility in Greek tragedy', *PCPS* ns 24, pp. 43–67.

Gould, J. P. (1980) 'Law, custom and myth: aspects of the social position of women in classical Athens', *JHS* 100, pp. 38–59.

Gould, J. P. (1987) 'Mother's Day. A note on Euripides' *Bacchae*', *Papers given at a Colloquium on Greek Drama in honour of R. P. Winnington-Ingram*, Supplementary Paper no. 15 of the Society for the Promotion of Hellenic Studies, pp. 32–9.

Humphreys, Sally C. (1983) *The Family, Women and Death* (London), chs 1–4.

Knox, Bernard (1979a) 'The *Hippolytos* of Euripides', *Word and Action* (Baltimore, Md, and London), pp. 205–30 (repr. from *YCS* 13 (1952)).

Knox, Bernard (1979b) 'The *Medea* of Euripides', *Word and Action* (Baltimore, Md, and London), pp. 295–322 (repr. from *YCS* 25 (1977)).

Lacey, W. K. (1968) *The Family in Classical Greece* (Ithaca, NY, and New York), ch. 7.

Lefkowitz, M. R. (1981) 'Women's heroism', *Heroines and Hysterics* (London), pp. 1–11.

Lefkowitz, M. R. (1986) *Women in Greek Myth* (London).

Lloyd, Michael (1985) 'Euripides' *Alcestis*', *G&R* 32, pp. 119–31.

Loraux, Nicole (1981) 'Le Lit, la guerre', *L'Homme* 21, pp. 37–67.

Nancy, Claire (1983) 'Euripide et le parti des femmes', *Les Femmes dans les sociétés antiques*, ed. E. Levy (Strasbourg), pp. 73–92.

Padel, R. (1983) 'Women: model for possession by Greek demons', *Images of Women in Antiquity*, ed. A. Cameron and A. Kuhrt (London), pp. 3–19.

Pomeroy, Sarah (1975) *Goddesses, Whores, Wives and Slaves: Women in Classical Antiquity* (New York).

Poole, Adrian (1987) *Tragedy: Shakespeare and the Greek Example* (Oxford), ch. 5.

Pucci, P. (1980) *The Violence of Pity in Euripides' Medea* (Ithaca, NY, and London).

Rabinowitz, N. S. (1987) 'Female speech and female sexuality: Euripides' *Hippolytos* as model', *Rescuing Creusa*, ed. Marilyn Skinner, *Helios* ns 13.2.

Reckford, Kenneth J. (1968) 'Medea's first exit', *TAPA* 99, pp. 329–59.

Reckford, Kenneth J. (1974) 'Phaedra and Pasiphae: the pull backwards', *TAPA* 104, pp. 307–28.

Sale, William (1977) *Existentialism and Euripides*.

Schlesinger, Eilhard (1968) 'On Euripides' *Medea*', *Euripides: A Collection of Critical Essays*, ed. E. Segal (New Jersey), pp. 70–89.

Segal, C. (1965) 'The tragedy of the *Hippolytus*: the waters of ocean and the untouched meadow', *HSCP* 70, pp. 117–69; repr. *Interpreting Greek Tragedy: Myth, Poetry, Text* (Ithaca, NY, and London, 1986), pp. 165–221.

Segal, C. (1978) 'The menace of Dionysus: sex roles and reversals in Euripides' *Bacchae*', *Arethusa* 11, pp. 185–202.

Shaw, Michael (1975) 'The female intruder: women in fifth century drama', *CP* 70, pp. 255–66.

Slater, Philip (1968) *The Glory of Hera: Greek Mythology and the Greek Family* (Boston, Mass.).

Vellacott, Philip (1975) *Ironic Drama* (Cambridge), ch. 4.

Visser, Margaret (1986) 'Medea: daughter, sister, wife and mother. Natal versus conjugal family in Greek and Roman myths about women', *Greek Tragedy and its Legacy* (essays presented to D. J. Conacher), ed. M. Cropp, E. Fantham, and S. E. Scully (Calgary), pp. 149–65.

Zeitlin, Froma (1985) 'The power of Aphrodite: Eros and the boundaries of the self in the *Hippolytus*', *Directions in Euripidean Criticism*, ed. P. Burian (Durham NC), pp. 52–111.

4

THE ARTICULATION OF
THE SELF IN EURIPIDES'
HIPPOLYTUS

Christopher Gill

In this chapter, I want to explore further a question which has
been much discussed in recent years, that of the best way to
bring out, in one's critical approach, the conceptions of character
and personality implied in Greek tragedy.[1] The topic I shall
focus on is that of 'the articulation of the self', as exemplified in
Euripides' *Hippolytus*. In using this phrase, I have two related
themes in view. One is the way in which, in this as in other Greek
tragedies, certain speeches can be read as being reflexive, as
expressing or even defining the 'self' of the speaker. (I shall
consider later what makes us regard certain speeches as reflexive,
and what kind of selfhood is expressed in this way.) The other is
the way in which these self-expressive speeches contribute to a
larger pattern of articulation, through which the play's central
argument or dialectic is constructed. As this dialectic unfolds, it
provides a framework of significance, within which we understand the reflexive stances of the figures and the kind of
selfhood they articulate.[2] The critical approach I have outlined
is one which could, I think, be applied to a wide variety of
dramatic forms. But the *Hippolytus* lends itself with a special
clarity to this type of approach. On the one hand, it contains a
number of speeches which are, in a variety of ways, reflexive in
style and which can plausibly be interpreted as expressions of
the selfhood of the speaking figure. On the other hand, as has
long been recognized, the play is organized (to an extent
unusual among Greek tragedies) around a single issue, that of
the nature of *sōphrosune*;[3] and the self-expressive speeches I
have in mind both contribute towards the articulation of that
issue and are in turn placed in a context of significance by the
play's central argument. I shall not be addressing directly the

76

themes of gender and eroticism that form the focus of this volume. But I hope it will become clear that there is a close relationship between the central figures' understanding of their selfhood and of their sexuality; and that both kinds of understanding need to be situated within the play's central dialectic if we are to appreciate their significance properly.

My interest in the idea of the 'articulation of the self' is not limited to its role as the organizing theme of a critical approach. I also want to raise the question whether this idea figured as part of the conceptual vocabulary of the culture from which the play derived. I shall suggest later in this essay that there is evidence, from a number of sources, which indicates that the Socratic technique of *elenchos* (intellectual cross-examination) was conceived as a process which involved the 'self-articulation', in a sense, of the participants. In particular, I see Plato's *Charmides* (treated here as a fictional recreation of Socratic *elenchos*) as strikingly analogous to the *Hippolytus*. In both cases, the exploration of the nature of *sōphrosunē* is conducted, in part, through self-reflexive comments on *sōphrosunē* by the participants; we appraise the quality of the comments (and of the people who utter them) in the light of the unfolding argument about *sōphrosunē* to which they contribute. My aim, in pointing out this analogy, is not to argue, as some have done, that the *Hippolytus* forms part of a debate about human psychology between Socrates and Euripides.[4] My aim is the more limited one of suggesting that the idea of the articulation of the self, or at least some version of this idea, may have formed part of the intellectual discourse of Athenian society at the time of the play's composition. If this is true, it gives an additional interest – and perhaps added validity – to the use of this idea as the focus of an interpretative approach to the play.

I will take up at a later stage the question of the possible connections between the *Hippolytus* and the intellectual concerns of the period. But I want to begin by considering an apparent objection to the kind of interpretative approach I have outlined. It is made in the course of a celebrated article by John Gould, in which he states his reservations about the interpretation of Greek tragic dialogue in terms of the expression of character, personality, or selfhood.[5] His general thesis is that in a Greek tragedy 'the play as whole [is] an image, a metaphor of the way things are, within human experience – not a literal enactment of "the way people behave"' (p. 62). It is this total image or metaphor which is 'humanly intelligible'; and the fact that the play as a whole is intelligible does not entail that each episode or figure within the drama is intelligible in the same way as is an event or person in real life.[6] During his discussion, Gould refers to two episodes in the *Hippolytus*, the dialogue between Phaedra and the Nurse (267ff.) and that between Hippolytus and Theseus (902ff.), which are often interpreted in terms of the disclosure of the character and state of mind of the participants. He argues rather that, in so far as these scenes communicate an 'image of human personality', they do so in a way that is crucially informed by the stylistic modalities of the dialogue, and by the formal conventions of the dialogue-types: specifically, those of the *stichomythia* of persuasion with its distinctively probing, gladiatorial manner, and of the oration or *rhēsis*, as a vehicle of accusation, appeal, or self-justification.[7] Gould's comments develop A. M. Dale's well-known claims that the determining factors in Greek tragic dialogue are 'the trend of the action' and 'the rhetoric of the situation', rather than the desire to bring out the psychological motivation and individual style of the characters involved.[8] Gould here underlines an important and evident truth: when Phaedra, at 373ff., presents a disquisition on human weakness in a deliberated, antithetical style, it is unnecessary (and critically dubious) for us to reconstruct the motivation that 'will plausibly account for Phaedra's making *this* speech at *this* moment'.[9] Formalized speech-making of this type is as much a convention of the Greek tragic genre as is the soliloquy or aside in Shakespeare, or the 'flash-back' or 'voice over' in a film; these are all ways in which a fictional figure's thinking or memory can be communicated to the audience, and none of them requires us to ask why *this* convention is used at *this* moment in the work.[10]

None the less, I have some reservations about Gould's claims, for reasons similar to those given by Simon Goldhill.[11] For one thing, although Gould goes a long way towards recognizing that different models of personality are implied by literary works of different periods and types (as his comments on Eugene O'Neill bring out),[12] there is still a tendency for him to contrast 'form' and 'character', *tout court*, as dramatic considerations, as though he is presupposing a single, determinate conception of character, which he takes to be either present in, or absent from, a particular text. But, in fact, when we ask how important 'character' is in a

78

given text, we need to be quite clear about what kind of conception of character we have in view. The kind of conception that matters, I take it, is the one that seems to be implied by the work itself. Establishing exactly what this is, and distinguishing this from 'our' conception of character (in so far as we are clear about what this is) is no easy matter. But clearly one important indicator of the way in which the psychology of the person is conceived is the type of vocabulary used in Greek tragedy to designate the processes of thinking and feeling (that is, such terms as *psuchē, gnōmē, phroneō, phrontizō,* and so on). And Goldhill is surely right to emphasize (what scholars such as Knox and Winnington-Ingram have helped us to appreciate) that we need to study such vocabulary as it functions within the dramatic context, coloured by, and forming a medium for, the moral and emotional conflicts of the play.[13] This type of enquiry raises methodological problems of its own, because it cannot be easily detached from the interpretation of the play as a whole. But it has the merit of keeping before our minds the question of the kind of conception of personality implied by the text, and of focusing our attention on some of the material relevant to this question.

Also, exploring this material helps to bring out a point which is not confronted fully by Gould. Although he insists that we cannot 'detach [a dramatic figure] from . . . the play's "world"', as articulated (in the case he considers) in 'the pervasive meta-phorical colouring of the whole language of the play' (p. 60), he does not emphasize equally the extent to which dramatic character can contribute towards making up the play's 'world' or 'language'. Goldhill formulates this point by drawing on Roland Barthes' distinction between the 'language' of character and that of discourse (the latter term meaning, I take it, the work's central dialectic and shaping action). As Barthes puts it: 'these two views [those of character and discourse] . . . support each other: a common sentence is produced which unexpectedly contains elements of various languages'. In this composite fictional language, *'The character and the discourse are each other's accomplices'.*[14] To put the point in the terms I used earlier, a play, as it proceeds, develops its own informing dialectic or argument, to which the various components of the play (character, language, physical action) contribute; and that dialectic increasingly forms a context of significance within which we understand the component elements of the play.

Let me try to apply this interpretative framework to the *Hippolytus*. It seems clear, as I noted earlier, that *sōphrosunē* is central to the informing dialectic of the play. Part of what this means is that we interpret the character of the dramatic figures in the light of what they say about *sōphrosunē*, and that we interpret what they say about *sōphrosunē* in the light of our impression of their character and of their understanding of what *sōphrosunē* consists in. In saying this, I am not suggesting that the play presupposes that *sōphrosunē* has a single, determinate meaning, which we can use as a normative reference-point by which to appraise the figures' understanding of the notion and in this way appraise their character. As Helen North's study shows, the term, *sōphrosunē*, together with its cognate verbal and adjectival forms, is conspicuously broad in meaning, in this and other periods;[15] and the play seems to explore and exploit this diversity of meaning.[16] There seem to be at least four senses involved: (i) (sexual) 'chastity' or 'purity'; (ii) 'virtue' in a slightly larger sense, though one that is sometimes difficult to distinguish sharply from that of 'chastity'; (iii) 'self-control', as shown in controlling desire or anger; and (iv) 'good sense' or practical wisdom, as shown in the successful management of one's life.[17] I do not think that this is a case of modern readers seeing a variety of senses in a term which would have had a single, uncomplicated meaning for the original Greek audience (although this is not to say that we can ever quite capture the feel that the term had for them, since no English term covers a similar range of meanings). Rather the drama *plays* on these differences, and does so in a way that critics have often found striking.

This is particularly clear in the case of two passages that the development of the action invites us to juxtapose, the end of Hippolytus' tirade against women and Phaedra's subsequent suicide-speech:

ἢ νύν τις αὐτὰς σωφρονεῖν διδαξάτω
ἢ κἄμ' ἐάτω ταῖσδ' ἐπεμβαίνειν ἀεί.

(667–8)

... ἵν' εἰδῇ μὴ 'πὶ τοῖς ἐμοῖς κακοῖς
ὑψηλὸς εἶναι· τῆς νόσου δὲ τῆσδέ μοι
κοινῇ μετασχὼν σωφρονεῖν μαθήσεται.

(729–31)

'Let someone teach women to be *sōphrōn* or allow me to go on trampling them down for ever' '... to make him realize that he shouldn't view my troubles with disdain; by sharing in this sickness of mine, he shall learn to be *sōphrōn*.' By *sōphronein*, Hippolytus seems to mean 'to be chaste' or, perhaps better, 'virtuous' (taking the English term in the slightly archaic sense of 'sexually proper', as in the phrase, 'a virtuous wife'). He presumably has in mind the kind of person who does not have illicit sexual desires rather than one who has them but keeps them under control.[18] Phaedra, on the other hand, in a clear echo of Hippolytus' phraseology, uses *sōphronein* rather to signify that Hippolytus should 'control himself', by moderating his feelings of anger and disdain. Hippolytus is to be made to unlearn his contempt for those in trouble (*kakois*), and, by sharing her 'disease' (the disgrace accruing from illicit sexual desire), learn to be more 'humane', which is perhaps another shade of meaning she attaches to *sōphronein*. Her usage of the term not only echoes the earlier one but, in effect, comments on it, colouring in retrospect our understanding of Hippolytus' usage and the attitude which it expresses.[19]

This process of accretion of meaning continues with the striking couplet that closes Hippolytus' speech of self-defence to Theseus:

ἐσωφρόνησε δ' οὐκ ἔχουσα σωφρονεῖν,
ἡμεῖς δ' ἔχοντες οὐ καλῶς ἐχρώμεθα.

(1034–5)

'She performed a *sōphrōn* act, although she wasn't *sōphrōn;* I am *sōphrōn*, but I haven't used this virtue well.' The lines resonate beyond their immediate context, and we are disposed to interpret them in the light both of what we take Hippolytus to mean, and of the unfolding dialectic of the play. Hippolytus seems to mean that Phaedra acted virtuously in killing herself, although – or, in a different way, because – she was not a virtuous person, in the sense of having chaste desires.[20] He, on the other hand, is *sōphrōn* because he has chaste desires, and also perhaps because he is showing self-control in not breaking his oath;[21] but he has gained no advantage, and has in fact been disadvantaged, by his possession of this quality.[22] At the same time, however, we may interpret his words in a rather different sense, and with a rather different valuation of the people concerned. When Hippolytus utters the paradoxical line 1034, we may think rather of the inner conflict Phaedra describes, in her monologue to the chorus, between her illicit sexual desire and her longing to be, as well as to seem, virtuous.[23] Also, after Phaedra's insistence that Hippolytus needs rather to *learn* to be *sōphrōn* – and after his violent and undiscriminating condemnation of women, which Phaedra might well take as showing an absence of *sōphrosunē* ('self-control' or 'humanity') – we may want to question his confidence, often reiterated elsewhere, that he is *sōphrōn*. Alternatively, we may want to say (like him, though in a different sense) that, *if* he has this quality, he has not used it 'well' (*kalōs*).[24] But I do not think that the passage disposes us to *replace* Hippolytus' meaning, or meanings, with the additional one we supply; much of the resonance of the lines derives from the fact that we recognize these different possible meanings and also recognize, from a certain point of view, their validity. Nor do I think that the play as a whole moves towards establishing any one sense of the term as superordinate or all-inclusive, any more than the play as a whole legitimates a single moral perspective from which to judge the figures as being (in some definitive sense) *sōphrōn* or not *sōphrōn*.[25] Rather, the resonant ambivalence of the lines contributes to the whole nexus of ambiguities, misunderstandings, and dislocations, of which the play's informing dialectic and ethos is made up.

In fact, I think this couplet forms one of a whole complex of passages which, through recurrent phrase-patterns, help to make up the play's distinctive character. The most common pattern is one which denotes a dislocation between outer act (or word) and inner mental state, or between underlying character or capacity and action (or impulse) in a given situation. The most famous examples of this pattern are these:

χεῖρες μὲν ἁγναί, φρὴν δ' ἔχει μίασμά τι

(317)

'My hands are pure, but my mind has a kind of pollution.'

ἡ γλῶσσ' ὀμώμοχ', ἡ δὲ φρὴν ἀνώμοτος.

(612)

'My tongue swore, but my mind is unsworn.' But these lines form part of a larger family of such antitheses:

... φρονεῖς μὲν εὖ, φρονοῦσα δ' οὐ θέλεις
παῖδάς τ' ὀνῆσαι ....

(313–14)

'You are sane; but, sane as you are, you don't seem to want to help your children.'

οἱ σώφρονες γάρ, οὐχ ἑκόντες ἀλλ' ὅμως,
κακῶν ἐρῶσι.

(358–9)

'Those who are *sōphrōn* [virtuous?] desire what is bad, although they don't want to.'

τὰ χρήστ' ἐπιστάμεσθα καὶ γιγνώσκομεν,
οὐκ ἐκπονοῦμεν δ'. ...

(380–1)

'We know and understand what is good, but we don't put this into practice.'

πόσους δοκεῖς δὴ κάρτ' ἔχοντας εὖ φρενῶν
νοσοῦνθ' ὁρῶντας λέκτρα μὴ δοκεῖν ὁρᾶν;

(462–3)

'How many men do you think there are who, though they're no fools, seem not to see the sickness in their marriage-beds?'

νοσοῦσα δ' εὖ πως τὴν νόσον καταστρέφου.

(477)

'Sick though you are, make your sickness work out well.'[26]

... θηρεύουσι γὰρ
σεμνοῖς λόγοισιν, αἰσχρὰ μηχανώμενοι.

(956–7)

'They go hunting, with fine words and vile plans.'
In a related pattern, we find the characterization of an action being radically qualified:

φίλως, καλῶς δ' οὐ τήνδ' ἰωμένη νόσον.

(597)

'Her attempt to cure this sickness was kindly meant but wrong.'

ὄλοιο καὶ σὺ χὤστις ἄκοντας φίλους
πρόθυμός ἐστι μὴ καλῶς εὐεργετεῖν.

(693–4)

'A curse on you and on anyone else who wants to do wrong to help friends against their will.'[27] Relatedly, we find phrases which contrast a figure's character with what they suffer; here are two, linked, examples (the latter also containing a qualified characterization):

ἢ δ᾽ εὐκλεὴς μὲν ἀλλ᾽ ὅμως ἀπόλλυται
Φαίδρα·

(47–8)

'Phaedra will keep her honour intact but die.'

... ὡς ὑπ᾽ εὐκλείας θάνῃ,
καὶ σῆς γυναικὸς οἶστρον ἢ τρόπον τινὰ
γενναιότητα·

(1299–1301)

'... so that he [Hippolytus] can die in honour, and [to reveal] your wife's maddening sting of lust, or, in a way, her nobility.'

These lines are interconnected by a number of verbal and thematic links, as well as by a recurrently antithetical, or at least qualifying, phrase-pattern.[28] They are also related to other passages, which convey similar dislocations in rather different verbal forms.[29] These lines are not, of course, to be treated as representing 'the voice of the author'; they are allocated to specific figures in specific dramatic contexts, and form an integral part of the dialogue. None the less, these lines play a special role in formulating the ethos of the play; in particular, the haunting repetition of antithetical phrase-patterns underlines the kind of dislocations articulated in the lines. Central to this ethos is the dislocation between character and action, or speech, and the related difficulty in giving a single, definitive characterization of actions, persons, or indeed of qualities (such as *sōphrosunē*). As a number of critics have emphasized, the mutual destruction which occurs in the play is not the result of an open and unambiguous confrontation between figures with radically opposed characters and ethical standpoints. Rather it is one in which various kinds of misunderstanding and miscommunication render the motives and characters of the central figures obscure to each other (and in this sense obscure the connection between character and action or word). In particular, at the heart of the play (and of its tragic quality) is the fact that Hippolytus and Phaedra largely fail to communicate to each other, or to others, the way in which they are both powerfully motivated by (versions of) the ideal of *sōphrosunē*, a failure which contributes crucially towards their destroying each other and themselves.[30] At the same time, there are significant differences between the views of *sōphrosunē* held by the different figures; and these differences are reflected in the divergent styles with which they express (or conceal) themselves. Some of the mis-communication derives from their divergent understanding of what *sōphrosunē* involves; and, in this sense, the play contains an 'argument' about the nature of *sōphrosunē*. But this is not an argument which anyone wins; no single view of *sōphrosunē* is validated by the complex causation and the outcome of the action. In this sense, the dramatic dialectic – like many Socratic arguments – is 'aporetic'.[31] Hence, as the recurrent phrase-patterns suggest, the tragic events result not only from the failure of the figures to articulate their *sōphrosunē* effectively but also from the ambivalence or indeterminacy of the quality itself.[32]

It is against this background of the play's informing ethos and dialectic that I want to place my study of the figures' self-articulation. The kind of 'selfhood' I am concerned with is one manifested in the figures' statements about themselves, and in their styles of discourse and gesture, when these are self-reflexive in character. In this drama such manifestations of selfhood are intimately connected with the figures' understanding of *sōphrosunē*, at least as far as Hippolytus, Phaedra, and the Nurse are concerned; and the self-understanding of these three figures is closely interlocked within the overall dialectical web of the drama.[33] The Nurse, as I shall suggest, sees herself essentially as an adjunct of Phaedra's existence, while her view of *sōphrosunē* constitutes a parasitic inversion of that of her mistress. Phaedra, on the other hand, sees herself as, in a sense, a 'failed' version of Hippolytus, as far as *sōphrosunē* is concerned. Thus, Hippolytus' view of himself, and of his *sōphrosunē*, forms the radiating centre for a nexus of forms of self-understanding. These features come out most plainly in two key speeches, Phaedra's account of her response to her passion (391–430) and Hippolytus' speech of defence to Theseus (esp. 991–1006, taken in conjunction with

1070–81), which I shall examine closely. But I want to begin by discussing in more general terms the interconnections between the self-understanding of these three figures.

Early in the play, we are given an image of Hippolytus' view of himself which remains valid throughout the play. He enters, a young man in hunting dress, surrounded by a group of admiring friends,[34] and, in a significant gesture, presents Artemis with a freshly picked garland, which he regards as a symbol both of his own chastity and of his special devotion to the huntress-goddess. The garland has been plucked from a 'virgin' meadow, cultivated only by *aidōs* ('shame' or 'reverence') with pure river water. The right to pluck such a garland belongs only to 'those for whom being *sōphrōn* is not a learned quality, but one which has been assigned as part of their nature in every respect for ever'.[35] Hippolytus thus presents *sōphrosunē* as a fundamental part of his nature, as something 'assigned' or 'given' to him (*eilēchen*), innate perhaps, but also, in principle, a lifelong property.[36] He also sees it as a property that is peculiarly, if not exclusively, *his*, and one which presumably underlies the privileged relationship he has with Artemis.[37] But he does not therefore take this property for granted, as being simply an intuitive response; nor does he maintain a reticent silence about it, as being something uniquely private or personal. The gesture of giving the garland and the associated presentation of himself as an exceptional devotee constitute an act of public self-display, just as does his conspicuous refusal to make any equivalent gesture to Aphrodite.[38] This stance is characteristic of Hippolytus throughout the play; his dialogue (as we shall see) is recurrently self-presenting, and the 'self' he presents is one which is peculiarly and exceptionally *sōphrōn*, that is, 'chaste', 'pure', and, in certain senses, 'virtuous', as in this opening scene.

Phaedra is also very much concerned with the public manifestation of herself as virtuous (and is very anxious to avoid presenting herself as 'base' or 'disgraceful'). Her statement of this concern (in the *rhēsis* to be discussed later) elicits from the chorus an expression of admiration for the 'fineness' of *to sōphron*, as being that which 'enjoys the fruit' (*karpizetai*) of a 'noble reputation' (*doxē esthlē*).[39] To this extent, her aspirations are similar to those of Hippolytus, allowing for the difference in the kind of *sōphrosunē*, and the kind of self-display, that is proper for a 'virtuous' wife and mother.[40] But her aspirations are frustrated and fail because, in the first instance, of the over-powering sexual urge that makes it impossible for her to say, as Hippolytus does, that *to sōphronein* (in the sense of 'chastity') is an integral and permanent part of her 'nature'. Hence, she is conscious of having within herself 'a kind of pollution' or 'sickness'; or, to put it more exactly, she is conscious of an inner conflict between 'herself' (conceived as the would-be virtuous wife) and the alien force or 'other' within her, the 'madness' or 'goddess' (*Kupris*) that is operating on her.[41] Her characteristic style in the drama is not, therefore, like that of Hippolytus, that of self-display (except in the special context of the self-revealing *rhēsis*, 391ff.), but rather that of concealment, 'covering up', and silence, modified, by the Nurse's pressure, into obliqueness and partial disclosure, then to a not wholly disallowed communication, and finally to a (written) lie that 'shouts' in order to suppress the truth about herself.[42]

Phaedra thus sees herself as an aspiring, and in the end a failed, version of Hippolytus, as regards their shared objective of being – and being seen to be – *sōphrōn*; and this fact seems to underlie her eventual hatred of him and also, perhaps, her passionate desire for him. Her last words (that he is to 'share her disease' and 'learn not to be disdainful of [her] troubles') respond to his gloating anticipation of her future covert disgrace, and express a wish to dislodge him from the stance of self-manifesting virtue she feels she can no longer share.[43] In her first appearance on stage, she expresses in lyrics her 'mad', transgressive desire to lead the kind of life that Hippolytus regards as constitutive of his *sōphrosunē*, the life of openness and visibility, purity and simplicity. And it may be that, as Froma Zeitlin suggests, we are to see her lust as taking the form of the desire to *be* Hippolytus rather than simply to be *with* him.[44] Perhaps this last inference presses psychologizing beyond what the text can bear.[45] But, in general, it is clearly central to the drama that, for both Hippolytus and Phaedra, their conceptions of *sōphrosunē* and of themselves are locked together in a close, intense way that, paradoxically, contributes to their mutual destruction.

If Phaedra's conception of herself is, in this respect, derivative of Hippolytus', the Nurse's is still more obviously derivative, and yet subversive, of Phaedra's. Early in the play, the Nurse presents herself as an adjunct to Phaedra, bound up in a painful but inescapable way with her mistress's continued existence.[46] Her subsequent adoption of priorities which are the reverse of Phaedra's (that is, trying to save her mistress's life at the expense of her honour)[47] is consistent with this presentation of herself. In working for this end, she not only tries to counter Phaedra's ethical stance with her own, antithetical stance, but also tries to subvert Phaedra's ethical position from the inside, so to speak, by skilful modification and inversion. Thus, in her response to Phaedra's *rhēsis*, she accentuates Phaedra's emphasis on 'keeping up appearances' (in spite of the onset of unchaste desire) and transforms it into a policy of systematic duplicity and covert self-gratification, rephrasing some of Phaedra's speech for the purpose.[48] Here and elsewhere she appropriates terms such as 'sensible', 'clever', and indeed *sōphrōn*, to commend such a policy;[49] although she is also capable of using *sōphrōn* in a way more calculated to appeal to Phaedra (meaning 'virtuous', or 'having chaste desires') in order to undermine the other's attempt to exercise *sōphrosunē* in the sense of 'self-control'.[50]

Her struggle with Phaedra is thus, in a sense, a struggle *within* Phaedra, and constitutes part of the latter's unsuccessful attempt to maintain her chosen course of action and ethical stance.[51] This struggle, which is in large measure about what is and is not to be made explicit, is also embodied in the relationship between their modes of articulation. While their characteristic styles are sharply contrasted (the Nurse's brutal explicitness confronting Phaedra's reticence and obliqueness), Phaedra twice half-allows the Nurse to act as her vehicle of disavowed explication.[52] It is one of the central paradoxes of the play that it is the Nurse's version of Phaedra's ethical stance to which Hippolytus is exposed through the Nurse's blunt, half-licensed explication,[53] that is, the version in which the points of contact between his ethic and Phaedra's are quite obscured. It is this exposure which triggers Hippolytus' violent tirade against women, which triggers in turn both Phaedra's criticism of his 'intemperance' and the counter-violence and 'shouting' of her lying death-note.[54] In this complex sequence of events, the three figures become so closely interlocked that what is said or done represents the result of their interaction (and of the misunderstandings and mis-communication in that interaction) rather than being a direct expression of the free choice and ethical stance of any one figure. This complexity represents on the level of plot the kind of paradox and dislocation I noted in the recurrent phrase-patterns of the play, notably those relating to the gap between character and word (or action), and between inner state and outward expression.

Within this larger pattern, I want to focus on parts of two speeches by Phaedra and Hippolytus (391ff. and 991ff.) in which we find with especial clarity the articulation of the kind of selfhood that is relevant to this dramatic nexus. In form, both speeches are *apologiai*, statements of self-defence, and have a tone of insistent self-justification; correspondingly, they constitute an assertion of the speaker's view of her or his moral character and conduct. Phaedra's speech, as has often been noted, articulates an ethical world-view in which the highest priority is given to the achievement of *eukleia* ('good name') and the avoidance of *duskleia* ('disgrace') for oneself and one's family.[55] This is, in a sense, a derivative or second-hand ethic, since it gives ultimate importance to what others believe; and this aspect of her ethic is underlined in the speech in a variety of ways. It comes out, for instance, in an emphatic couplet:

ἐμοὶ γὰρ εἴη μήτε λανθάνειν καλὰ
μήτ' αἰσχρὰ δρώσῃ μάρτυρας πολλοὺς ἔχειν.

(403–4)

'I would not want my fine actions to pass unnoticed or my shameful ones to have many witnesses'; in her repeated stress on being silent about, or concealing, her illicit desires, and on her fear 'of being caught out disgracing my husband';[56] and, above all, in the compelling image of her nightmare, that of being 'seen' in the mirror of time which 'reveals those among men who are bad' (428–30). This last image, especially, encapsulates the second-order, 'reflected', quality of her ethical concern, which is, as some critics suggest, very much that of a woman who wants to fulfil her role in a world whose order is established by male authority.[57]

However, it is important, and not altogether easy, to define Phaedra's ethical stance exactly. Phaedra does not *only* want to 'keep up appearances' (regardless of what underlies those appearances); she dissociates herself emphatically from the hypocritical wives (τὰς σώφρονας μὲν ἐν λόγοις, 'virtuous only in words', 413) who live in this way. It is her heartfelt wish to *be* the kind of person whom others will properly regard as a 'virtuous' wife; she genuinely wants to meet the standards society sets for her.[58] Hence, as she tells us, she has attempted to conquer her illicit desire by *sōphronein* (presumably meaning 'self-control', that is, *trying* to be virtuous, 398–9). Her indignation against those who seek to subvert the standards she respects (the 'nobles' to whom 'disgraceful things seem fine') is emphatic, and is one of a number of strongly personal judgements she makes about the importance of maintaining social standards.[59] Relatedly, in her account of her response to her passion, she consistently identifies 'herself' (through first-personal verb-forms, for instance) with the virtuous woman who resists the passion, or at least who makes decisions in the consciousness that she cannot resist it. The passion itself, by contrast, is not presented as being 'her', or even 'hers', but as an external force, an 'other': it is something that 'wounds' her, a 'sickness', 'folly', or 'the goddess of love' (*Kupris*).[60] There is an inherent instability in this stance, in that Phaedra defines herself in a way that completely excludes something (her passion) that is clearly, in some sense, part of her; and, later in the play, this instability becomes explicit.[61] But in this speech, at any rate, Phaedra maintains consistently a certain mode of self-presentation, identifying 'herself' with the person who acts 'virtuously' and in line with what society expects.[62]

In the case of Hippolytus, we can find comparable passages of self-articulation in the first part of his speech of defence to Theseus and in the subsequent dialogue (991ff. and 1070ff.). Although, as Gould points out, these speeches are informed by rhetorical strategies (and by 'the rhetoric of the situation'),[63] this does not mean that they do not also constitute a means of self-articulation by Hippolytus. Indeed, Hippolytus' understanding of his own *sōphrosunē* is an essential part of the play's central dialectic, and thus of the situation generated by the dialectic at the point in the play. Also, Hippolytus' picture of himself in these speeches, together with the style of his self-presentation, is very much in line with what we find elsewhere in the play. Whereas for Phaedra *sōphrosunē* is associated especially with keeping up appearances (though also with maintaining the standards of conduct that 'appearances' require), for Hippolytus *sōphrosunē* is conceived as something which derives from his own nature rather than from an attempt to meet social standards. His *sōphrosunē* is expressed in his relationships (with gods, *philoi*, etc.,

996ff.), and especially in the consistency with which he maintains these relationships ('I am the same person to my friends whether they are present or absent').[64] But what underlies that consistency is not simply the desire to achieve accepted standards of conduct but an 'innate' or 'integral' *sōphrosunē*,[65] and an 'inner' purity that renders him immune from the impulses other men need to resist. Responding to the accusation of rape, he insists not only on the purity of his body (which is all the case really requires) but also on the purity of his inclinations. He has no desire even to see representations of the sexual act, let alone to perform it, because he has a 'virgin mind' (*parthenon psuchēn*, 1006).

This is the strongest point of contrast between Hippolytus' self-presentation and Phaedra's. There is no tension between 'him' and his passion; his deepest desire is to act in accordance with his ethical ideal.[66] But his insistence on the innerness of his *sōphrosunē* does not prevent him from wishing, like Phaedra, to make a public display of his *sōphrosunē*. Of course, the immediate context of his speech goes some way towards explaining this wish; since he is accused of an unchaste act, he needs to show others that he is chaste. But does this need alone explain his claim that, in the whole wide world (indicated with a cosmic gesture – 'you see this sun and earth'), 'there is *nobody* more *sōphrōn* than me' (993–5)? Significantly, the worst fate he can envisage, if he is proved to be 'bad by nature', is that he should die 'without fame or name' (*akleēs anōnumos*), utterly unnoticed (1028–31). Again, in the subsequent dialogue with Theseus, what gives him most pain is the thought that 'I seem evil and am supposed to be such by you'.[67] It is the pain of misrecognition that prompts two wishes (which are both, in different ways, reminiscent of Phaedra's phraseology): that the house itself could speak and bear witness of his innocence, and that he could 'stand opposite and look at [himself]', so as to act as a fellow-mourner for his troubles. The echoes of Phaedra's lines partly serve to underline the differences between them: Phaedra lives in dread of what the house might utter and of the prospect of seeing herself caught in the 'mirror' of public censure, while Hippolytus positively wants the house to tell its secrets and longs for another self to 'reflect' his grief (which is largely the grief of someone who is not properly reflected in the 'mirror' of public appraisal).[68] At the same time, however, the echoes underline their shared preoccupation with the confirmation, through public 'reflection', of their view of themselves as *sōphrōn*.[69] Like Phaedra, and in some ways still more emphatically, Hippolytus wants both to *be sōphrōn* (as he understands this) and to *be seen* as such; he wants not only to have 'inner' *sōphrosunē* but also to exhibit this innerness in the public domain, and the display, as well as the innerness, seems integral to his understanding of himself.[70]

In my reading of these passages, I have tried to emphasize how the speeches function as a means of self-articulation by the figures concerned, and also to show how the 'selves' thus articulated fit into the play's larger dialectic, its exploration of the nature of *sōphrosunē*, and of the way in which *sōphrosunē* is – and is not – communicated. In the remainder of this chapter, I want to reflect further on the significance of these passages within the play as a whole, and also to consider in more general terms the kind of self-articulation contained in these passages. For both these purposes, I want to draw on some intellectual texts of the period, which can help us both to define the central emphases of the speeches, and to analyse the kind of self-articulation they embody.

My reading of these passages suggests not only that it is a matter of importance, for both figures, to communicate their *sōphrosunē*, but also that *sōphrosunē*, as they understand this, depends in a quite crucial way on such communication. For Phaedra, clearly, *sōphrosunē* consists in acting in a way that manifests to one's society the fact (and it is important that it *is* a fact) that one is meeting social standards of virtuous conduct. For Hippolytus also, despite his emphasis on the 'inner' and 'natural' quality of his *sōphrosunē*, the public expression of the quality is seen as an integral part of its possession, and one whose deprivation causes deep distress. The attitudes embodied in these speeches intersect with a number of central themes of intellectual debate of the time, in so far as we can reconstruct this, including the question whether a virtue such as *sōphrosunē* depends on nature (*phusis*) or on the kind of teaching and habituation that ensures conformity with the laws or conventions (*nomoi*) of society.[71] They relate especially to a question discussed in a number of fifth-century texts, whether (as Antiphon puts it) one should act in the same way when alone and unobserved as when one acts with witnesses, and thus risks 'disgrace and punishment'; that is, whether what is just by nature is the same as what is just according to the laws of society, which purports to govern the whole range of one's actions and desires.[72] Democritus' view on this question is that 'one should not feel more shame before other men than before oneself', and that such 'self-respect' should be established 'as a law (*nomos*) for one's *psuchē*'.[73] The ethical stances, and personal styles, of the central figures in this play can plausibly be placed within this debate. Phaedra's assumption that a virtue such as *sōphrosunē* depends on the sanction of public opinion, and Hippolytus' assumption that it depends rather on one's own inner nature, but that this 'innerness' merits the reward of public recognition, can thus be situated within a framework of ethical thinking that goes beyond the play itself.

However, in placing the attitudes adopted by the central figures in this wider context of significance, it is important not to lose contact with the informing ethos of the play itself. If we were to follow through the implications of some of the ideas of the period (especially, Democritus' stress on the importance of 'self-respect'), we might be inclined to read the play as containing a critique of Phaedra's second-order ethic. In such a reading the eventual decision to destroy Hippolytus by her lying accusation in order to save her own reputation and that of her children might be taken as a natural consequence, and an implied criticism, of this ethic. Hippolytus' more self-related ethic might, in such a reading, emerge as morally preferable; and the fact that he keeps his oath not to reveal Phaedra's passion, even at the cost of his own life, might be taken as indicating his moral superiority.[74] Such a reading has its attractions; but there are also serious objections to it. For one thing, any attempt to draw a sharp contrast between their two ethics needs to be qualified by the fact noted earlier of Phaedra's strongly personal commitment to her ethic of social conformity, and by Hippolytus' desire for social recognition of his personal ethical stance.[75]

More importantly, this type of reading seems to cut across one of the informing themes of the play, articulated in its plot as well as in recurrent phrase-patterns: namely the dislocation between character and act or word brought about through miscommunication and misunderstanding. Consistent with this theme is the fact that Phaedra's 'shame ethic' only issues in her lying death-note as a result of a tangled web of circumstances, to which the Nurse's misrepresentation of Phaedra's state of mind and Hippolytus' misguided response also make crucial contributions. To say that the final avenging Phaedra is not the same person as the earlier Phaedra (the Phaedra who is preoccupied with her own *sōphrosunē*) would be to go too far.[76] But it is true, none the less, that her revenge is not presented as the predictable reaction of that earlier figure, but as one in which her character (as disclosed in the monologue of 373ff.) is only partly reflected. Similar considerations might also apply in the case of Hippolytus. I suggested earlier that he could be judged (by the standards of Democritus' ethic of 'self-respect') as morally superior to Phaedra. But if one applied those standards more strictly, one might be inclined to see in his persistent desire for public recognition of his purity an indication that his ethic is less 'inner' and more socially grounded than it seems. And one might go on to see in his undiscriminating denunciation of women (616ff.), and his gloating anticipation of Phaedra's future discomfort (659–62), evidence of an underlying weakness in his moral character and understanding. The speech might be taken as showing that for Hippolytus it is not enough simply to *be sōphrōn* (by his standards); he has to *dramatize* his *sōphrosunē* by rhetorical self-dissociation from those who lack it and by underlining his stance as a morally superior observer of others' faults. Perhaps there is something in this suggestion; but it is important also to note that the speech is marked, among Hippolytus' utterances, by its generalizing crudeness and personal viciousness, and that the context invites us to take it as the passionate, even hysterical, response of a man in a state of shock.[77]

In other words, the play is not so shaped as to show how certain types of defective character and attitude naturally generate disastrous consequences for themselves and others. Rather it underlines, through the central action and the recurrent phrase-patterns, the paradoxical and unpredictable way in which these figures' commitment to *sōphrosunē* (as they understand this notion) contributes to their mutual destruction. Also, the *Hippolytus*, like other Greek tragedies, does not invite us only to appraise its figures and their ethical positions, but also to engage with them sympathetically, even when we have reservations about those positions.[78] Correspondingly, a reading which places the figures too firmly in a moral schema, especially one based on ethical statements drawn from outside the play, runs the risk of misrepresenting the ethos of the play, which is at once distinctive and characteristic of the tragic genre in its emphasis on the paradoxes and moral ambiguities of human existence.[79]

The kind of self-articulation we find in the play (and also the kind of ethical 'statement' the play makes through such self-articulation) can be defined further by reference to another contemporary intellectual project, that of the Socratic *elenchos*, as exemplified in Plato's *Charmides*. Any reconstruction of the methods of the historical Socrates is necessarily conjectural; but I want to give special prominence to those passages in the Platonic dialogues where the Socratic *elenchos* is presented as an investigation of the interlocutor's mind (parallel to a medical investigation of his body), in which he is invited to 'examine himself' and to 'give an account of himself'. Typically, the interlocutor is asked to state his understanding of a given virtue (one which he can reasonably be supposed to possess) and in this way to put 'himself' into words in a way which enables Socrates to examine his understanding of the virtue in question.[80] Eric Havelock has argued persuasively that it is this aspect of the Socratic project which is the object of comic parody in Aristophanes' *Clouds*, especially in the *'encouchement'* or 'bed-bug' scene; and that this feature of Socratic method was therefore taken by Aristophanes to be one which Athenian audiences in the 420s BC would find recognizable and a source of amusement.[81]

If we accept the implications of this type of evidence, it follows that the response to the Socratic *elenchos* involves a kind of 'articulation of the self'; and, although the process involved is, on the face of it, a purely intellectual one (one is asked to define a given virtue, for instance), it is also clear that the process is thought to reveal the 'self' in a relatively broad sense. As Nicias puts it in the *Laches*, once someone starts a dialogue with Socrates, he cannot stop 'being dragged around in argument' until he has been forced to 'give an account of himself (*didonai peri hautou logon*), of how he lives now and how he has lived his life so far' (187e9–188a2). It seems clear in the *Charmides*, for instance, that the kind of definition offered of the virtue in question is intended to disclose the character of the interlocutor, and to indicate the depth or shallowness of his understanding of the virtue. Thus, the definitions offered by Charmides ('doing everything in a quiet and orderly manner' and 'being ashamed') are clearly meant to reflect his immature, 'good boy', understanding of the virtue. Similarly, Critias' attempts at definition, together with some of the dramatic by-play of the dialogue, seem designed to reflect his aristocratic (not to say, snobbish) apprehension of it, as well as his rather shallow pretensions to intellectual sophistication.[82] Thus, in the *Charmides* as well as the *Hippolytus*, the process of self-articulation is conducted in a way that involves different styles of reflexiveness: Charmides' diffident modesty (as evidenced by his reply to whether or not he possesses *sōphrosunē*) is implicitly contrasted with Critias' ostentatious, but shallow, self-confidence.[83] Indeed, the extent to which the Socratic method, as recreated in such works as the *Charmides* and *Clouds*, shares with the *Hippolytus* an interest in self-articulation through dialogue (embodied in the content as well as the style of reflexive utterance) may suggest that the idea of 'the articulation of the self' played an unusually prominent role in the thought-world of the period.

I think it is worth pursuing the question of the similarities and dissimilarities between the *Hippolytus* and *Charmides*, in order to define with greater precision the kind of self-articulation we find in Euripides' play, and the way in which this fits in with the 'dialectic' of the work as a whole. As my comments indicate, a Platonic dialogue such as the *Charmides* has something of the atmosphere of a pre-Menandrian 'ethical' comedy, in which we feel relatively confident in appraising the character of the figures (as being modest, boastful, and so on).[84] Also, the unfolding dialectic gives us some degree of confidence in appraising the figures' definitions of *sōphrosunē* and, relatedly, in appraising the depth and shallowness of thinking that underlies these. In the *Hippolytus*, this is true only in a much more qualified way. It is true, as I have already suggested, that the unfolding dialectic of the work invites us to 'place' the figures (as regards their understanding of *sōphrosunē*) in a larger ethical framework, and also to feel reservations, of various kinds, about the quality of their understanding.[85] But it is also true, as I have argued, that any inclination to arrive at a definitive, unequivocal set of judgements on the figures is counteracted by the para-doxical and ambivalent ethos of the play and by the sympathetic engagement established between audience and central figures.[86] These factors make it difficult to (so to speak) 'discard' any of the figures from our concerns (and difficult also to discard their ethical stances and reflexive styles), regardless of the reservations we feel about these; whereas in the *Charmides* we have more confidence in doing so.[87]

However, it is important not to overstate the differences between the two works in this respect. Although the *Charmides*, as its argument unfolds, invites us to discard the formulations of *sōphrosunē* offered by the interlocutors, it does not proceed to offer a definitive formulation of the virtue; it is thus, like most early (and some late) Platonic dialogues, aporetic in character. The aporetic character of this dialogue, as of other Socratic dialogues, is sometimes taken to be purely formal; and it is often supposed that a solution to the difficulties is implied in the argument (namely, the Socratic paradox that virtue is knowledge).[88] It is true, of course, that the argument gives a special status to certain lines of enquiry (in this dialogue to the idea that *sōphrosunē* consists in knowing what one does and does not know); but this line of enquiry, like the others, is inconclusive and is, I think, genuinely unconcluded.[89] The Socratic project, in other words, is to *press* the argument, and to explore its problematical and paradoxical implications; indeed, the so-called Socratic 'doctrines' are, arguably, to be understood as means to advance such a procedure.[90] To defend this claim fully would take me outside the scope of this chapter; but it is worth stating it in order to bring out a further respect in which Euripides' play may reflect its contemporary milieu.[91] While both the *Hippolytus* and the *Charmides* explore the nature of *sōphrosunē*, and do so through the presentation of different modes of self-articulation (and different understandings of the 'self' so articulated), neither work attempts to present a definitive model of *sōphrosunē* or of the ideal self; and, in this respect, both works (if we can take the *Charmides* as exemplary of Socratic method) may be representative of one side at least of intellectual debate in the late fifth century.[92]

NOTES

1   I also contribute to this debate in 'The question of character and personality in Greek tragedy', *Poetics Today* 7:2 (1986), pp. 251–73, 'The character/personality distinction', in C. B. R. Pelling (ed.), *Characterization and Individuality in Greek Literature* (Oxford, 1990), pp. 1–31, and in a forthcoming book on *Character, Personality, and the Self: A Study in Greek Literature and Philosophy*.

2   The relationship between selfhood and articulation is one I also
    pursue in 'Two monologues of self-division: Euripides, *Medea*
    1021–80 and Seneca, *Medea* 893–977', in M. Whitby, M. Whitby,
    and P. Hardie (eds), *Homo Viator: Classical Essays for John Bramble*
    (Bristol, 1987), pp. 25–37, and in 'Snell, Adkins, and the Greek
    concept of the person', an unpublished paper given to the Hellenic
    Society in London, 1988.
3   On the connotations of this untranslatable term, pp. 80–2.
4   See, most recently, T. H. Irwin, 'Euripides and Socrates', *CP* 78
    (1983), pp. 183–97, with references to earlier discussions.
5   John Gould, 'Dramatic character and "human intelligibility" in
    Greek tragedy', *PCPhS* 24 (1978), pp. 43–67.
6   The assumption, which Gould seems to make, that we do *not*
    encounter similar problems in interpreting people in real life, has
    now been usefully questioned by P. Easterling, 'Constructing
    character in Greek tragedy', in Pelling (n.1) pp. 84–7. As she points
    out, referring especially to E. Goffman, *Frame Analysis* (Cambridge,
    Mass., 1974), our understanding of people in real life depends on
    the interpretative 'frame' in which we place them, and on the
    extent to which the conventions of their discourse are ones which
    make them 'intelligible' to us.
7   Gould (n.5), pp. 54–8.
8   Euripides, *Alcestis*, ed. A. M. Dale (Oxford, 1954), pp. xxiv–xxix,
    and *Collected Papers* (Cambridge, 1969), pp. 139–55.
9   Gould (n.5), p. 56; Gould compares the equally rhetorical
    pronouncements of Medea in E. *Med.* 214ff.
10 On the relationship between cinematic and literary conventions of
    narrative, cf. S. Chatman, 'Characters and narrators', *Poetics Today*
    7:2 (1986), pp. 189–204.
11 S. Goldhill, *Reading Greek Tragedy* (Cambridge, 1986), hereafter
    RGT, pp. 172ff.; cf. 'Goldhill on molehills', *LCM* 11:10 (December
    1986), pp. 163–7, and 'Character and action: representation and
    reading', in Pelling (n.1).
12 Gould (n.5), pp. 44–6.
13 Goldhill, *RGT*, pp. 175ff.; cf. B. M. W. Knox, *The Heroic Temper:
    Studies in Sophoclean Tragedy* (Berkeley, Calif., 1964), chs 1 and 2,
    and R. P. Winnington-Ingram, *Sophocles: An Interpretation*
    (Cambridge, 1980), esp. ch. 2. It is a defect of studies of individual
    psychological terms (even a meticulous study such as D. B. Claus,
    Toward the Soul: An Inquiry into the Meaning of 'Psyche' before Plato
    (New Haven, Conn., 1981), or of groups of terms studied in
    isolation from the drama (such as T. B. L. Webster, 'Some
    psychological terms in Greek tragedy', *JHS* 77 (1957), pp. 149–54),
    that the importance of the dramatic context is not fully brought
    out.
14 Goldhill, *RGT*, pp. 173–4, citing R. Barthes, *S/Z*, trans. R. Miller
    (London, 1975), p. 178.
15 H. North, *Sophrosyne: Self-knowledge and Self-restraint in Greek
    Literature* (Ithaca, NY, 1966).

16 As does Sophocles' *Ajax*; cf. Goldhill, *RGT*, pp. 193ff.

17 To allocate these different senses to specific usages is to risk effacing the important ambiguities of meaning which the term has in the play. But here is a crude classification of the *primary* meanings of the term in different contexts (lumping together verbal, adjectival, and noun forms, of which the most common are the adjective, *sōphrōn*, and the infinitive, *sōphronein*).

   (i) 'chastity': 80, 413, 494, 1034, 1100, 1402.
  (ii) 'virtue': 358, 431, 667, 995, 1007, 1365.
 (iii) 'self-control': 399, 731, 1034.
 (iv) 'good sense': 704, 1013 (1035).

Obviously, to explore the resonance of the term fully in the play, one would need to situate it in a vocabulary of related terms, including *semnos, sophos, phronein, gnōmē, suggnōmē, aidōs, eukleia, kalos,* etc., each of which would also exhibit its own complexity of meaning.

18 Contrast his more complex usage in 1034, discussed on pp. 81–2. Presumably, even Hippolytus does not demand, as a precondition of *sōphronein*, the kind of *absolute* sexual chastity he regards as his own special quality (79–80, discussed on p. 86, cf. 1002–7).

19 Cf. Goldhill, *RGT*, pp. 132–3, who notes D. Grene's attempt, in his translation of *sōphronein* in 731 ('learn of chastity in moderation'), D. Grene and R. Lattimore (eds), *The Complete Greek Tragedies,* vol. III (Chicago, 1959), to bring out the reference back to 667–8; and, for *sōphronein* as 'be humane', 'pity', cf. North (n. 15), p. 108. See also G. Berns, 'Nomos and Physis (an interpretation of Euripides' *Hippolytos*)', *Hermes* 101 (1973), pp. 165–87, esp. pp. 177–85, who underlines the irony in the idea that Hippolytus, who insists that *sōphronein* must derive from nature not learning (79–80) should be made to *learn* to be *sōphrōn*.

20 Cf. W. S. Barrett (ed.), *Euripides: Hippolytos* (Oxford, 1964), ad loc.: 'What she did was to perform a single act ... her suicide, that subdued [her passion] once for all'. On this reading, *sōphronein* denotes a crude type of self-control (a type Phaedra herself envisages in 398–402, following the failure of her attempt to subdue her passion by will-power, *sōphronein,* 399). Conceivably, however, Hippolytus may mean simply that she behaved in a *sōphrōn* way because she was prevented (by him) from acting on her unchaste desires.

21 Cf. 656ff.; it is his 'reverence' (*eusebes*) that makes him keep his oath, but the effort of self-control involved in suppressing his indignation is evident in these lines; contrast the unforced, 'natural' quality of his chastity, 79–80, 1002–7, discussed on pp. 86, 90–1.

22 Thus, in yet another sense of *sōphronein,* that of showing prudence or good sense in the management of one's life (1013, and perhaps also 704), Hippolytus, in not using his *sōphronein* well, proved *not* to be *sōphrōn.* Froma Zeitlin suggests another nuance in 1035, 'The power of Aphrodite: Eros and the boundaries of the self in the

CHRISTOPHER GILL

Hippolytus', in P. Burian (ed.), *Directions in Euripidean Criticism*
(Durham, NC, 1985), p. 200 n. 80. Hippolytus realizes that
Phaedra overheard his angry (intemperate) speech (616–68) and
hence that, in this respect, he has not used his capacity for
sōphrosunē (self-control?) as he should have done.

23 Lines 398–9 and context, discussed on pp. 86–7, 89–90.

24 See 616ff., esp. 664–8, 729–31; also 995, 1007, 1100–1, 1365, as
well as 1035.

25 Hence, we can see the force of Artemis' judgement that Aphrodite
destroyed Hippolytus because 'she was pained by [his] being
sōphrōn' (1402), while also recognizing the force of Aphrodite's own
inclusion of Hippolytus among 'those who are arrogant'
(*phronousin ... mega*, 6); cf. Berns (n. 19), pp. 174–5. A. Schmitt,
'Zur Charakterdarstellung des Hippolytos im "Hippolytos" von
Euripides', *Würzburger Jahrbuch für die Altertumswissenschaft* 3
(1977), pp. 17–42, seems to me to go too far in suggesting that the
play moves towards establishing a single, negative, judgement on
Hippolytus' self-ascribed *sōphronein*. (See, for example, 29: 'Damit
scheint mir über die wahre Natur von Hippolytos' "sophrosyne"
kein Zweifel mehr möglich: Sie ist eine aus der Leidenschaft
kommende Verblendenheit.')

26 My translation attempts to capture what I take to be an intended
ambiguity in καταστρέφου between 'subdue' your sickness and
'work it out' (i.e. satisfy your sick desires), the interpretations
considered as alternatives by Barrett (n. 20), ad loc.

27 There is a double antithesis here, between πρόθυμός ('wants', 'is
keen to') and ἄκοντας ('against their will'), and between μὴ
καλῶς ('[do] wrong') and εὐεργετεῖν ('help', 'do good to').

28 See, esp., the parallelism between 317 and 612, with *phrēn* as the
subject of the second, antithetical, clause in each case; the similar
characterizations of the 'sensible' (who none the less fail to act on
their 'good sense') in 313 (*phroneis eu*), 358 (*sōphroneis*), and 462
(*echontas eu phrenōn*), the phrasing of 358–9 being also echoed
in first-personal form in 380–1; *nosos* is a link between 463, 477,
597, 730, and 1300 (*oistron*), thus connecting different patterns
of antithesis and qualification; and dying with *eukleia* is a link
between 47–8 and 1299. For further such qualified
characterizations, see 331, 505–6, and the related ambiguities of
709, 718, and 721 (on the latter passages, see Reckford and Segal
refs in n. 76 below).

29 Notably 385–7 on the two-fold (*dissai*) types of *aidōs* whose distinct
character Phaedra would like to be made transparent through
distinct names; and 925–31, Theseus' wish for two-fold (*dissai*)
voices to render transparent the inner character of the true and
false friend. The former passage contains the radical qualification
of character that figures in 597 and 693–4 (but here applied to a
quality, *aidōs*, or possibly pleasure); both passages contain the
disjunction between inner and outer that figures in 317, 612, and
956–7. See further on these passages Zeitlin (n. 22), pp. 83–4,

100

Goldhill, *RGT*, pp. 134–5, also Claus and Willinck (refs in n. 55 below) and Kovacs (ref. in n. 59 below).

30 Cf. B. M. W. Knox, 'The *Hippolytus* of Euripides', *YCS* 13 (1952), pp. 3–31 (repr. in B. M. W. Knox, *Word and Action* (Baltimore, Md, 1979), pp. 205–30), R. P. Winnington-Ingram, '*Hippolytus*: a study in causation', in *Euripide, Fondation Hardt Entretiens* VI (Vandoeuvres-Genève, 1960), pp. 171–91, H. C. Avery, 'My tongue swore, but my mind is unsworn', *TAPA* 99 (1968), pp. 19–35, and C. Segal, 'Shame and purity in Euripides' *Hippolytus*', *Hermes* 98 (1970), pp. 278–99.

31 I.e. inconclusive; cf. p. 97 on this.

32 Cf. Goldhill, *RGT*, pp. 125–6, 134–7, and Zeitlin (n. 22), esp. pp. 80ff.

33 Although Theseus is sometimes also associated with the theme of *sōphrosunē* (as being someone who *fails* to show 'self-control' over his anger at Hippolytus' alleged rape, 885–98, cf. 1320–4), he seems to me not to be so closely interlocked with the other figures in this respect, and I will not discuss him here.

34 54–5; cf. 987 and 1179–80.

35 ὅσοις διδακτὸν μηδέν, ἀλλ᾽ ἐν τῇ φύσει
    τὸ σωφρονεῖν εἴληχεν εἰς τὰ πάντ᾽ ἀεί,

                                              (79–80)

36 On this view of the virtue, and on the points of similarity and difference with philosophical ideas about the acquisition of virtue, see Berns (n. 19), pp. 165–9, and discussion on pp. 92–3.

37 See 82–7, esp. *monō(i)* (84), although the more generalized phrasing of 79–80 allows for the notion of a *class* of such privileged (*sōphrōn*) devotees.

38 Cf. A. Schmitt (n. 25), pp. 24–7, though noting my reservations about Schmitt's overall view (n. 25).

39 See esp. 403ff., 421–30, discussed on pp. 89–90; the chorus's response (431–2) confirms her view of the importance of the public manifestation of virtue.

40 Cf. n. 18 above.

41 See 317, 394, 398–401; cf. Segal (n. 30), p. 281, and discussion on p. 90.

42 See esp. 243–6, 279, 297–300, 317ff., 345ff., 393–7, 498ff., 706ff., 877–80; cf. refs in nn. 30 and 32 above.

43 728–31 (cf. 660ff.), discussed on pp. 80–1. As noted earlier (esp. n. 19 above), she also wants him to *learn* to be *sōphrōn* in another sense ('humane'); and in this respect she does not regard him as a complete exemplar of *sōphrosunē*.

44 See 208ff. (taken with 73ff.), noting esp. the similarity between 208–11 and 77–8, and the reiterated expressions of desire to do what Hippolytus does, as well as being where he is; cf. Goldhill, *RGT*, pp. 124–5, and Zeitlin (n. 22), p. 110.

45 In view of her subsequent radical contrast between her (*sōphrōn*) self and her lust (seen as 'mad', 'diseased', and as the work of *Kupris*

in 391ff.), it might perhaps seem misguided to see her lust as an *expression* of the desire for *sōphrosunē*. The objection, I should make plain, is not to 'psychologizing' as such (cf. my response to Gould on pp. 78–9) but to the kind of psychologizing that does not respond to the psychological concerns implied in the text. Cf. n. 69 below.

46   186–8, 253ff.

47   See esp. 490–8, 500–2; Phaedra later describes this policy woundingly as characteristic of someone who 'wants to do wrong to help friends against their will' (693–4, cited on p. 84).

48   See esp. 465–6:

> ... ἐν σοφοῖσι γὰρ
> τάδ᾽ ἐστὶ θνητῶν, λανθάνειν τὰ μὴ καλά.

a cunning modification of Phaedra's 403–4:

> ἐμοὶ γὰρ εἴη μήτε λανθάνειν καλὰ
> μήτ᾽ αἰσχρὰ δρώσῃ μάρτυρας πολλοὺς ἔχειν.

To this extent, Gould's claim that 'it is the shaping pressure of rhetorical form which determines the movement of the speech more than any sense that *these* arguments are native to the Nurse, or that they are chosen to penetrate the defences of *this* opponent' ('Dramatic character', p. 56), needs qualification; 467–9, which he cites in this connection, form part of the Nurse's modification of Phaedra's ethic, cf. Segal (n. 30), p. 281, n. 2.

49   See 462–3 (also 477, cf. n. 26 above), and 465–6 (n. 48 above). Later (695ff.), I take it that when the Nurse says ... οὐκ ἐσωφρόνουν ἐγώ. (704), she means primarily, 'I didn't act sensibly', that is, in line with the amoral pragmatism of 700–1, 'I didn't succeed'; although a secondary sense, more in line with Phaedra's usage (cf. n. 50 below), might be, as Barrett takes it, 'I went too far', i.e. 'I failed to show proper self-restraint'.

50   Line 494 and context; cf. Phaedra's account of her attempt to use *sōphrosunē* ('self-control') to preserve her reputation (*eukleia*) in 398–9 and 413ff.

51   See esp. 503–6, and n. 61 below.

52   345–52 and 500–24; for Phaedra's (and the Nurse's) style of explication, see refs in n. 42 above; the second passage (500–24) shows that the Nurse is capable of adopting Phaedra's style of obliqueness to further her own objective of acting as the mouthpiece of Phaedra's desires.

53   The Nurse's actual proposition is elided from the drama; but its character as a (misleading) explication of Phaedra's secret is clearly signalled in the language of 565–600.

54   See 728–31, discussed on pp. 80–1, and 877ff.

55   See, for example, C. W. Willinck, 'Some problems of text and interpretation in the *Hippolytus*', *CQ* 18 (1968), pp. 11–43, esp. p. 20 and context, and D. Claus, 'Phaedra and the Socratic paradox', *YCS* 22 (1972), pp. 223–38, esp. 230, and refs in following notes.

56   As she graphically puts it, 'it is this very thing [fear of such

disgrace] that is killing me', i.e. driving me to commit suicide (419), a declaration which follows her expression of hatred and amazement at those who can commit adultery in secret and still 'look in their husband's face' and not be afraid that 'the timbers of their house will speak' of their offences (413–18).

57 Cf. Goldhill, *RGT*, pp. 126–7, Zeitlin (n. 22), pp. 99–100; on the centrality of the image of the mirror in the play's exploration of forms of self-knowledge, see also J. Pigeaud, 'Euripide et la connaissance de soi', *Les Etudes classiques*, 44 (1976), pp. 3–24, esp. 14ff., and C. A. E. Luschnig, *Time Holds the Mirror: A Study of Knowledge in Euripides' Hippolytus* (Leiden, 1988).

58 In comparison with Amphiaraus, in Aeschylus' *Seven Against Thebes*, who prefers to *be* best rather than *seem* so (592), Phaedra wants *both* to be good (as she understands this) *and* to seem so; Zeitlin (n. 22), p. 100, also cites the passage to make a rather different point.

59 See esp. 'to me' (403), 'I knew' (405), 'may she die terribly' (407), 'I hate' (413), 'this very thing' etc. (419), 'they say' (and, inferentially, 'I accept') 'that this alone competes in life (i.e. enables one to win life's competitions): the possession of a just and good character (or mind, *gnōmē*, 426–7)'. Willink (n. 55) over-assimilates Phaedra's position to that of the 'successful adulteress' of whom she is 'inwardly envious' (24), or that of the Nurse; D. Kovacs, 'Shame, pleasure, and honor in Phaedra's great speech (Euripides, *Hippolytus* 375–87)', *AJP* 101 (1980), pp. 287–303, esp. 300–2, appreciates better the sincerity and integrity of her position, but overlooks its limitations, on which see discussion on p. 93.

60 See 392–4, 398–402; for the use of first- and third-personal forms to define what is and is not 'oneself', cf. Gill (n. 2).

61 See 502–6:

καὶ μή σε πρὸς θεῶν — εὖ λέγεις γαρ, αἰσχρὰ δέ —
πέρα προβῇς τῶνδ'· ὡς ὑπείργασμαι μὲν εὖ
ψυχὴν ἔρωτι, τἀσχρὰ δ' ἢν λέγῃς καλῶς,
ἐς τοῦθ' ὃ φεύγω νῦν ἀναλωθήσομαι.

'No, by the gods – for your shameful advice is given well – do not go on in this way. I am so well worked over ["tilled", like a field] in my *psuchē* by desire that, if you speak well of shameful things, I shall be expended ["used up"] on that which I am now running away from.'

While Phaedra still sees 'herself' as the virtuous person at risk and not as the 'desire' which is operant on her, the speech as a whole, and especially the metaphors ('tilled', 'used up'), disclose that the rigid separation between 'her' and 'desire' is being undermined, as is the related adherence to the standards by which she defines her virtue.

62 Her autobiographical account underlines the point that she holds the same values that she believes her society holds: she regards as a *nosos* ('sickness') what she knows is regarded as *noson ... dusklea* ('a

disgraceful sickness'), 394 and 405. The account of 'the path of [her] *gnōmē*' (391) is in line with the kind of *gnōmē* which she knows men say 'alone competes in life' (427). Claus (n. 55), pp. 230 and 236–7, underestimates the extent to which the values of a 'shame-culture' can be personally felt, and, correspondingly, to which a person can identify her 'self' (in a relatively stable way) with the kind of self approved by those values.

63 Cf. Gould (n. 5), pp. 57–8, and discussion above, esp. n. 8.

64 Line 1001; this line, together with 997–1000, clearly contains a barbed, though covert, allusion to the duplicity (and lack of *sōphrosunē*) he attributes to Phaedra as a result of the Nurse's proposition.

65 See, emphatically, 79–81 (and nn. 35–6 above), the recurrence of the 'nature' theme in 995 (*sōphronesteros gegōs*), and the repeated phrase *ei kakos pephuk' anēr* (1031, 1075, 1191) – which Hippolytus, of course, denies.

66 Contrast 1002–6 (and 78–80) with 392–4, 397–402, discussed on p. 90, and also 317. ('My hands are pure, but my mind, *phrēn*, has a kind of pollution.')

67 1071–2; the repetition (*phainomai dokō te soi*) presumably emphasizes the pain he feels in seeming to be such a person.

68 1074–5, cf. 418 and context; 1078–9, cf. 428–30.

69 Cf. Zeitlin (n. 22), pp. 95, 99–100. Gould (n. 5), p. 57, tries to counter psychologizing readings of these utterances of Hippolytus, seeing in 1078–9 only 'a brilliantly conceived theatrical image which uses the form to convey his total isolation'; but the kind of psychologizing he has in view is not quite the sort attempted here (or, as I think, by Zeitlin), in which the 'psychology' of the drama is seen as embedded in its verbal forms and gestures.

70 Cf. the opening scene, esp. 78ff., 653–5, and his frequent affirmations of virtue, before and after this has been revealed by Artemis (1100–1, 1191–3, 1242, 1365, 1383–4, 1455).

71 Cf. North (n. 15), pp. 86–8, Berns (n. 19), pp. 169–73, and, more generally, W. K. C. Guthrie, *A History of Greek Philosophy*, vol. III (Cambridge, 1969), ch. iv. A related question is whether *sōphrosunē* consists in the kind of unforced expression of a virtuous character (as Hippolytus thinks, 79–80 and 1002–6) or in the conscious process of restraint of desires of which one disapproves (the *sōphronein* identified by Phaedra in 398–9). See, for example, an expression of the latter view in Antiphon (87) B58 and 59, H. Diels and W. Kranz, *Die Fragmente der Vorsokratiker* 6th edn, vol. II (Berlin, 1952) (= DK), trans. K. Freeman, *Ancilla to the Pre-Socratic Philosophers* (Oxford, 1948), pp. 151–2; cf. Schmitt (n. 25), p. 25 n. 39, and Zeitlin (n. 22), p. 200, n. 80.

72 See Antiphon, DK (87) B44, fr. A, cols. 2–3, trans. Freeman, *Ancilla*, p. 147.

73 Democritus, DK (68) B264 (also B84 and B244), trans. Freeman, *Ancilla*, pp. 102, 113, and 115 (cf. Segal (n. 30), p. 285); see also

Critias' *Sisyphus*-fragment, DK (88) B25, trans. Freeman, *Ancilla*, pp. 157–8.

74 See esp. 716–31, 1060–3 and context; cf. Segal (n. 30), pp. 281–3, 288–92, Winnington-Ingram (n. 30), pp. 183–5, and E. R. Dodds, 'The *Aidōs* of Phaedra and the Meaning of the *Hippolytus*', *Classical Review* 29 (1925), pp. 102–4.

75 This reading is also criticized by Kovacs (n. 59), esp. pp. 300–3 (cf. D. Kovacs, *The Heroic Muse: Studies in the Hippolytus and Hecuba of Euripides* (Baltimore, Md, 1987), and Claus (n. 55), pp. 234–5, on the rather different grounds that 'The poet has given us no inducement to look behind the glittering shame-culture values that lie on the surface of the play' (Kovacs (n. 59), pp. 301–2). I agree that the poet should not be seen as placing the figures in a determinate ethical schema which is quite distinct from that presupposed by the figures themselves; but I think this tragedy (like others) is much more ethically exploratory and questioning than Kovacs supposes (cf. nn. 25 and 32 above) and therefore it should not be seen as endorsing a given ethical framework in the way that Kovacs envisages; see further discussion on pp. 94 and 96.

76 This claim is made, in effect, by K. J. Reckford, 'Phaedra and Pasiphae: the pull backward', *TAPA* 104 (1974), pp. 307–28, esp. p. 317, who sees the Phaedra of this play as, at this point, assuming the character of the Phaedra of the first Euripidean *Hippolytus*, the 'bad woman "who has taken evil daring upon herself"'. This seems to overstate the case; closer to the truth are the suggestions made by Segal, 'Shame' (n. 30), p. 289 (cf. also some of Reckford's remarks in pp. 316–17), that Phaedra, responding to the situation produced by the Nurse's disastrous intervention, becomes more like the Nurse in her ethical stance (e.g. in using prevarication and deceit to preserve her reputation, 709ff., esp. 716–21, cf. 465–6); and also that she takes up the brutal note in Hippolytus' misguided attack on female lack of *sōphrosunē* in formulating her own response to this attack (728–31, cf. 664–9, discussed on pp. 81 and 88, and 719–21, cf. 661–2).

77 Despite Hippolytus' self-characterization at 664–5 as a continual critic of women (noted by, for example, Schmitt (n.25), p. 22), Hippolytus' characteristic mode, as we have seen, is that of presenting himself as *sōphrōn*. This is sometimes coupled with incidental discrimination between himself and those who are not *sōphrōn* (as he understands this), e.g. in 79–81 and 997–1001 (cf. nn. 37 and 64 above), but it is not elsewhere coupled with *blanket* criticism of women (or of any other group) for not being *sōphrōn*; nor is it coupled elsewhere with the cruel gloating tone of 661–2 (cf. 668). The more complex and humane tone of 1034 (also 1407 and 1409) is also rather exceptional, and these lines are marked as responses to exceptional circumstances; but they are perhaps no *more* exceptional than his response to the Nurse's proposition.

78 Cf. Gill, refs in n.1 above. As in some other tragedies, the dramatic situation disposes us to have a sense of privileged access to the

main figures: we feel that we understand Phaedra as Hippolytus, certainly, and the Nurse, possibly, do not (given the Nurse's coarser ethical stance) and that we understand Hippolytus as Theseus does not; and this promotes sympathetic engagement with these figures regardless of our ethical misgivings about them.

79 On the characteristically tragic ethos, cf. R. B. Rutherford, 'Tragic form and feeling in the *Iliad*', *JHS* 102 (1982), pp. 145–60, and Goldhill, *RGT*, pp. 31–2, 285–6.

80 See, for example, Plato, *Charmides (Chrm.)*, 155e–159b, 160d–e, *Laches (La.)*, 187e, 188b–c, *Protagoras*, 352a–c, 331c, 333c; cf. the account of Socratic method in *Apology* 29d ff.

81 Eric Havelock, 'The Socratic self as it is parodied in Aristophanes' *Clouds*' *YCS* 22 (1972), pp. 1–18, esp. 11–14, on *Clouds* 694ff. The *Clouds* was performed in 423BC (in a version subsequently revised), *Hipp.* in 428BC.

82 *Chrm.* 159b, 160e, 162ff., esp. 163b–c, 164d ff., 169d; cf. T. G. Tuckey, *Plato's Charmides* (Amsterdam, 1968, repr. of Cambridge, 1951), pp. 20ff., North (n.15), pp. 156–8, Berns (n.19), pp. 169–70. See further, for the implications of such dialogue for our understanding of the Socratic project, J. Annas, 'Self-knowledge in early Plato', in D. J. O'Meara (ed.), *Platonic Investigations, Studies in Philosophy and the History of Philosophy*, vol. 13 (Washington, DC, 1985), 111–38.

83 *Chrm.* 158c–d and refs in n.82 above.

84 On the 'ethical' quality of Menandrian comedy, cf. Longinus 9.15, and see further C. Gill 'The *ethos/pathos* distinction in rhetorical and literary criticism', *CQ* 34 (1984), pp. 149–66, 163, esp. n.79.

85 E.g. as regards the 'second-order' quality of Phaedra's ethic, and Hippolytus' insistence on the public display of his *sōphrosunē*; cf. discussion above, esp. nn.71–4.

86 Cf. discussion above, esp. nn.78–9.

87 In *Chrm.*, and in other Platonic dialogues, such 'discarding' is formalized in the work by the shift from one interlocutor to another (e.g. from Charmides to Critias), and by the increasing tendency of the argument to address itself to theses supplied by Socrates himself rather than his interlocutors.

88 See, for example, Tuckey (n.82), pp. 101–2; this approach to the Socratic dialogues is taken furthest by T. H. Irwin in *Plato's Moral Theory* (Oxford, 1977), ch. III.

89 *Chrm.* 166c–167b and ff.; Annas (n.82), pp. 134–6, brings out the full impact of the shift from analysing *sōphrosunē* as self-knowledge to analysing it as knowledge of knowledge and suggests reasons why the latter line of enquiry is (genuinely) inconclusive.

90 The idea that the early Platonic dialogues (and perhaps the later ones too) are to be taken as genuinely aporetic and in this sense 'sceptical' has been recently explored by, for example, P. Woodruff, 'The skeptical side of Plato's method', *Revue Internationale de Philosophie*, 156–7 (1986), pp. 22–37, and D. Davidson, 'Plato's philosopher', *London Review of Books* (1 August,

1985), pp. 15–17; these discussions develop some of the implications of G. Vlastos's 'The Socratic elenchus', *Oxford Studies in Ancient Philosophy* I (1983), pp. 27–58, and 'Socrates' disavowal of knowledge', *Philosophical Quarterly* 35 (1985), pp. 1–31.

91 For some analogous suggestions, as regards the tragic genre and its contemporary intellectual context, cf. Goldhill, *RGT,* ch. 9.

92 I am grateful to the participants in the London Classical Society seminar for their comments on the paper on which this essay is based, and I have tried to correct an unclarity in my position which that discussion brought out. I am grateful especially to Anton Powell for stimulating both the oral and the written versions of this essay.

5

MALE HOMOSEXUALITY IN EURIPIDES

William Poole

I know of no topic in classical studies on which a scholar's normal ability to perceive differences and draw inferences is so easily impaired; and none on which a writer is so likely to be thought to have said what he has not said, or to be charged with omitting to say what he has said several times.

(Dover, 1978, p. vii)

The main purpose of this chapter is to give a comprehensive account of all the passages in which Euripides refers or may reasonably be thought to refer to the subject of male homosexuality, whether in respect of characters who actually appear in his plays, or by way of mythological or other casual allusions. This will culminate in an attempt to discover what can be known about the *Chrysippus,* now unfortunately lost, the one play by Euripides in which homosexual love was the dominant theme. So far as I am aware, this has not been done before, and commentators, when incidentally referring to the subject, have generally taken the view that Euripides was unsympathetic towards pederasty. For instance, in a book composed fifty years ago for the intelligent layman, Gilbert Murray wrote:

It is interesting, however, to observe that there is in Euripides no trace of sympathy for the one form of perverted indulgence on which the ancient tone was markedly different from ours. It is reserved for the bestial Cyclops and Laius the accursed.

(Murray, 1936, pp. 37–8)

I should also like to say something about two separate but related topics: one is Euripides' treatment of male beauty,

108

particularly beauty of an effeminate type, irrespective of the gender of the person who is attracted by it; and the other is Euripides' attitude to male friendship where there is no discernible homosexual component. In addition I want to comment on one or two pre-Euripidean passages which seem to me to have been insufficiently noticed by people who have wished to maintain that homosexual feelings are disregarded in the Homeric and Hesiodic texts.

First, I must make my position clear on two fundamental questions. I agree with Dover that Greeks of the fifth century BC were well aware that people differ with regard to what we would now call their sexual orientation, and that this applies to dispositions as well as to behaviour. By way of illustration, there is a probably satyric fragment (*Trag. adesp.* 355N) consisting of the following dialogue: 'Is he more inclined to women or to men?' 'Wherever beauty is added, he is equally versatile.' Or again, Pindar, after describing the handsome Hippocleas as the object of attention of youths, older men, and young girls alike, adds (*P.* X 59f.): 'Love for different types of person afflicts the hearts of different people.' The Greeks knew that erotic attraction to members of one sex neither precluded nor required erotic attraction to members of the other, and they would have had no difficulty in recognizing the fact that individuals are distributed throughout the length of Kinsey's seven-point spectrum.

Second, I share Dover's view that the openness with which the subject could be discussed in the fifth century militates strongly against postulating the existence of latent or repressed homosexual feelings, though I shall want to invoke an important exception. But this position must be carefully distinguished from the view, which I do not hold, that Greek writers were bound to be explicit about homosexual feelings in order to be sure of being understood to refer to them at all. As Cicero (*Tusc.* IV 71) was to put it later: 'Who can doubt concerning the abduction of Ganymede what the poets mean, or fail to understand what it is in Euripides' play that Laius speaks of and desires?' The same social conditions which made it easy to talk about and find acceptable expression for such feelings also made it easy for such feelings to be recognized when not made absolutely explicit. And herein lies a difficulty: for what remains inexplicit may be so either because it can be taken for granted without needing to be stated or because it has no existence at all.

Let me begin my enquiry with a brief look at some of the testimony relating to Euripides' life. As in the case of other early poets, much of this biographical material is patently unreliable and anecdotal, being often based on the demonstrable misuse of what the poet himself wrote or what was written about him by others: in our case Aristophanes is clearly a fertile source of misinformation. However, I do think that some of his jokes (e.g. *Ran.* 946f., 1045ff.) are more effective if it is assumed that Euripides' domestic life was turbulent or in some other way unsatisfactory. Athenaeus (XIII p. 603e) describes Euripides as a lover of women, in contrast to Sophocles whom he calls a lover of boys, and Euripides in the *Life* is credibly reported to have had two marriages and at least three children. However, Aelian (*Var. Hist.* XIII 4) states that Euripides as well as Pausanias was a lover of the poet Agathon when the latter was a bearded 40-year-old, and elsewhere (*Var. Hist.* II 21) that he composed his *Chrysippus* to gratify Agathon. Gellius (*NA* XV 20) hedges his bets:

> He is said to have had an inordinate hatred of nearly all women, whether it was because his nature recoiled from intercourse with women, or because he had had two wives at the same time, something which Athenian law permitted for those who were weary of their marriage.

Others state that his two marriages were successive, and that both his wives were unfaithful. The *Suda* asserts:

> Some people relate that it was not by dogs but by women that he was torn to pieces one night while making his way inopportunely to visit Craterus the *eromenos* of King Archelaus, for he was very much given to passions of this kind: others say that it was on his way to the wife of Nicodicus of Arethusa.

His fate has clearly been assimilated either to that of Actaeon or to that of Pentheus or Orpheus. There is soberer testimony concerning other aspects of Euripides' life, but his sexual activities have been irretrievably sensationalized.

The most extended and explicit portrayal of homosexual passion in the extant plays occurs in the *Cyclops*. The scene in question is both comic and sinister. The choral ode which precedes it begins (495ff.) in gentle mockery of the kind of

religious language we find in the parodos of the *Bacchae* (73ff.):
'Blessed is the man who exults in the delightful gushing juice of
the grape, spread out after revelry [reading ἐπίκωμος: text
uncertain], with his arm round a dear companion.' Does this
indicate support merely, or affection? The word ὑπαγκαλίζειν
and cognates is used elsewhere by Euripides both with protective
(*Hcld.* 42, *Tr.* 757) and with sexual (*Hel.* 242) overtones. The
latter might seem less likely here, because the chorus go on to
evoke the image of a voluptuous girl on the bed. However, they
then make their imagined reveller ask the question (502) 'Who
will open the door for me?' which is also capable of a sexual
interpretation (e.g. Ar. *Eccl.* 990); so we should probably envisage him as ready to choose between the boy and the girl,
which mirrors Polyphemus' situation later on (581ff.). The
satyrs now (511ff.) express pretended admiration for Polyphemus'
beauty in the manner of a wedding hymn invoking the bridegroom. Odysseus and Silenus come out of the cave with Polyphemus, who in his drunken elation wishes to be joined by his
brothers (531). Odysseus makes several attempts to dissuade
him from this course of action, which threatens to ruin the
escape plan; but eventually it is Silenus who succeeds by urging
that there will be more drink to go round if it is not shared by so
many (540). It is clear that in this play Polyphemus has no
permanent sexual partner, and earlier (323ff.) he has referred
to the pleasures of masturbation to illustrate his self-sufficiency,
which makes him indifferent to or defiant of Zeus and the other
gods.

Now there is a competition among rogues: Polyphemus thinks
that he is not getting his fair share of the drink (552); Silenus
unwisely pretends that the noise of his own surreptitious drinking is the result of his being kissed by Odysseus who, he claims,
desires him because he is beautiful. Polyphemus has made his
Homeric pledge to eat Noman last (550), and now invites
Odysseus to become his wine-pourer (566), considering Silenus
to be unjust in this role (560), as well he might, in view of the fact
that Silenus greedily drains his cup at a single gulp (565).
Odysseus urges Polyphemus to drink even more intemperately
(570) so as to bring on sleep. Eventually Polyphemus reaches
such a pitch of intoxication that he sees heaven and earth
mingled together, with the throne of Zeus and all the other gods
(578ff.). He mistakes the hairy satyrs for Graces, but would

rather seek relief with Silenus as his Ganymede, thus neatly turning the tables on the father of the satyrs, who had been the first to introduce the idea of pederasty into the dialogue. When Polyphemus says (583f.) that he takes more pleasure in boys than in women, the use of the word πως suggests bewilderment at the conscious realization of his predicament rather than the expression of a rooted sexual preference. At any rate, he drags the reluctant and terrified Silenus into the cave, and a veil is drawn. The satyrs tell Odysseus to follow and rescue their father, while sleep supervenes to prevent the final outrage (597f.).

The grotesque fooling of this scene is succeeded by what many modern readers would regard as the barbaric burning out of Polyphemus' eye. Euripides, however, makes no attempt to arouse pity for the blinded Cyclops, who is merely a figure of fun; and there is no serious examination of the moral implications of the situation. In his tragedies, and *Hecuba* would be the obvious one to compare, Euripides does not take the view that vengeance, even when inflicted on a grossly wicked person, is morally the last word.

In an earlier scene than the one I have just described, when Polyphemus is in a less advanced state of drunkenness, there occurs a passage (420ff.) which, as editors have remarked, has parallels elsewhere in Euripides. Fragment 907N has been assigned by Matthiae (1813–37), rightly in my view, to the satyric *Syleus*. Although this fragment consists of only two lines, enough is known of the plot of the play from which it comes to enable us to identify situational and verbal parallels with the *Cyclops* passage. In both plays the foreground character, Polyphemus or Heracles as the case may be, has been indulging in gluttony and drinking. In both he behaves with outrageous arrogance towards the other people present, and his callous drunken enjoyment contrasts with the weeping of others, Odysseus' shipmates (*Cyc.* 425) or Syleus' daughter (fr. 694N), as the case may be. In both he engages in barbarous singing, and the word ἄμουσα is used both times. In both he has drinking companions, Syleus (fr. 691N) and probably later his daughter in the lost play. Finally, in both, can it be doubted, there is an attempt at sexual seduction, which may or may not have been successful. *Trag. adesp.* 418N, probably satyric, is a fragment of a scene resembling these; but since it may not be by Euripides, and is certainly heterosexual, I shall refrain from discussing it here.

But there is a third play by Euripides which contains a scene with these same characteristics. This is the *Alcestis,* and the scene is that between Heracles and the slave (747ff.). Again we have the gluttony, the drunkenness, and the arrogance, with Heracles as the foreground character; and again there is the barbaric singing, and this time the whole phrase ἄμουσ᾽ ὑλακτῶν ('barking out barbaric songs') recurs (760). Again there is the weeping of the household in general (762), and of the speaking slave in particular (768). But there are further parallels, as there is more text to compare. In both plays the foreground character is garlanded (*Cyc.* 517f., 558f., *Alc.* 759), the verb θερμαίνειν *(Cyc.* 424, *Alc.* 758) is used to describe the intoxicating effect of the wine on him, and in addition Heracles in the *Alcestis* is likened to a pirate, λῃστήν τινα (766), while Origen describes his behaviour in the *Syleus* (p. 575 Nauck) as λῃστρικῶς, which may go back to something in Euripides' text. One major item only is lacking in this catalogue of similarities: where in the *Alcestis* is the attempted seduction? The answer has to be that Heracles embarks upon a seduction of the slave. If not, why does he invite the slave to drink alone with him (795), and why does his advice to the slave to live for the day and enjoy the good things of life culminate in an injunction (790f.) to honour Cypris who among gods gives the greatest delight to mortals? We can make ourselves hear the wheedling tone in the actor's voice when, having said to the slave 'Obey my words if you think I am speaking wisely', he adds (794) οἶμαι μέν: 'I think you do.' If we could attend the first performance of the play under Euripides' supervision, the staged action would make it clear whether or not my hypothesis is correct, and we would know, for example, whether the slave is of an age to be the appropriate object of homosexual seduction. The textual evidence which can be brought to bear on this point is exiguous: at line 747 he says that he has placed food before many strangers from all manner of countries; but since the house is noted for being hospitable (πολύξεινος (569)), it should not have taken him too long to achieve this. At line 769 he describes Alcestis as having been a mother to him and to the whole household, a sentiment which I find more suitable in the mouth of a youth than in that of an older man. Lines 779ff. also suggest that he is lacking in worldly experience. Finally, Heracles' invitation to honour Cypris cannot be addressed to someone who is markedly old. None of these textual points is decisive, although there appears to be nothing that rules my interpretation out; and the earlier part of the scene seems to me excessively long and purposeless if this hypothesis is not accepted. At any rate, though occupying the place of a satyr play, this is a tragedy; and the slave quickly pours cold water on Heracles' designs by acquainting him with the truth about the domestic situation.

Finally, I would draw attention to two things. First of all, in the *Cretan Women,* one of the other plays of the same production, a central character, Aerope, had been seduced by a servant (Schol. Soph. *Aj.* 1297). Second, later writers carry a tradition that either Apollo or Heracles was the lover of Admetus, though none earlier than Callimachus (*Hymn* II 47f.) and Rhianus (fr. 10P) in the case of Apollo, or than Plutarch (*Amat.* 761e) in the case of Heracles. If these mythological variants were current in Euripides' time, clearly he could not make use of either of them in our play without vitiating his idealized picture of the marriage of the central characters; but it might have given him the germ of the idea for the little scenario which I have sought to rescue from oblivion. Can line 842, where Heracles says that he must perform a service (ὑπουργῆσαι χάριν) for Admetus, be used as evidence that Euripides did have this particular variant at the back of his mind (cf. for this verb in a sexual sense Pl. *Symp.* 184d, Amphis fr. 20.5K)? It should be noted that Pheres taunts Admetus on account of his good looks (*Alc.* 696ff.) which make women willing to die for him.

Wine is, of course, often associated with sex in ancient writers, and at *Bacchae* 773 someone actually says that without wine there would be no sex. This association is particularly marked in Euripides when there is something illicit or extravagant involved in the sexual relationship. Apart from the scene in the *Cyclops* already discussed, we have Heracles in the *Auge* (fr. 265N: childbirth in a temple), Macareus in the *Aeolus* (Schol. Ar. *Nub.* 1371f.: fraternal incest), Laius in the *Phoenissae* (21ff.: disobedience to an oracle), and Xuthus in the *Ion* (551ff.: a girl seduced at a religious festival). Mention of this last example leads me from a case of homosexual seduction where the aggressor is thwarted to one which exists only in the mind of the putative victim. At *Ion* 517, Xuthus on entering greets Ion with the words ὦ τέκνον – the point would have been sharper if Euripides had made him say ὦ παῖ – which Ion does not understand and does not seek to get elucidated. This style of address does not necessarily imply natural parenthood, but may be used when the speaker feels protective towards or in a position of authority over the addressee and there is a large age difference between them, as for example in the case of the tutor at *Electra* 567, the Nurse remonstrating with Phaedra at *Hippolytus* 350, or the chorus addressing Eteocles at Aeschylus *Septem contra Thebas* 686. Ion's reply (518) shows that he is bewildered. But when Xuthus asks (519) to be allowed to kiss his hand and embrace his body, Ion thinks that the stranger has taken leave of his senses. In all his four speeches from 519 to 525 Xuthus uses the verb φιλεῖν or words from the same root. At 521, allowing for textual uncertainty, he asks whether he can really be out of his senses if he desires to kiss the boy, having found τὰ φίλτατα. It should be noted that this phrase is also used by Sophocles (*Ph.* 433) to describe Patroclus in relation to Achilles. At 522, Xuthus tries to touch Ion who at 524 threatens to kill him when he persists in seeking to make physical contact. At 526 Ion says that he is not in the habit of restoring ignorant and mad strangers to their senses, using the word ἀμούσους which we have already encountered in other relevant contexts (to which might be added fr. 663N). Only then at 527 does Xuthus indicate that Ion is about to kill his own father, using the word πατρός, and all is revealed. Xuthus has been acting in the belief, based on an oracular response, that he is Ion's natural father; but what construction has Ion been putting on the stranger's behaviour all this time? He believes, surely, that Xuthus has been making homosexual advances to him, and in the temple precincts at Delphi, moreover. Both are mistaken; but under the new misapprehension Ion becomes able without impropriety to touch Xuthus (560), and they can each use the word φίλος to characterize their supposed relationship (571, 613). I have no doubt that Ion is of an age to arouse homosexual feelings in others. He is a young man of perfect growth (780), but without sexual experience (150). He is on the border between youth and manhood, being described frequently as both νεανίας and παῖς, the latter largely under the influence of the dispute over his parentage which goes on throughout the play. Hermes says (53) that his body has reached a sufficient degree of manhood for him to be made treasurer of the god by the Delphians, but his youth is also stressed by his mother at 354. Creusa, after recognizing him as her son, refers to his cheeks (1460; not his beard, cf. *IT* 1366) when embracing him, and immediately goes on to add that in him Erechtheus is young once more (ἀνηβᾷ, 1465). Also, of course, Ion may be supposed to have some physical resemblance to his mother, whom Xuthus presumably still finds attractive.

There are three heterosexual examples in the extant plays of Euripides where two characters, on their first significant encounter with one another, are involved in misunderstandings where one of them thinks that unwelcome sexual demands are being made. The closest parallel to our passage is *Electra* 563ff., where Electra for a moment believes that the tutor is trying to force her into physical contact with the unknown young man who confronts her, and whom she has not yet discovered to be her lost brother Orestes. Again the words τὸν φίλτατον (567) are not correctly understood by the supposed victim, and again she has to be assured by her interlocutor (569) that he is indeed in his right mind, and that there is an innocent explanation of his conduct. (The passage was first correctly read and explained by J. Jackson, 1955, p. 173.) Earlier in the same play (216ff.) Electra herself had mistaken the motives of the two strangers when they first emerged from cover – note especially the reference to illicit touching (223) – and later in the same scene (341ff.) she has to intervene to remove the unjust suspicion from the mind of her husband that her conversation at the gate with the two young strangers is motivated by a desire to gain some sexual advantage from the situation; and they in turn are asked to forgive her husband's boorishness.

At *Iphigenia in Aulis* 819ff. the callow and unworldly Achilles, having paid a graceful compliment to the appearance of the woman who has come out of the tent to talk with him, recoils from Clytemnestra's invitation to him to touch her hand as being an affront to Agamemnon, and is horrified by her reference to the beginning of a happy marriage (832). It is quickly established that it is her daughter whom she thinks he is going to marry; but her misapprehension of the situation turns out to be more serious than his.

Finally, at *Helen* 541ff. Helen begins by rushing for sanctuary to the tomb of Proteus, deceived by the savage appearance and tattered clothes of the man who stands before her into thinking not that he has sexual designs on her himself, but that he is an agent of Theoclymenus who is indeed seeking to manoeuvre her into marriage against her will. But as recognition of the apparently impossible fact that it is her husband who is confronting her forces itself upon her mind, it is Menelaus' turn to take fright under the illusion that she must be a phantom. At 566f. he rejects the real Helen's claim to be his wife, and her desire to touch his clothes, and prays to Hecate to send him kindly visions. Of course it is the other Helen who is the real phantom. We are surely entitled to infer from these passages taken together that Euripides was capitalizing on a widespread popular belief that strangers, especially when met with alone, could be sexually threatening to youths and women alike.

I turn now from these pleasantries to something much deeper. It seems clear to me that Pentheus' downfall in the *Bacchae* is partly brought about by the fact that he finds the Stranger sexually attractive. This is, of course, only one ingredient in a complex relationship, but it is a not unimportant one. Dionysus deliberately assumes an oriental and effeminate type of beauty which certainly goes back as far as the *Edonians* of Aeschylus (fr. 61R), but which Euripides appears to have regarded as insidiously corrupting to those who fall under its power, irrespective of their gender, and sometimes though not always to its possessor himself. Their cousin Actaeon is pointed out (337f.) as a terrible example of the fate that awaits those who set themselves against one of the Olympians. Cadmus makes no allusion to the sexual dimension of this episode because he does not know of its relevance to Pentheus' condition. Pentheus arrives in a state of unhealthy excitement: ὡς ἐπτόηται (214), says Cadmus: 'What a state he's in.' This word is sometimes used by Euripides and other writers to describe an emotional disturbance which has a sexual component (*IA* 585, *Cyc.* 185). The earliest example that I would want to adduce of this usage in relation to homosexual feelings occurs at Hesiod, *Works and Days* 441ff., where the poet advises the landowner to employ a sturdy 40-year-old labourer who will keep his mind on the job and no longer have an eye for his age mates. For ploughing and sowing such a person is preferable to a younger man, because the latter will get excited over his age mates (μεθ' ὁμήλικας ἐπτοίηται, 447). Could the word ὁμῆλιξ itself connote the presence of homosexual feelings (cf. *Od.* XV 197, discussed on p. 130)?

117

To return to the *Bacchae*. Pentheus soon embarks on a physical description of the Stranger (233ff.), based only on hearsay, which stresses his Lydian origin, his scented fair hair, and his seductive dark eyes, mentioning at the end the rites he is making available to young girls. He returns (352ff.) to the Stranger's effeminate appearance, which is used, he says, to defile the beds of women. When the Stranger is brought in and Pentheus at last has a chance to see him face to face, what are the first words, after turning from the servant, that he addresses directly to him? 'You're not bad-looking' (453). He quickly adds by way of qualification – is it an afterthought? – 'As far as women are concerned.' He then lingers over the Stranger's physical appearance: his long hair, his pale skin and indoor complexion, the beauty by means of which he pursues love. The hair he describes as full of desire (πόθου πλέως, 456); but is not he too now πόθου πλέως, smitten by a desire which he cannot acknowledge even to himself? This is part of a more general failure by Pentheus to recognize that he has within himself the capacity to respond to the Dionysiac rites which outwardly he is so strenuously resisting. At 477 he asks the Stranger what the god is like to look at, having first established (469f.) that he is no mere dream image, and receives what he regards as evasive answers designed to stimulate his curiosity further. At 493 he wishes to cut off the Stranger's delicate hair, thereby making physical contact with him; later (928ff.) it will be the Stranger who arranges Pentheus' hair as part of a more fundamental reversal of their roles. Pentheus, who has furtively lusted after the effeminate beauty of the Stranger, will himself be dressed as a woman to incur the mockery of the Thebans, and death at the hands of their womenfolk. At first (821ff.) Pentheus is reluctant to do this, but is persuaded of the necessity for the disguise to avoid being killed on Mount Cithaeron if seen there as a man (823). But only the invasion of his mind by Dionysus (850ff.) makes it possible for him to accept this. By the next scene (925ff.) he has reached the point of exulting in his physical resemblance to his mother and her sisters. There is some concealed sexual imagery in Pentheus' exchanges with the Stranger, notably at 800 where he says: 'I am at grips with the Stranger' (συμπεπλέγμεθα ξένωι), a metaphor from wrestling, but one which can have sexual connotations (as at fr. 326N, Pl. *Symp.* 191a, and Soph. fr. 618R, from the *Troilus*, where the

verb is used of Peleus' union with Thetis beneath the waters). At
969 Pentheus says to the Stranger, 'καὶ τρυφᾶν μ' ἀναγκάσεις.'
Consciously he imagines himself borne on a litter like a child in
the arms of his mother, and editors rightly quote *Ion* 1375f. as a
parallel for this usage of the verb. But the words could mean
'You will make me behave dissolutely'. In the previous line he
had talked about his ἁβρότητα, a word which can also have
sexual associations (as at *Tr.* 820, *Bac.* 493, Pindar *P.* VIII 89,
Soph. *Tr.* 523).

Pentheus' sensuality is unfocused, and not directed towards
one specific object. He wishes to see things done by others rather
than to do things himself. The wish to which he gives strongest
expression is to see the women on Mount Cithaeron engaging in
sexual relations with the Stranger. He ends up by becoming a
woman himself, and allowing the Stranger to do what he likes
with him (934, σοὶ γὰρ ἀνακείμεσθα δή, 'I'm in your hands now').
At 223 he speaks of the women serving the beds of men
generally, but at this stage all he wants to do is to hunt them off
the mountain. His own sexual feelings have not yet been fully
aroused. When they are, it is clear that they are directed much
more strongly towards the Stranger than towards the women.
There is no erotic evocation of the attractions of the women, as
there was to be half a century later in the *Oineus* of Chaeremon
(fr. 14Sn.), and as there is of the Stranger. Only the women have
gone to Cithaeron (32ff.), and there are no other males involved
in their rites. Although Cadmus and Tiresias go dancing on the
mountain (191), they are clearly the only males in Thebes to do
so (195ff.). But they do not mingle with the women, and are
unseen by the first messenger; Cadmus has to go back to
Cithaeron to collect the body of Pentheus when he hears from
someone else what his daughters have been doing (1222ff.). At a
turning point in the play (811) the Stranger for the first time
asks Pentheus if he would like to see the women on the
mountain. Pentheus is enthusiastic about this, and says that he
would like to see them drunk to their own detriment. He also
now first has the idea of concealing himself in the pine forest.
When the Stranger tells him (939f.) that, on seeing the Bacchae
chaste contrary to his expectation, he will regard him as fore-
most among his friends, Pentheus is too far gone to comment.
At 956 the Stranger calls Pentheus a crafty spy on the maenads,
picking up a word which he had used forty lines earlier only

when Pentheus was out of hearing; and the motif of the spy in disguise will be seized on by the chorus (980ff.) when urging the Bacchae to destroy him. Pentheus is now fully in the Stranger's power, and imagines he can already see them, like birds snared in a thicket, occupying their beds (957f.). Things do not work out the way Pentheus had planned. It is the Stranger who sees and inspects Pentheus before they leave for Cithaeron. At 1058ff. Pentheus expresses frustration at not being able to see the maenads practising their immorality (αἰσχρουργίαν); and at 1075 his own conspicuous visibility will precipitate his downfall and dismemberment. Pentheus' humiliation and death are brought about by his unacknowledged yearning to participate in the rites of Dionysus, which is distorted by an erotic attraction to the human embodiment of Dionysus himself.

Just over two centuries after the production of this play the cult of Dionysus began to be introduced into parts of Italy and at Rome itself. Livy (XXXIX 13) reports that originally only women were admitted to the cult, but in due course changes were made: men also were admitted, initiations became much more frequent, and the rites took place by night instead of during the day. As a result erotic practices developed which were predominantly homosexual (*plura uirorum inter sese quam feminarum esse stupra*), and those who were reluctant to participate (*minus patientes dedecoris*) were made into sacrificial victims. Nothing was forbidden to the worshippers, and men who were unwilling to go along with the sexual practices were concealed in caves on the pretext of having been carried off by the gods (*raptos a diis homines dici*). The cult spread very rapidly, and eventually initiations were restricted to those under the age of 20. The closest Euripides comes to anything like this is in the Cyprus ode (*Bac.* 402ff.), where the chorus yearn to go to a place where desire reigns, and where the practice of orgiastic rites is permitted (414f.).

The kind of effeminate male beauty with which the Stranger is endowed in the *Bacchae* is portrayed as a source of corruption in other plays of Euripides, especially in ones written towards the end of his life. In many cases the passions it arouses are heterosexual. Alexander is a salient example, reinforced by the fact that his beauty is joined with the oriental luxury of Phrygia. At *Tr.* 987f. Hecuba says to Helen: 'My son's beauty was outstanding, and when you saw him your mind was turned to

Cypris.' She then goes on to describe Aphrodite as the beginning of folly (ἀφροσύνης). Even in his name play, where he is a wronged and sympathetic character, and where he speaks (fr. 54N) of wealth and luxury as a poor education for manliness, his judgement of the goddesses and the destruction it will bring are clearly foreshadowed. Again, Aegisthus (*El.* 945ff.) is represented as deriving his insolence from his usurpation of the royal palace, but also from his innate beauty. Electra, after pretending to recoil in maidenly modesty from discussing the topic, indicates that he used his beauty for the seduction of women, and rejects the idea of a husband with the face of a girl who is merely decorative on the dance floor, in favour of someone more virile whose children will be real warriors. She has already gone on at some length (930ff.) about the benefits to children of having virile fathers. It will be recalled that Aegisthus is portrayed as womanish in the *Oresteia* (Aesch. *Ag.* 1625, *Cho.* 304f.), though there Aeschylus has in mind his cowardly disposition – a foil to the aggressive hardihood of his wife – rather than his good looks.

The beauty of athletes, which of course need not be of this soft-featured type, is also disparaged at fr. 282.10f.N where they are described as ornaments of the city in their youth, while in their old age they are like worn out garments. (The word ἄγαλμα, literally something to take delight in, is, it seems to me, often applied by Euripides to people who have the beauty characteristic of a statue, as at *Hec.* 560.) This occurs in a long diatribe against athletes, questionably attributed by Athenaeus to the first *Autolycus*, a satyr play. On the other hand Helen (*Hel.* 205ff.) mourns her supposedly dead brothers as twin ornaments of their country, and they assist in the happy resolution of the plot at the end. The dead Phaethon's athletic accomplishments are painfully recalled (fr. 785N) by his mother Clymene, and since he had been a reluctant bridegroom, he may also have been portrayed as having had outstanding beauty like his namesake (Hes. *Th.* 986ff.). When in the *Theseus* (fr. 386N) Hippolytus, about to become a victim of the Minotaur, describes himself as a profitless delight to his father's house, his use of the word ἄγαλμα would have more point if he is already endowed with the beauty which will captivate Phaedra later on. Similarly, the words addressed to the dead hero by his mother (*Sup.* 1163f.) would have added poignancy if he was beautiful like

Parthenopaeus. At *Electra* 387f. Orestes describes men with good physique but devoid of intelligence as mere decorations of the marketplace, in contrast with Electra's farmer husband. The ignorant Taurian shepherd, seeing the handsome Orestes and Pylades sitting on the seashore, at first mistakes them for the Dioscuri or statues of a sea god (*IT* 272ff.). When the Euboean sightseers watch with admiration the athletes from all over Greece disporting themselves on the shore at Aulis, they mention Nireus (*IA* 201) simply as the most beautiful of the Achaeans without further comment. It will be recalled that at *Iliad* II 671ff. he is a weakling and brings only three ships with him from Syme. In Euripides he is linked to the preceding hero described by the chorus, who is Odysseus, the architect of the plot to bring Iphigenia to Aulis, and followed by Achilles, whose athleticism is extolled, but whose beauty is not referred to either here or anywhere else in the play; not even in the dialogue between Agamemnon and Clytemnestra where his merits as a bridegroom are being enumerated (695ff.). His divine ancestry (699) and the land he inhabits (713) are both mentioned, but not his beauty. Nor is it mentioned in Agamemnon's letter to his wife (98ff.) where he is attempting to persuade her to bring their daughter as a bride to Aulis; nor when Achilles boasts (959f.) of the number of girls who are eager to marry him; nor when at his parents' marriage Chiron prophesies (1062ff.) the future military exploits of their son. Moreover, he in turn is eventually attracted to Iphigenia not by her beauty but by the nobility of her nature (1411f.; contrast *IT* 19ff.), and he is described as already bearded (909). However, at 209 it is stated that he has been brought up by Chiron (cf. *El.* 448ff.), whom he regards (926f.) as a man of piety, so that, as Agamemnon puts it (709), he should not learn the habits of bad men. In this connection it should be noted that Dio of Prusa (LVIII 4) attests Chiron as one of the lovers of Achilles, and this may go back to Sophocles' satyr play of that name, which Euripides may therefore be covertly attacking, since that play is known to have been set at least partly in the vicinity of Chiron's cave.

A similar role as innocent educator of youth is assigned to Orpheus in the *Hypsipyle*. At the end of the recognition scene (fr. 64.95ff.), Euneus explains to his mother how after Jason's death he was taken to Thrace by Orpheus, where he was taught to play the lyre, and his brother Thoas was instructed in the arts of war.

There is no suggestion that Orpheus might have taken advantage of the opportunity to initiate the boys into homosexual practices, and no reference to the tradition that he rather than Laius was the inventor of pederasty (Phanocles fr. 1P). Nearly all the other allusions to him in Euripides are to his powers of persuasion or to his asceticism, but in the catalogue of Argonauts (*Hy.* 1 III 6ff.) he immediately follows Achilles' father Peleus, and uses his lyre to give the time for their strokes to the rowers.

The beauty of Achilles must have featured prominently in the *Scyrians,* an early play, where he is disguised in girl's clothes and brought up at the court of King Lycomedes on Scyros, in ignorance of his own identity. There he makes the king's daughter Deidamia pregnant. A fragment probably belonging to this play (fr. 880N) says that men should be esteemed for their action in war, not among women, and he is eventually recruited for the Trojan expedition. We do not know how Euripides handled the inherent implausibilities in this situation. Later writers (Niceph. *Progym.* Westermann, 1843, p. 365) make his beauty rival that of young girls in its power to attract male lovers, but it is highly unlikely that this was the line taken by Euripides either in the *Scyrians* or in the *Telephus,* where he was also a character. Indeed, in none of the extant plays is his beauty referred to, unlike that of his mother (*Andr.* 1278); and in the surviving plays and fragments Patroclus is nowhere mentioned.

However, pathos is derived from the mangled beauty of Achilles' son Neoptolemus, murdered by the Delphians (*Andr.* 1154f.; contrast 1235ff. on the death of Achilles himself). Similarly, the chorus lament (*Hip.* 1343f.) over the young flesh and fair hair of the mutilated Hippolytus; but once Artemis appears on the scene, there is no further reference to his beauty because of the need to concentrate attention on his chastity. It has been urged by Dodds and others that the use by the Stranger of the word νεανίας *(Bac.* 974) in relation to Pentheus marks the point at which our sympathy begins to turn towards him. I do not accept this. The Stranger clearly views Pentheus as a young warrior in conflict with a god. In any case the word has already been used of Pentheus (274) by Tiresias, who has just been attacking his youthful impetuosity and immaturity. The word is used again (1254) by Agaue of the young Thebans who are Pentheus' hunting companions, but she immediately goes on to say that all he can do is to make war on God. However, at 1185ff.

her delusion that she is carrying the head of a young calf with soft hair suggests to me that Pentheus was beautiful as well as young, and this does evoke our pity for him after he has been dismembered. By contrast, at *Orestes* 1029f. Electra mourns at the prospect of the untimely loss of her brother's youth, though he is not beautiful, but emaciated by disease (34f.).

In Adrastus' funeral speech over the Seven who died at Thebes, Parthenopaeus is depicted (*Sup.* 888ff.) as an exemplary resident alien in Argos. The concluding couplet about him (899f.) says somewhat startlingly that he had many male lovers and as many female ones (reading ἴσας), but he was careful to do no wrong (μηδὲν ἐξαμαρτάνειν). Collard (1975), following Dindorf (as reported in *OCT* app. crit. ed. Diggle), wishes to delete this couplet as an interpolation. First of all, the manuscript has ὅσας ('what a lot of females'), for which several emendations have been suggested, of which I would regard ἴσας as acceptable (Diggle (1981) compares fr. 990N). Second, the next character sketch, that of Tydeus, has undoubtedly suffered serious textual disturbance, but that is not a very good reason for believing that it begins here, since the speech is constructed of clearly separate units. Third, Collard condemns the reference to Parthenopaeus' sexual lifestyle as 'inconsequential stuff'. But is it any more inconsequential, even coming as it does at the very end of the character sketch – a fact to which Collard seems to me to attach undue importance – than Capaneus' avoidance of gluttony (864f.) or Hippomedon's rejection of the Muses (881ff.)? On the other hand ἐξαμαρτάνειν, to which I shall return, appears to have been a favourite word of Euripides, occurring about twenty times; and wc nccd the lines to give point to the allusion to Parthenopaeus' beauty (889). Aeschylus (*Sept.* 533ff.) had already portrayed him as a boy just emerging into manhood, but savage none the less in a way that belied his name. In the *Phoenissae* a rather similar picture is presented. At 145ff. he is long-haired and fierce-eyed, with a well-armed following, his shield (1104ff.) depicting his mother at the Calydonian boar hunt, and Antigone prays that Artemis with her arrows will violently destroy him (151ff.). There is in fact (1153ff.) a brutal account of the destruction of his beautiful features caused by the warrior Periclymenus. His birth and future exploits were doubtless foretold in the exodos of the *Meleager*: his mother Atalanta is a major character in the play, and fr. 537N predicts the cannibalism of Tydeus. Returning to μηδὲν ἐξαμαρτάνειν (*Sup.* 900), we may ask whether it implies total sexual abstinence on the part of Parthenopaeus, or merely correct conduct in sexual matters, such as the avoidance of force in relation to women, and the granting of his favours as an *eromenos* only to those who are worthy of them. (One is reminded of fr. 138N; though, since this comes from the *Andromeda*, the application is unlikely to be homosexual.) It should perhaps be connected with a number of passages, mostly from early plays, where Euripides speaks of two kinds of love, one chaste or moderate, the other uncontrollable and destructive. The former is accepted or even welcomed by characters and chorus alike, while they pledge themselves to steer clear of the latter, or pray to be spared its devastating effects (cf. fr. 331N from the *Dictys*, 388N from the *Theseus*, *Sth.* 19ff., *Med.* 627ff., *Hip.* 525ff., all early; fr. 929a Sn., of unknown date; *Hel.* 1102ff., *IA* 543ff., both late).

Mention of Hippomedon's rejection of the Muses and a soft life in favour of the outdoor pursuits of hunting and shooting, which are implicitly commended by Adrastus, leads me to consider a famous debate between these two lifestyles, as exemplified by the brothers Amphion and Zethus in the *Antiope*. Zethus, who speaks first, takes issue with his brother for his womanish appearance (fr.185N), which makes him unsuited to the judicial and warrior roles of a citizen. He is useless to the state and no good to his friends, his nature being subservient to pleasure (187N). Amphion, who had begun the scene by exhibiting the power of his lyre (225N, 1023N), replies (199N) that it is wrong to reproach him for his weak and effeminate body, since good sense is preferable to a strong arm. We are reminded here of a fragment (290N) of the *Bellerophon*: 'I always fear a strong and foolish man less than a weak and clever one.' Amphion continues (198N) by saying that a man with possessions but no experience of beauty at home can never be called blest (ὄλβιον), but only a fortunate (εὐδαίμονα) guardian of his wealth. Good counsel has a place in war also (200N). Horace (*Ep.* I xviii 39ff.) gives the impression that at the end of the debate Amphion capitulated to his brother. Perhaps he merely agreed to drop the argument. It is scarcely conceivable that an outright victory for Zethus could be the last word on the subject by any poet, let alone Euripides; and from what we know of Pacuvius' translation (Pac. Ia R^2) we can be certain that the emphasis of the debate shifted from poetry to wisdom and virtue. (Cicero *Fin.* I 4 says that the translation was very close to the original, like Ennius' version of the *Medea* where we can verify his accuracy.) Euripides must have considered that there was a place for both types of man in a well-ordered city. At any rate Hermes in the exodos (*Antiope* 84ff.) predicts the achievements of Amphion's lyre in the building of Thebes, and also his Phrygian marriage; but fails to mention its disastrous outcome, which springs from the presumably inherited beauty (as well as the number) of his children.

Before leaving the subject of effeminate beauty, we should note finally the contemptuous refusal of Orestes (*Orestes* 1527f.) to kill someone he regards as neither woman nor man; and this may be because the slave in question is a eunuch, as I am inclined to think, or merely because he is a coward (cf. *Andr.* 591, *IA* 945, both in relation to Menelaus; *Alc.* 723, 732).

We can gain a clearer impression of the unusualness of Euripides' portrayal of male beauty as something insidious, which a noble character may conspicuously lack, by contrasting Pindar's treatment of the same theme. For Pindar, Achilles and Patroclus are the outstanding model of a pair of homosexual lovers who perform joint or separate exploits for their own or one another's glory (*O.* IX 70ff., X 16ff.). But more generally he links physical beauty to the beauty of athletic or martial achievement (*O.* VIII 19f., IX 64, IX 94, X 99ff.; *N.* III 19ff., V 4f., XI 13ff.; *I.* VII 22f.). Moreover, the type of male beauty which Pindar delights in depicting is robust and virile, as can be seen from his portrait of Jason arriving in the marketplace of Iolcus (*P.* IV 78ff.), to take one example of many. The difference in sensibility could not be more marked.

If male beauty, especially when accompanied by soft or luxurious living, is usually disparaged by Euripides, male ugliness or deformity is sometimes commended. At *Orestes* 917ff., in the debate in the Argive assembly over the fate of Orestes, the farmer who works his own land is described as unprepossessing; but he speaks against the stoning of Orestes as proposed by the glib and reckless orator who precedes him, and advocates crowning Orestes for wishing to avenge his father by killing a wicked and godless woman. Euripides may well think that this goes too far, but it is surely in the right direction. The farmer is reminiscent of Electra's husband, and is praised among other things for leading a blameless life and being the type of person who is the salvation of the city. And in the same play Orestes himself astonishes Menelaus on account of his deformity (ἀμορφία (391)), brought about by the disease which is wasting his body. There is another example in the *Oedipus* where Jocasta commends the lame and blinded Oedipus as her future husband on the grounds that good looks are of no value compared with good sense (fr. 548N), and virtue in a husband is more profitable than beauty (cf. his own words, Soph. *OC* 576ff.). She must regard such a husband as good-looking even if he is not actually so (fr. 909N). Oedipus, who in Euripides' version has already been blinded by the servants of Laius (fr. 541N), has just solved the Sphinx's riddle, and is about to receive his reward. Similarly, a character in the *Ino* says (fr. 405N) that many people prefer an aristocratic marriage for the sake of the children, even if the partner (gender unspecified) is deformed.

In a debate with her daughter (*El.* 1041ff.) Clytemnestra asks the bizarre question: 'If Menelaus had been secretly abducted (ἤρπαστο) from his home, would it have been right for me to kill Orestes to rescue my sister's husband, and how would your father have put up with this?' We need not pursue her argument further, but it seems to me that fair-haired Menelaus is imagined in the humiliating situation notoriously occupied by his wife Helen as part of Euripides' general hostility to this Spartan hero throughout his work. At *Orestes* 1531f. Menelaus is scorned by Orestes for taking pride in his shoulder-length golden hair, and at *Orestes* 348ff. the chorus describe him as strutting onto the stage with great splendour (πολλῆι ἀβροσύνηι, or whatever we should read here). He is always depicted as a bully to the weak, a coward in the face of the strong, or sometimes the not-so-strong, and an inconstant and quarrelsome friend. Even in the *Helen* he cuts a poor figure until the escape plan is well under way.

At *Medea* 244ff. Medea complains that when vexed by domestic troubles a man can go out and assuage his heart's distress by turning either to his companions (ἥλικας) or to a particular friend, whereas a woman has only one person she can look to, her husband. Most manuscripts have ἥλικα, but the easy correction on metrical grounds was made long ago by Porson before it was discovered to have any manuscript authority. However, Wilamowitz (1875, pp. 206–7) launched the influential

idea that line 246 was an interpolation by a Byzantine schoolmaster, who is assumed to be toning down the sexual implications of the previous line; and this idea has found its way into
modern texts. But there can be few lines less likely to have been
the work of a prudish schoolmaster. By φίλον Medea means an
eromenos, and her point is much more strongly made if there is
an explicit multiple antithesis to her words πρὸς μίαν ψυχήν in
the next line.

I turn now to incidental allusions in the plays to myths which
have or may have a homosexual content. The most obvious hero
to start with is Ganymede, whom we have already encountered
in connection with the Cyclops. At *Troades* 820ff. the beauty of
his menial task, as he delicately moves about pouring wine for
Zeus and filling his cups, is considered vain when set against the
burning of his native land. At 834ff. the beautiful calm of his life
among the gods is contrasted with the violent destruction of the
city where he exercised as a youth. At 844ff. the reproach to
Zeus of which the chorus will no longer speak refers not, I think,
to his abduction of Ganymede as such or to their homosexual
relationship, but to his lack of compassion for the city which had
provided him with such a cupbearer. We have a similar use of
the myth at *Iphigenia in Aulis* 1049ff. where Ganymede, 'the
darling bedfellow of Zeus', pouring the wine at the wedding of
Peleus and Thetis, is poignantly juxtaposed with the imagined
scene of the sacrificial knife awaiting Iphigenia, and her mock
marriage. The gods can enjoy themselves, but mortals must
suffer. There is one more brief allusion to Ganymede in the
Phrygian's monody at *Orestes* 1390ff., where the theme of his
youthful exercising mentioned at *Troades* 834ff. is again taken
up, this time with a specific reference to his horsemanship, an
accomplishment which Euripides seems to have regarded as
especially appropriate for Trojan princes (*Tr.* 1209ff., fr. 935N).

There is, as Willink (1986) points out, no allusion here to the
Homeric story of the marvellous horses given by Zeus as a
consolation prize to Tros for the loss of his son, recorded in *Iliad*
V 261ff. and the Homeric *Hymn to Aphrodite* 210ff. There is in
fact Homeric reticence concerning the homosexual element in
the Ganymede story, though it appears to me to be clearly
implicit in what *is* said. Theognis (1345ff.) and Ibycus (Page,
1962, 289) are the earliest writers who make the erotic theme
overt. At *Iliad* XX 231ff. Homer calls him the most beautiful of

mortal men, and says that it was on account of his beauty that he was carried off to be the wine-pourer of Zeus, and to live among the gods. But why is it important to have a beautiful wine-pourer, unless he is sexually desirable (cf. the case of Clitus, *Odyssey* XV 250f.)? This is a genealogical passage with only two digressions: the one we are considering now, and another about miraculous horses. The story of the horses in *Iliad* V alludes fleetingly to and surely presupposes the fuller account which happens to be recorded for the first time in the later *Hymn to Aphrodite*. There and in *Iliad* XX Ganymede is explicitly linked with Tithonus and Anchises, three handsome Trojan princes who each acquired an Olympian lover. The almost godlike beauty of the race is stressed (*Hymn* V 200ff.), and the link with Tithonus is again made by both Ibycus and Euripides (*Tr.* 845ff.).

I must here digress to point out what I believe to be another example of deliberate Homeric reticence with regard to a homosexual relationship, this time in the *Odyssey*, between Telemachus and Pisistratus. At III 397ff. in Pylos Nestor installs Telemachus in his sleeping place, on a jointed bedstead, 'and beside him (πάρ) Pisistratus of the good ashen spear, leader of men, who was the only one of his sons in his palace who still remained unmarried'. That formulation with πάρ alone or in composition occurs about twenty-five times elsewhere in Homer to describe people sleeping together in pairs (e.g. *Il.* I 611, Zeus and Hera; IX 663ff., Achilles and Patroclus, separate from one another, but each with his own concubine; XXIV 676, Achilles and Briseis: contrast 673 where Priam and the herald sleep separately and there is no πάρ; *Od.* X 11, the Aeolids in incestuous couples. The sole exception is *Od.* XIV 523 describing the makeshift hospitality on Eumaeus' crowded floor, where a bed has been placed for Odysseus by the fire and the young men lie beside him, while Eumaeus himself prefers to sleep apart with the swine).

Finally, when the two youths have reached Sparta we read (IV 304ff.) that their host Menelaus 'slept in an alcove of the lofty hall, and beside him (πάρ) long-robed Helen lay, godlike among women'. The immediately preceding lines do not specify the sleeping arrangements of the two young men with such particularity as at Pylos, and in themselves would leave the question open; but when a similar scene is resumed after the lapse of a few days at the beginning of book XV, Athena finds them still in bed as when we left them. After she has spoken to the sleepless Telemachus, he wakes his companion (XV 44f.) by kicking him with his foot (λὰξ ποδὶ κινήσας). (This passage is clearly modelled on *Il.* X 154ff., but the differences are instructive. There the fathers of the two young men go through the Greek camp to arouse Diomedes in the middle of the night. It is Nestor who awakens him, using a similar form of address; and the same phrase occurs to describe the method by which he does so. But Nestor is standing beside Diomedes who is lying not on a bed but outside his tent on an oxhide with a rug under his head.) However, it is still night time, and Pisistratus wisely tells his companion to stay until morning; the latter does not get up, or put on his clothes, until he catches sight of Menelaus (59ff.).

Telemachus is tall, dignified and handsome (XVIII 217ff.), with beautiful eyes inherited from his father (XVI 15, XVII 39; I 208, XIX 417), a feature which among Homeric mortals he shares uniquely with Patroclus (*Il.* XXIII 66); and he is just embarking on the responsibilities of manhood (XIX 160f., 532ff., XXII 426f.). It is reasonable to infer (XVIII 175f., 269f.) that he has started to grow a beard, and I take him to be the *erastes*. He first encounters Pisistratus serving meat and pouring wine for his father's guests (III 40f.), but by the time they reach Sparta he is calling him 'my heart's delight' (IV 71) in a tête-à-tête from which other people are meant to be excluded. (There are six other Homeric instances of the formula (ἐμῶι) κεχαρισμένε θυμῶι. One is quite colourless: Agamemnon to Diomedes (*Il.* X 234); two reveal the feelings of divinities towards their protégés: Athena to Diomedes (*Il.* V 826), and Dionysus to the steersman (*Hymn* VII 55); and in the remaining three, strong affection between mortals is involved: Sthenelus to Diomedes (*Il.* V 243), Achilles to Patroclus (*Il.* XI 608), and Briseis to the dead Patroclus (*Il.* XIX 287), a scene highly charged with emotion.) At the final parting (*Od.* XV 195ff.) of the two young men, Telemachus describes them as age mates (ὁμήλικες), and refers to the friendship of their fathers. It seems to me that the word is here being used to characterize a stronger relationship than that expressed by ξεῖνοι or φιλότητος above; so perhaps, like the Latin *frater*, it could have been used in early poetry to convey the fact that they were homosexual lovers. Clearly they share a bed both at Pylos and at Sparta, but Homer abstains from giving further details. I have found no trace of this homosexual relationship in any subsequent writer, but I assume that it formed part of the oral tradition on which Homer drew.

Returning to Euripides, at *Helen* 1465ff. there is mention of the nocturnal revels in Sparta at the festival in honour of Hyacinthus, killed by Apollo who had challenged him to a discus-throwing contest. In this ode the whole of the first antistrophe is written in a somewhat elliptical style, but a myth of thwarted love must underlie the middle section of it. The optimistic strophe invokes the ship that will bring Helen home to long-deferred happiness with her husband in Sparta. But what she will find when she gets there, as described in the antistrophe, is more sombre. For the reference to Hyacinthus is sandwiched between allusions to the Leucippides and Hermione. The daughters of Leucippus were either abducted by or tragically betrothed to Helen's lost brothers, while the bridal torches for her daughter Hermione's wedding have not yet been lit. There is no other prehellenistic literary evidence for Apollo as the lover of Hyacinthus, though Pausanias (III xix 4) mentions a painting by Nicias the son of Nicomedes, who was contemporary with Alexander the Great. But there are fifth-century vase-paintings depicting Zephyrus as the boy's lover. So Hyacinthus could have been killed by Apollo either through a tragic mistake, or out of vindictive jealousy. The reference to Apollo ordaining the cult (1475) perhaps favours the first view.

At *Cyclops* 10ff. Silenus describes at great length the troubles that he and his satyr sons have gone through to rescue Dionysus from the Tyrrhenian pirates, obviously a boastful exaggeration. What motive for the pirates' seizure of Dionysus did Euripides expect his audience to have in mind? In the seventh Homeric *Hymn* the motive is clearly to gain a ransom from his family and friends, who are assumed to be wealthy (11f., 28ff.). In other versions of the story they want to sell him into slavery, where of course his sexual attractiveness would be a definite asset. In the Homeric *Hymn*, though his smile of superiority (14) is reminiscent of the Stranger's (*Bac.* 438f.), his beauty is of a contrasting type, though none the less alluringly portrayed. He is described as a young man in his prime, with beautiful black waving hair, and a purple cloak round his powerful shoulders (3ff.). But in Hyginus (*Fab.* 134), where Dionysus is described as *impubis* and there are other differences from the version in the *Hymn*, the motive of the pirates is simply rape (*cum eum ... uellent ob formam constuprare*; cf. also Serv. D. Verg. *Aen.* I 67). Hyginus' account is largely dependent on that of Ovid (*Met.* III 582ff.), unless they have a common source. But Ovid does not mention the motive of rape, though he describes Dionysus as *uirginea puerum forma* (607). However, like other unusual mythological variants which Hyginus preserves, this one may go back a long way, possibly to a satyr play on the subject belonging to the earlier part of the fifth century. At *Cyclops* 112 Silenus describes the pirates' action with the words Βρόμιον ἀνήρπασαν. ἁρπάζειν and related words, when they have a human being as their object, are generally used by Euripides to designate violent seizure intended to result in serious harm to the victim, such as rape or murder or being eaten. (For exceptions where it is used in a rescue context cf. *Ion* 1598, *Hel.* 246, *Or.* 1634, *Bac.* 288, 524.) The *Cyclops* is pervaded throughout by the unsatisfied sexual desires of the satyrs and of other characters, and a homosexual reference here would be entirely appropriate. However, I am unable to decide whether Euripides intended one, since there would have to have been an explicit version of the myth already in existence to make the reference intelligible to Euripides' audience, and we have no evidence of such a version.

Drinking parties are a setting in which we might expect homosexual allusions to occur. At *Rhesus* 359ff. (date and authorship disputed) the chorus ask whether ancient Troy will ever again spend all day in the drinking of healths and in love coteries (θιάσους ἐρώτων), in singing and passing round the cups to produce intoxication, once the sons of Atreus have gone back over the sea to Sparta. This is a play very much dominated by males, the only female character being the *dea ex machina*, and I think that an Athenian audience would be bound to take the chorus' reference in this lyric as being primarily to homosexual love. In fr. 631N from the *Plisthenes,* a play about which very little is known, the noise produced by the game of *kottabos* is a harmonious song of love which resounds in the house. This is also from a male-dominated play, and Athenaeus makes it clear that the allusion is to *eromenoi* at whom lovers aim their *kottaboi.* A parody of this proceeding occurs in a fragment of the *Oineus* (562N) where the head of the old man himself is the target. The protracted drinking scene in the *Cyclops* has already been dealt with.

The unbridled lust of tyrants, which may encompass young victims of either gender, is sometimes mentioned as one item in a catalogue of their abuses of power. In this connection I have already referred to Aegisthus in the *Electra*. At *Sup.* 442ff. Theseus only directs his attack on absolute rulers at their lust for young virgins. What young men have to fear is being killed by assassination if they are of independent spirit, or in wars prosecuted to maintain the ruler's power. Fragment 626N from the *Plisthenes* consists of advice to a young man on how to avoid the usurpation of power by a potential tyrant and on other civic matters, and may have formed part of a longer speech which urged caution against the exercise of sexual appetites. No wonder Ion in his attack on tyranny as against the simple life of a temple servant says (*Ion* 625ff.) that he would rather be a contented citizen than a tyrant, who takes delight in the company of evil friends, and hates good men through fear of assassination. However, fr. 362N from the *Erechtheus* is a long speech by a father who is about to depart for a battle where he expects to be killed, and who has generally been assumed to be Erechtheus himself, in which he gives advice to his young son on the duties of a good ruler. He offers detailed guidance (18ff.) on the boy's choice of friends: prefer the society of older men; detest intemperate habits; base pleasures bring only brief delight. He instructs the young man (24ff.) not to luxuriate in excess, or pursue immoral sexual passions (αἰσχροὺς ἔρωτας) for free citizens. Humiliating the children of the honest poor reaps a violent harvest. The general tone of this passage leads me to believe that Euripides had homosexual seduction predominantly in mind. However, it is to be noted that in his work as a whole far more space is given to sexual violence against women than against boys. The speech concludes with a handclasp and a caution against excessively affectionate farewells, which may produce effeminacy of spirit (32ff.). This directly mirrors a remark by Praxithea in her great speech in the same play (fr. 360.28ff. N) that when a son is sent into battle by a mother's tears, it makes him effeminate.

It is a curious feature of Euripides' language that he never uses the words ἔρως παίδων to refer to the homosexual love of boys, but always to the desire by childless people for offspring,

WILLIAM POOLE

where a poet more careful to avoid stylistic rugosities might have
preferred to use τέκνων, which in fact only occurs once in this
application (*Arch.* 46). There are two certain instances with
παίδων (*Med.* 714f., *Ion* 67), plus a third if *Ion* 1227f. is genuine,
which I agree with Herwerden (as reported in *OCT* app. crit. ed.
Diggle) in doubting; but in addition we actually have the phrase
παίδων ἐραστής (*Sup.* 1088) in a non-homosexual sense. It is true
that in all these cases the surrounding context makes the
meaning unambiguously clear, and that the use of the words
ἔρως or ἐραστής signifies the intensity of the longing suffered
by childless people, just as at fr. 358N the words ἐρᾶτε μητρός
signify the primacy and irreplaceability of filial love, and are not
intended as an exhortation to emulate Oedipus. Nevertheless I
detect here a not uncharacteristic insensitivity in Euripides to
linguistic nuance, which may shade over into an unease in his
audience concerning the feelings which the words in isolation
would most naturally be thought to represent. However, in the
one passage where the verb ἐρᾶν has παιδός for its object (*Hip.*
1303) the reference is erotic, but it applies to Phaedra's passion
for the son of Theseus.

Euripides put a high value on male friendship which lacked a
homosexual dimension. Heracles and Theseus, who are likened
to a father and son (*Her.* 1401), Heracles and Iolaus,
Hippolytus and his companions are all obvious examples; the
effeminacy and submissiveness with which Heracles feels himself reproached by Theseus (*Her.* 1412f.) relate, of course, only
to his broken spirit. There are a number of passages where male
friendship is stated to be more valuable than wealth or power or
blood ties (e.g. *Her.* 1425f., *Or.* 804ff., 1155ff.). It is valued for
its innate affection as well as for any practical assistance which
one friend may bring to the other, or any sacrifice he may be
prepared to make.

There are two pairs of young men whose relationship in
Euripides I have yet to examine before going on to the
Chrysippus. Xenophon in his *Symposium* (VIII 30f.) makes Socrates
assert that Ganymede was carried up to Olympus by Zeus not for
his body but for his soul. He then cites Homer for this view, not
very convincingly. He adds that Homer made Achilles take
vengeance for the death of Patroclus not because he was
his boyfriend (παιδικοῖς) but because he was his companion
(ἑταίρωι). I make no comment on this, since, as I have indicated,

134

the relationship between these two heroes is not touched upon by Euripides. Xenophon then continues:

> And Orestes and Pylades, and Theseus and Pirithous, and many other demigods, the best among them, are cele-brated for having shared in the accomplishment of the greatest and noblest deeds, not because they slept together but because of their mutual admiration.

The first inference we are entitled to draw from this passage is that some people in Xenophon's time, if not at the dramatic date of the dialogue (420 BC), took the opposite view; though there is no early extant literary evidence in either case, unless a homosexual attachment underpins the pact of loyalty between Theseus and Pirithous inscribed at the entrance of their descent to Hades (Soph. *OC* 1593f.). Was Euripides one of these people?

For Theseus and Pirithous there is little to build on. Plutarch (*De aud. poet.* 28a) relates that in the first *Hippolytus* Euripides made Phaedra reproach Theseus on the ground that it was because of his illicit affairs (παρανομίας) that she fell in love with Hippolytus. It has been conjectured by Mayer (1883, p. 68) that among Theseus' παρανομίαι a homosexual relationship with Pirithous may have been included, which Phaedra's own shame-lessness led her to vilify. It is further suggested that at the opening of the play, as in the *Phaedra* of both Seneca (91ff.) and Sophocles (fr. 686–7R), Theseus and Pirithous were away to-gether in the Underworld and believed to be dead. However, nothing in the surviving fragments of Euripides requires us to accept either of these hypotheses, and Phaedra could simply have been referring to her husband's many affairs with women, some of which were subsequent to her marriage, and some of which involved the use of force. In the *Pirithous* the author (Euripides or Critias) used a version of the myth (like that found in Hyg. *Fab.* 79) in which both heroes were rescued by Heracles from the Underworld as the result of a special favour, but if this was in any way connected with the fact that they had formerly been lovers, the surviving fragments again provide no evidence.

In the case of Orestes and Pylades I would also return a negative verdict. There is a very close bond of affection between them, but nothing that compels us to believe that they are or have been lovers, though undoubtedly there must have been members of Athenian audiences willing to put this construction on their relationship. Euripides could easily have made this explicit if he had wanted to, and one must wonder whether his failure to do so reflects a deep reluctance to present a homosexual attachment in such a positive way. Pylades tends Orestes in his madness and sickness (*IT* 307ff., *Or.* 800, 879ff.); they stand by each other in adversity when most other people are against them (*El.* 82ff., *IT* 919); they show their affection by embracing (*Or.* 800); each is unwilling to live without the other, and both are prepared to die together or for one another (*IT* 607f., 673ff., *Or.* 1069ff.). When asked (*IT* 497) if they are brothers born of the same mother, Orestes replies: 'By affection (φιλότητί γ'), but not by blood.' However, Orestes appears to have a beard (*IT* 308, *Or.* 290; contrast *El.* 1214ff., unless Wilamowitz (as reported in app. crit. of *OCT* ed. Murray) was right to assign this speech to Electra), and he would therefore have to have been the *erastes*. Pylades was certainly the younger of the two (*IT* 920, 231f.). Their apparently final farewells (*IT* 708ff., *Or.* 1082ff.) are moving, but in the end I remain unpersuaded.

And so to the *Chrysippus*. It is impossible to give a scene by scene reconstruction of the play; but a plausible context for most if not all of the principal fragments can be indicated, and important restrictions can be placed as regards which version of the story Euripides is likely to have followed. Some can be ruled out at once. For example, we are told (Schol. Eur. *Ph.* 66) that 'some people relate that Laius was killed by Oedipus because both of them were in love with Chrysippus'. Or again, 'Praxilla of Sicyon says that Chrysippus was ravished by Zeus' (Page, 1962, 751). Or again, 'Chrysippus the son of Pelops whom Theseus ravished at the games' (Hyg. *Fab.* 271; text uncertain). It is clear from our surviving witnesses that only Laius was involved as the lover of Chrysippus in Euripides' play.

In approaching our task we must in general give primary weight to those witnesses who claim to be deriving their information from Euripides himself, as against mythographers and other writers who specify either no source or a source other than Euripides. But a caution is needed with regard to the testimony of one of our main witnesses, Accius. Assuming, as I shall, that his *Chrysippus* was a version of Euripides' play, and not of one of the other Greek tragedies on the subject (about which virtually nothing is known) such as the one by Diogenes of Sinope, it is still possible that not everything that he preserves corresponds with something in Euripides. The surviving fragments of his *Bacchae* and *Phoenissae* make it clear that his translation is not always literal and contains additions of his own (e.g. 237, 243f., 585, 597f. R^2); and there is other evidence which makes it certain that Republican tragedians, even when basically following one original, felt free to introduce material from another source. For example, the opening of Accius' *Telephus* (609f. R^2) does not correspond with the opening of Euripides' play (fr. 696N), and is in my view a translation of the opening of his *Scyrians* (fr. 681a Sn.); both at any rate are invocations of Helen. So when using the remains of early Roman tragedy to reconstruct lost Greek plays, we have to be aware that contamination is a serious possibility. Similarly, writers of Attic comedy produced plays on mythological subjects which parodied tragic originals. Strattis around 400BC wrote a *Chrysippus* which I have little doubt was based on that of Euripides. His *Phoenissae* contains a parody of part of Jocasta's attempt to reconcile her two sons (Str. 45K = *Ph.* 460f., Str. 46K = *Ph.* 546f.), and there are clear instances in other plays of his dependence on Euripides. But unfortunately we cannot gain much of an idea of the kind of use that comic poets made of their originals. So when we read a fragment of his *Chrysippus* (Str. 52K) referring to the management of a horse on a short rein, this does not in itself imply that in Euripides' play Laius had taught Chrysippus how to drive a chariot, as attested by Apollodorus (III 44), since metaphors from horsemanship are pervasive in Greek poetry. Again, the fact that the word κοχώναι (buttocks) is attested for Strattis' play (Str. 53K) tells us nothing we should not expect from a comic treatment of our theme. The remaining citation (Str. 51K) may well form part of a parody of Pelops' curse.

There are three accounts of the legend of Chrysippus by contemporaries or predecessors of Euripides about which we have some detailed knowledge, though it has to be remembered that he could have been as easily influenced to react against them as to imitate them. These are the accounts of Pisander, Aeschylus, and Hellanicus. Hellanicus can be dismissed from consideration at once. In his version (Schol. *Il.* II 103) Chrysippus is the son of Pelops by a former wife – not, as in other versions, a bastard son born later – and his stepmother Hippodamia suborns her sons Atreus and Thyestes to kill him out of fear that he will succeed to the throne because of the inordinate affection which his father has for him. When Pelops finds out, he curses and exiles Atreus and Thyestes. (A somewhat similar story is told in Schol. Eur. *Or.* 4.) There is clearly no place for Laius in this narration, and Chrysippus must be above the age when he could be expected to be an *eromenos*.

In the introduction to his edition of the *Seven against Thebes*, Hutchinson (1985, pp. xviii ff.), correctly in my view, infers from the attestation of the word χυτρίζειν in the *Laius* of Aeschylus (fr. 122R) that that play centred on the birth and exposure of Oedipus. Support for this view which he does not mention comes from a fragment of Plato's comedy *Laius* (64a E) where a woman in labour, who must surely be Jocasta, is exhorted to take courage and be of good heart. Since the *Laius* was the first play of Aeschylus' tetralogy, there can have been no dramatization of the abduction of Chrysippus. However, I share Lloyd-Jones' view (1973, pp. 119ff.) that the solemn oracle of Apollo three times forbidding Laius to beget children (Aesch. *Sept.* 745ff.) must have been motivated by something previously done by Laius, and this can only have been his abduction of Chrysippus, though it is to be noted that Pindar also (*O.* II 38ff.) gives no explanation of the oracle that Oedipus would kill his father. I also agree with Lloyd-Jones that Laius' act must have been a violation of hospitality, as in the case of Paris in the *Oresteia*, since we can safely assume from Aeschylus' treatment of Achilles and Patroclus in the *Myrmidons* (fr. 134a–138R) that he would not have expressed disapproval of a homosexual relationship to which Chrysippus had consented. I would further suggest the possibility that in the *Laius* Tiresias evoked in the chorus recollections of this past event, in the same way as Cassandra does (Aesch. *Ag.* 1090ff.) with regard to the banquet of Thyestes.

Pisander, who has been thought by Webster (1967, pp. 111ff.) and others to provide the skeleton of Euripides' plot, related (Schol. Eur. *Ph.* 1760) that Hera sent the Sphinx from Ethiopia against the Thebans because of their failure to punish the impiety of Laius in abducting Chrysippus from Pisa. Chrysippus stabbed himself to death out of shame. Laius was the first man to practise this lawless passion (ἀθέμιτον ἔρωτα). The detail of Laius being the first pederast was certainly used by Euripides, as we know from Aelian (*NA* VI 15). However, this, when taken in conjunction with frr. 840 and 841N, which show Laius hesitating over whether to seduce the boy, makes it certain that no version of the story in which a homosexual relationship between Laius and Chrysippus is already established before the play opens can be regarded as a source for Euripides' plot. This excludes both Pisander's version and also the highly romantic account given by Dositheus in his *Pelopidae* (Ps.-Pl. *Paral.* 313e), which Hartung (1843–4, I, pp. 135ff.) and others have favoured as being dependent on Euripides.

There is no explicit mention of Chrysippus in the extant writings of Euripides outside his name play. The opening of the *Antigone* (frr. 157–8N) recounted the prosperity and subsequent misfortune of Oedipus, but probably went back no further in the story; the opening of the *Oedipus* (fr. 539a Sn.) does indeed mention that the conception of Oedipus was against the will of Apollo, but we do not know what, if any, reason was given for the oracle. At *Phoenissae* 13ff. (cf. also 1598f.) Jocasta relates that after a long period of childlessness Laius consulted the oracle of Apollo, who told him that if he begot a son he would be killed by him; but under the influence of lust and wine Laius disregarded the oracle. At 379f. she refers to her illicit childbirth as the beginning of the divine destruction visited upon the race of Oedipus. At 867ff. Tiresias tells Creon that the land has been sick since the time when Laius begot a child against the will of the gods. At 1611f. Oedipus says that he has received the curse from Laius and handed it on to his children: only a god could have made him behave so destructively towards himself and his sons. There is no backward reference to Chrysippus in any of this (contrast Soph. *OC* 964f.), and if these two plays belonged in the same production, we may find this omission surprising.

We very much need to know the date, or at least the approximate period of his life, at which Euripides wrote the *Chrysippus*, since a number of the decisions about its contents that we have to make are affected by our answer to this question. The corrupt and lacunose production record which is preserved among the mass of material prefixed to some of the medieval manuscripts of the *Phoenissae* invites us to assign the *Chrysippus* to a late date. We know that the *Phoenissae* was produced after the *Andromeda* (412) and before the *Orestes* (408), and the didascalia can be and has been easily supplemented so as to yield the information that *Oenomaus, Chrysippus,* and *Phoenissae,* together with a satyr play which was not preserved, formed part of the same production.

This does not correct all the errors in the text, such as the non-existent archon Nausicrates, but it would result in a connected trilogy covering an unusually long stretch of mythological history. However, I think that Webster (1967, p. 102) was right to reject this testimony as unreliable, but for more reasons than he gave; although I do not feel thereby bound to accept his further hypothesis (p. 163), on the basis of Schol. Ar. *Ran.* 53, that the *Phoenissae* was produced together with the *Antiope* and the *Hypsipyle*.

First of all, neither the *Oenomaus* nor the *Chrysippus* contains any resolutions in its undoubted extant iambic trimeters. In the case of the *Chrysippus*, from which very few trimeters survive, this may not be significant; but in the case of the *Oenomaus*, from which there are twenty-four, I think it is. Putting these two plays back in time removes them from the very crowded last years of Euripides' life to a period where his work is more thinly spread. If *Chrysippus* is an early play, fragment 1027N cannot well be its opening words, as Turner (on *P. Oxy.* xxvii 2455) supposed, since the beginning of its third line, ἀνήρ γενόμενος, contains a metrical phenomenon which is unexampled until quite late in Euripides' life (not earlier than *Her.* 493, *IT* 1371, fr. 56.1N; and with the same participle *Tr.* 504, *Ion* 1576, 1582). Moreover, the fragment expresses the sentiment that one should refrain from disgraceful conduct while still a boy, because of the consequences for one's old age if one does not; but since Chrysippus' virtue, as we shall see, is not yet under siege, this opening is not so appropriate as has sometimes been thought, at any rate if spoken by Chrysippus himself. Fragment 972N, 'The gods have many types of stratagem with which to lay us low, being stronger than we are', has also been suggested by Webster (1967) as a possible opening for the play; but there are many other contexts in which this fragment could have occurred, as can be seen from the similar sentiment expressed in the *Archelaus* (fr. 254N).

The material prefixed to the *Phoenissae* in the medieval tradition includes some items which are extraneous to the play itself, though relevant to an understanding of its antecedents, such as the oracle given to Laius (though in a form which does mention the rape of Chrysippus); the riddle of the Sphinx (though not the version used by Euripides in his *Oedipus*, fr. 83A) together with its solution; and a narration of the

Chrysippus story which, as I shall argue, could well be the plot summary of Euripides' play. The name of the *Phoenissae* is only inserted into the corrupt didascalia by conjecture, but perhaps the record really belongs with the material relating to the *Chrysippus*. In that case we are free to supply a different third play title, and in order to maintain a connected trilogy I suggest that it should be the *Thyestes*, which was certainly produced before 425 BC (Ar. *Ach.* 433). In fact this makes a more coherent sequence, since the *Oenomaus* has obviously much more to do with the history of the Tantalids than of the Labdacids.

It seems to me on the whole likely that a version of the Chrysippus myth occurring in a manuscript of Euripides would reflect the treatment in his play. It should be noted that the *Chrysippus* immediately followed the *Phoenissae* alphabetically in the book of plot summaries (*P. Oxy.* xxvii 2455 fr. 17) thought by some scholars to be the work of Dicaearchus. It is too short as it stands to be the missing summary from that collection in its entirety, but it might be an abridgement of it. There are some not very decisive verbal parallels with other plot summaries: we have the participle παραγενόμενος (line 32 Murray), which occurs at least half a dozen times in the other summaries; we have ἐθεάσατο (32), and the aorist participle occurs three times elsewhere in the collection, including once (*Hip.* arg. 7) in reference to Phaedra catching sight of Hippolytus and falling in love with him; the phrase τοῦ δὲ μὴ τοῦτο ποιῆσαι βουληθέντος (34) is paralleled by μὴ βουλομένου δὲ ἐκείνου (*Alc.* arg. 10); the participle μαθών (36) occurs three or four times in the other summaries; and finally the verb ἀναιρεῖν, which we have twice (37, 38), occurs perhaps not surprisingly about eight times elsewhere in the collection. Our plot summary in the form in which it has come down to us contains some inelegancies, such as ἔμαθε καὶ μαθών (36), and there are no references to stage entrances and exits; but the use of the word θρηνοῦντος (35) in particular (cf. θρηνεῖν *Andr.* arg. 14 applied to Peleus mourning over the body of Neoptolemus) convinces me that we have the summary of a tragic plot, and if so, then it must surely be the *Chrysippus* of Euripides. At any rate, unlike most other versions of the myth, it includes nothing that could not have occurred in our play, though it may well omit some things of importance that did. The plot is a simple one, with only three major characters discernible, Laius, Chrysippus, and Pelops;

and this suits an early play, unlike for example the involuted and eventful drama narrated by Dositheus.

It is uncertain who speaks the prologue, or who comprise the chorus; but the action of the play presumably takes place in the vicinity of the palace at Pisa, which Pelops had inherited after the death of his father-in-law Oenomaus, though, as we shall see, he clearly controls a great deal of the Peloponnese besides. Locating the abduction here accords with the testimony of Athenaeus (XIII 602e) and Apollodorus (III 44); and Laius is thus guilty of a breach of hospitality, as he was in Aeschylus. Whether he could have reached Pisa from Thebes in five days, as Plutarch (*Amat.* 750b) maintains, I do not know. The statement in the opening sentence of the plot summary that he caught sight of Chrysippus on the road would then refer to the effect the boy had on Laius when he first set eyes on him, before the action of the play starts (cf. *Hip.* 26ff. for the similar effect made by Hippolytus on Phaedra); and already this is enough to make him forget his native land. His passion would have been able to grow stronger during his stay in Pisa.

From an examination of the fragments themselves one scene comes into focus more clearly than any other. This is the scene containing frr. 840 and 841N, in which Laius describes the conflict between his passion and his reason. As has been generally recognized, this is very reminiscent of Medea and Phaedra in similar situations, and Albinus in quoting fragment 841N in fact makes the connection with Medea. For me this is the clinching argument for a date around 430 BC, since we do not find this kind of inner conflict represented in any of Euripides' later plays (the closest parallel is with Agamemnon in the *IA*). Plutarch, after quoting fr. 841N, immediately goes on to quote two more fragments (*Trag. adesp.* 379, 380N), in which the same conflict is portrayed using nautical metaphors. Wilamowitz (as reported in Kannicht and Snell, 1981, p. 115) and Mette (1967–8) have suggested that all three may well belong to the same speaker, and I agree. In that case Laius begins by telling someone that he understands the counsel being given to him, but his nature drives him on inexorably. He goes on to make the point that to know what is good but to be unable to put it into practice must be an evil sent by the gods. He then says that he is giving way to his passionate feelings, like an anchor hook set in the sand which can no longer resist the sea swell; he is like a ship under sail just launching itself with a favourable wind, and the cables can no longer hold.

To this scene I would also assign Acc. 267R[2], 'It is better to retard than to hasten wrong doing'; and it is surely this scene, or the next one I shall discuss, that Cicero (*Tusc.* IV 71) had in mind. The person addressed by Laius in fr. 840N as the giver of advice cannot be Pelops or Chrysippus, and may be a slave or perhaps the chorus leader. For the futility of offering counsels of restraint to a mortal under the sway of a strong sexual passion cf. fr. 340N from the *Dictys*, fr. 665N from the *Stheneboea*, *Medea* 28f., *Hippolytus* 395f., all early; *Troades* 1015; and possibly fr. 962N, which Hartung (1843–4) wished to attribute to our play, and fr. 1042N. Fragment 1079N may afford a counter example where the advice was heeded. When such counsel is offered to a god (*Ion* 436ff., *Antiope* 11ff.) he always ends up by protecting the offspring of his passion (but cf. *Her.* 339ff., which evokes only a limited response). Our play appears to be unique in that the person being counselled is actually present on the stage, unless this was also the case in the *Dictys*; although Phaedra is present at *Hippolytus* 722f., the counsel which she rejects is by this time not directed towards getting her to resist her passion. Fragment 842N will be spoken by Chrysippus in the scene where Laius first propositions him and the boy rejects his offer: having wisdom and courage, he would rather be ugly than beautiful and base. Fragment 928N, if it is part of our play, could also belong here: 'It is dangerous to acquire beauty that goes beyond moderation.' For a similar sentiment cf. *Helen* 262f. It is interesting to note that there is no suggestion in the surviving fragments that Chrysippus derives his beauty from his father, in whom it is so conspicuous in both Pindar (*O.* I 26ff.) and Sophocles (fr. 474R). Of course, there can in our play be no reference to any homosexual relationship between Poseidon and Pelops; but there is equal reticence in the only other passages where Euripides mentions his feasting among the gods (*Hel.* 388ff., *IT* 388). Since Laius is the first pederast, there are no clear moral norms to guide his conduct; but he presumably asks Chrysippus to accompany him to Thebes, and makes it sufficiently obvious what he really wants. It would be possible, and perhaps better, to imagine the fragments embodying Laius' inner conflict as coming after rather than before the confrontation with Chrysippus; the interlocutor of fr. 840N would then have firmer ground on which to counsel restraint: but having failed to be persuaded Laius proceeds to violence.

Acc. 262R^2 has a very Euripidean ring: 'No one was without a weapon, and whatever he had to hand he would hurl, whether it was iron or a lump of rock.' Webster has compared two similar passages, fr. 495.11ff.N from the *Melanippe Bound*, and *IT* 308ff.; but the closest parallel occurs at *Andromache* 1152ff. which describes the murder of Neoptolemus at Delphi: 'And as he fell to the ground, who did not wield a sword, who did not bear a rock, hurling and clattering? And the whole of his beautiful body was marred by savage wounds.' The prototype for such passages is *Iliad* XXII 369f. on the death of Hector. All three Euripidean passages come from messengers' speeches, and in all of them young men are beset by people of inferior status who wish to kill or capture them. Warmington (1961, II pp. 402–5) suggests that our fragment occurs when Laius is kidnapping Chrysippus and other people are trying, unsuccessfully, to rescue the boy. The question then arises: how do they eventually recover his body alive or dead? A second scene of very much the same kind would seem to be required for this, otherwise what is to prevent Laius from carrying the boy off to Thebes, from where as in Hyginus (*Fab.* 85) a war would be needed to regain him?

There is also another difficulty: when does the sexual consummation take place? There has to be an opportunity for this, even though of course it will not be described in detail. It is impossible that the founder of pederasty should have failed to accomplish his purpose. I suggest the following scenario: Laius manages to carry off the reluctant boy in his chariot, as depicted in vase-paintings, but without the knowledge of Pelops. This accords with λάθραι τοῦ ἑαυτοῦ πατρός 'without the knowledge of his father' (35) in our plot summary. After driving for a while, Laius, overmastered by his passion, stops in a secluded spot on the pretext of needing refreshment, and rapes the boy. (A similar story is told by Apollodorus (*Epit.* II 8) concerning Myrtilus and Hippodamia, but there Pelops arrives in time to save his wife.) Meantime Chrysippus' disappearance has been noticed and Pelops sends out a search party. Before the fugitives can resume their journey, their pursuers are upon them. An undisciplined fight breaks out in which Chrysippus is mortally wounded, but Laius escapes in his chariot. Here belongs fr.

844N which describes Laius urging on his horses, as Webster (1967) realized. All this is recounted to Pelops in due course in a messenger's speech. Fragment 843N, on the uncertainty of men's fluctuating fortunes, in which I take the master addressed to be Pelops rather than Laius, could occur at the beginning of this speech (cf. Soph. *Ant.* 1155ff. for a similar sentiment similarly placed).

We now come to Acc. 264 and 266R^2 which belong closely together. They could occur in a long speech of Pelops lamenting the loss of his son, either before the messenger's arrival, or else after he has heard the bad news. Acc. 264R^2 refers to Pelops' belief that Atreus and Thyestes would have been willing to share their wealth with their illegitimate brother after Pelops' death. (I prefer Ribbeck's (1871–3) emendation *alternabilem* to the manuscript reading *aeternabilem*.) For some reason Webster (Trendall and Webster, 1971, III 3.16–18) asserts very positively that in this play Chrysippus is a son of Hippodamia, but I do not understand why he should be so sure of this. At any rate in Acc. 266R^2 Pelops says that if Chrysippus survives he will give him Sparta and Amyclae. This is reminiscent of the partitioning of the Peloponnese in the plays about Temenus and his descendants, and of Megara's account (*Her.* 462ff.) of the intended apportionment by Heracles of his territories to his three sons. Webster thinks that Pelops is offering prizes at the Olympic games. They have to be at Olympia, because Nemea, where the seizure of Chrysippus took place according to Hyginus (*Fab.* 85), is too far away from Pisa, though it does lie between Thebes and Argos, as we recall from the *Hypsipyle*. But Webster's view of this fragment is objectionable on two other grounds. First, *si superescit* must surely mean not 'if he wins', but 'if he survives', as it certainly does in the passage from Ennius (*Ann.* 514S) which Festus also quotes to illustrate this linguistic usage. And second, one does not give away cities as prizes in Greek athletic contests, not even to a Chrysippus. I believe that there were no games in this play.

Acc. 268R^2 is spoken by Pelops and the chorus who hear Chrysippus' voice as he is brought in dying, in much the same way as Hippolytus is (*Hip.* 1342f.). There are other passages in Greek tragedy where people's voices are heard off-stage when they are at the point of death (e.g. *Med.* 1271ff., Aesch. *Ag.* 1343ff.). Pelops, like Theseus in the *Hippolytus*, takes a final farewell of his son, from whom he may now learn for the first time all that has happened. He regards Laius as responsible for Chrysippus' death (though it is very unlikely that Laius wounded him intentionally with his own hand), and utters his famous curse. (For a similar curse of childlessness invoked by an angry father, this time against his own son for a sexual offence with the father's mistress, cf. *Il.* IX 448ff. In Euripides' *Phoenix* the son is innocent, but is blinded nevertheless.) It is not necessary for Laius to have been present to hear this curse, as Webster (probably basing himself on Ael. *NA* VI 15) assumes (cf. *Hip.* 887ff., *Tr.* 766ff., Soph. *OC* 421ff.). The *Chrysippus* would thus end, like a number of other early plays of Euripides, such as *Stheneboea, Medea, Hecuba*, not with a *deus ex machina* but with human beings in irreconcilable conflict.

I am unable to suggest a convincing location for fr. 1183M because of the defectiveness of the text. There are a number of situations where it would be appropriate for silence to be observed.

We are left with fr. 839N. This was imitated by Ennius (*Trag. inc.* 365f. J) and by Pacuvius in his *Chryses* (Pac. 86ff. R^2), where it immediately follows a scene in which the unfavourable interpretation of an omen is vehemently rejected by one of the characters. There is of course no room for such a scene in our play. Long anapaestic utterances of this type embodying general reflections seem to be more characteristic of Euripides' earlier plays than of his later ones, though fr. 913N from the *Auge* is a significant exception. The position of the fragment in our play is not altogether clear. Kranz (1933, p. 202) compares it with *Medea* 1081ff., which comes straight after the monologue expressing the conflict between Medea's reason and her passion in which she finally resolves to kill her children. But the content of the two anapaestic passages is very different. More probably, as Webster believed, fr. 839N is uttered by the chorus after the messenger's speech, offering as a consolation to Pelops for the loss of his son the thought that when we die our elements return to the earth and the ether from which they came, in the same way as Amphiaraus in the *Hypsipyle* (fr. 60.89ff.) consoles Eurydice for the loss of her son Opheltes with the thought that, though individuals must die, life still continues.

Our fragment contains three basic ideas: that ether and earth are the parents of all living things (lines 1–7); that what was sprung from earth goes back to earth, and what was sprung from ether goes back to the pole of heaven (8–11); and finally, that nothing that comes into being perishes, but reveals a different form through the separation of its parts from one another (12–14). This thought was easily adapted by Lucretius (I 250ff., II 991ff.) to the requirements of his atomistic philosophy; but Vitruvius (VIII praef. 1) was aware in summarizing it that Euripides had derived it for the most part from Anaxagoras, who taught the doctrine (A73, 84, 109 D-K) that ether is a life-sustaining fire in the upper regions, and also (B17 D-K) that 'birth and death are not properly regarded by the Greeks: for nothing comes into being or is destroyed, but is the result of the mingling or separation of existing constituents. Therefore birth should rightly be called mingling, and death separation' (cf. also B2, 5, 10 D-K). The idea that our flesh and blood are absorbed back into the earth, while our breath, or our ashes, or perhaps even our mind, goes up into the ether recurs elsewhere in Euripides (*Sup.* 531ff., 1140f., *Or.* 1086ff., *Er.* 71f., fr. 971N; cf. also *Hel.* 1014ff., *Ph.* 808f.). By a fine imaginative extension this idea is applied to the destruction of Troy (*Tr.* 1319ff.), where the city and its houses will fall nameless to earth, while the dust will fly like smoke into the ether, making the Trojan women homeless; the name of the land will vanish, as its elements are dispersed; unhappy Troy is no more. But it is the first half of our fragment, describing the procreation of men, plants, and animals, that provides the clearest indication of its significance within the play. There is a similar description in fr. 484N, where Melanippe tells on the authority of her wise Centaur mother Hippo how heaven and earth had at first one form; but when they became separated from one another, they gave birth to the whole range of living creatures. But here it is heaven, not ether, which is the male procreative principle, though Euripides does treat ether and heaven as interchangeable elsewhere (e.g. fr. 981N), and even equates ether with Zeus (fr. 877, 941N). Amphion in the *Antiope* (fr. 1023N) sings of ether and earth the mother of all things; at fr. 908b Sn. it is ether which nourishes and bestows breath on mortals; at fr. 330N ether is responsible for changes in the seasons, and for birth and death; and elsewhere Euripides speaks of ether as embracing earth (*Bac.* 292f., frr. 919, 941, 944N; contrast *Or.* 1375ff. where it is ocean as opposed to ether which does this). The place of ether in

Euripidean cosmology gave rise to several jokes in Aristophanes (as at *Thesm.* 14ff., *Ran.* 891f.); yet as early as the *Heliades* Aeschylus had written (fr. 70R) that 'Zeus is ether, earth, heaven, everything and whatever is beyond these'.

But the Euripidean passage of which we are most strongly reminded by fr. 839N is fr. 898N on the power of Aphrodite, from an unknown early play. This in turn is clearly modelled on Aesch. fr. 44R from the *Danaides*, where I agree with the view that Aphrodite is speaking in support of Hypermestra who because of her love for Lynceus has accepted marriage rather than obey her father by killing her husband. The image of the mutual love between heaven and earth, and of earth being pierced and watered by heaven to produce fruitfulness and nourishment for mortals, recurs substantially in both these passages and in the *Chrysippus* fragment. All this suggests that in our play the chorus are advocating fertility and marriage as a higher goal than the sterile and violent passion of Laius, who will only manage to beget a son destined to be his murderer. It will be recalled that at *Cyclops* 578ff., just before his attempted homosexual seduction of the supposed Ganymede, Polyphemus sees in his drunken stupor heaven and earth mingled together; and he uses virtually the same verb as is used of their procreation at fr. 898.11N and Anax. B17 D-K; but like Laius he turns away from this image and from the gods whom he has defied in pursuit of an illusory happiness. All this points to the possibility that our play contained the earliest example known to us in Greek literature of a debate between exponents of heterosexual and homosexual values. The former will have urged the strength of the bond which ensures the continuance of all life through successive generations; what arguments Laius was permitted to use in his defence, other than pleading the irresistible force of his passion, we do not know. He could have advanced the view that homosexual love enhances military comradeship, as Aeschylus had perhaps done in the *Myrmidons*, and as Plato was certainly to do later (*Symp.* 178e); or that it is a spur to the education of the young; but, as we have seen, there is little reason to believe that Euripides made use of these motifs in other plays (but cf. fr. 897N, 663N).

The *Chrysippus* as I have reconstructed it is certainly not a play which we should expect to have been composed to gratify an *eromenos*, as Aelian (*Var. Hist.* II 21) declares that it was, except as an object lesson in what to avoid; though on my dating it would be chronologically just about right for Agathon. But this should not trouble us. An anecdote such as that of Aelian need be neither true nor plausible, and the quotation in fact continues: 'Whether this is true or not I cannot positively assert, but it is at any rate widely reported.' In addition two other plays are stated in the *Life* of Euripides to have been produced as a result of personal crises. The *Archelaus* is said to have been written to gratify the king of Macedonia shortly after Euripides went to live there in exile, and this has been generally accepted; the play is certainly a very late work. But also the *Hippolytus* – presumably the first one – in which he castigated the shamelessness of women is said to have been prompted by the discovery of his first wife's infidelity; and this we need not believe. At any rate, what comes across most strikingly from the surviving fragments of the *Chrysippus* is the depiction of Laius' inner struggle to fight against his natural inclinations, and the disastrous consequences of his failure to do so. This is strongly reminiscent of Phaedra's fight against her passion for the son of Theseus in the second *Hippolytus*, and I have drawn attention to other similarities between these two plays. I cannot help wondering whether this, when taken in conjunction with the portrayal of male beauty as both alluring and corrupting, and also perhaps with the triangular relationship which may underlie the allusions in Aristophanes (*Ran.* 944, 1408, 1452f., fr. 580K) and in the *Life* to Cephisophon, might not reflect a strong but reluctant attraction towards homosexual attachments on the part of the man who wrote the *Chrysippus*.

REFERENCES

Collard, C. (ed.) (1975) *Euripides: Supplices. Edited with introduction and commentary by C. Collard*, Groningen, 2 vols.
Diggle, J. (1981) *Euripides, OCT II*, Oxford.
Dover, K. J. (1978) *Greek Homosexuality*, London.
Hartung, I. A. (1843–4) *Euripides Restitutus*, Hamburg, 2 vols.
Hutchinson, G. O. (ed.) (1985) *Aeschylus: Septem contra Thebas. Edited with introduction and commentary by G. O. Hutchinson*, Oxford.
Jackson, J. (1955) *Marginalia Scaenica*, Oxford.
Krantz, W. (1933) *Stasimon*, Berlin.
Lloyd-Jones, H. (1973) *The Justice of Zeus*, Berkeley, Calif.
Matthiae, A. (1813–37) *Euripidis Tragoediae et Fragmenta*, Leipzig.
Mayer, M. (1883) *De Euripidis Mythopoeia capita duo*, Berlin.

Mette, H. J. (1967–8) *Euripides. Die Bruchstücke* (= *Lustrum*), Göttingen, vols 12 and 13.

Murray, G. (1902–13) *Euripides*, OCT, Oxford, 3 vols.

Murray, G. (1936) *Euripides and His Age*, London.

Page, D. L. (ed.) (1962) *Poetae Melici Graeci. Edidit D. L. Page*, Oxford.

Ribbeck, O. (1871–3) *Scaenicae Romanorum Poesis Fragmenta. Secundis curis recensuit O. Ribbeck*, Lipsiae, 2 vols.

Trendall, A. D. and Webster, T. B. L. (1971) *Illustrations of Greek Drama*, London.

Warmington, E. H. (1961) *Remains of Old Latin* II, London.

Webster, T. B. L. (1967) *The Tragedies of Euripides*, London.

Westermann, A. (1843) *Scriptores poeticae historiae Graeci*, Brunswick.

Wilamowitz-Moellendorff , U. von (1875) *Analecta Euripidea*, Berlin.

Willink, C. W. (ed.) (1986) *Euripides: Orestes. With introduction and commentary by C. W. Willink*, Oxford.

6

THE STRUCTURAL PROBLEMS OF MARRIAGE IN EURIPIDES

Richard Seaford

I

> But fight at the ships together. And whoever of you is struck and meets death and his fate, let him die. For it is not unseemly for a man to die fighting for his country; but his wife is safe and his children after him, and his household and his portion of land unharmed, if the Achaeans go away with their ships to their dear fatherland.

This is Hektor encouraging his troops in the *Iliad* (15.494–9). Death in battle is made acceptable by the thought of the continuity of the household (*oikos*). As an ancestor a man remains in a relation with his progeny, a relation concretely manifested in the cult of the dead.[1] Hence the peculiar horror of the oaths and curses that refer to the destruction not only of the man but also of his offspring and household. Hektor in fact loses the continuity of his household as well as his life. As is predicted in the *Iliad*, and enacted in Euripides' *Trojan Women*, his son is killed and his wife sold into slavery. His *oikos* is annihilated by violence.

Violence was not the only threat to the continuity of the *oikos*. The danger of disappearance through lack of a male heir is a familiar worry in the city-state, which legislated in various ways to prevent it.[2] But there is yet another danger, and this will be the main concern of this chapter: the threat presented to the continuity of the *oikos* by the fact that it is not normally self-reproducing. The means of the continuity of the household is marriage, which, as patrilocal, generally requires the introduction of a woman from another household. Almost every marriage is therefore a conjunction of two households, and as

151

such contains the possibility of competing claims. The wife may be in an ambiguous position, between her family of origin and her family by marriage. It is an ambiguity which the ritual of the wedding seems designed to prevent, with its elaborately symbolic removal of the bride from her parental home in a cart to the home of her husband. In Boeotia, for example, the axle of the cart was burnt, 'signifying', as Plutarch puts it, 'that the bride must remain, since her means of departure has been destroyed'.[3] The rites of incorporation of the bride into her new home seem to have centred on the hearth. In taking up a position at the hearth she is envisaged as a suppliant, entirely dependent on her new master.[4] At a later stage of what is in a sense the same process her child will, a few days after birth, be attached to its father's hearth in the ritual at the hearth called Amphidromia. The bride changes not only household but also domestic cult.[5] It is perhaps in the light of this separation of the woman from her family of origin that we should see the distinction[6] in the second book of Thucydides between the exhortation to soldiers (11.2) 'not to appear worse than your fathers' and the exhortation to widows (45.2) 'not to be worse than your natures'. The woman is systematically denied the past continuity of her household of origin.

Although the wife may, of course, in fact retain links with her natal family, symbolically she is, in the wedding ritual, irreversibly transferred from her family of origin to the household of her husband, with whom she is united 'for the ploughing of legitimate children' (as the formula has it), in the hope of sons who will succeed their father in the *oikos*. I will look at various ways in which, in the plays of Euripides, this model of transferral, monogamy, and continuity may be imagined as threatened. Section II concerns cases in which marriage or sexual union represents a danger to the girl's family of origin. Section III concerns cases in which the wife puts her husband above her family of origin. Section IV concerns cases in which the wife puts her family of origin above her family by marriage. In all these cases the problem is in one way or another the failure of transferral: the woman remains implicated in two different lineages, a contradiction which may endanger the continuity of one or the other of them. In the remaining cases continuity is threatened by the failure of the other important element of the model, monogamy: the problems arise from the man's relationship

152

with another woman (V) or the woman's relationship with another man (VI).

These problems are neither invented nor discovered by Euripides. They inhere in his mythical material, versions of which must predate even the city-state. But the development of the city-state is, as we shall see in the next section, not without its effect on marriage and the household. It may be, therefore, that Euripides' selection and treatment of myths, and in particular the frequency in his work of the themes discussed in this chapter, reflect to some extent the social changes accompanying the development of the city-state. This suggestion might receive support from a study of the various deviations from the mono-gamic model in Greek mythology as a whole on the one hand and specifically in the mythical products of the city-state on the other. Here, though, I am concerned with Euripides (but will occasionally refer, mainly in the notes, to other tragedians, as well as to Menander). Plays mentioned without author are by Euripides.

II

The sexual union of a girl may endanger her natal family in various ways. She may assist a male intruder against her natal family, as in the story of Ariadne assisting Theseus dramatized in the *Theseus*, or of Jason and Medea dramatized in Sophokles' *Kolchides*. Another kind of danger is presented by a daughter who has no brothers. In the *Danae*, Danae's father Akrisios has no sons. It is presumably he who says (fr. 318 Nauck), 'A woman, leaving her paternal home, belongs not to her parents but to her husband. But the *male* kind remains permanently in the house as a defender of the paternal gods and tombs.' According to Apollodorus (2.4.1), Akrisios, being without sons, enquired of the oracle how to get them, and the god replied that his daughter would give birth to a son who would kill him. This is presumably the oracle referred to in fragment 330a of Euripides' play. The household with female but no male offspring has no successors, or rather the successors come from another house-hold, the house of the daughter's husband. And so the daughter's son may, to the extent that he belongs to an alien household, be imagined as representing a threat to the family of origin. This is, I think, the problem expressed, in the extremist logic of myth, by the oracular response to Akrisios. How can it be solved?

Apart from the unsatisfactory method employed by Akrisios, who locked his daughter up, there are three main solutions, which I will exemplify from Homer. One is to produce a son from another woman. Helen produced only a daughter (Hermione) for Menelaos, and so he had a son (Megapenthes) by a slave-girl (*Od.* 4.11–14). Another solution is to marry the daughter to a man who does not belong to another kinship group. Such a man will fall into one of two categories. Either he belongs to the same extended family as the girl, or he is an outsider whose links have been cut off from his own family.[7] To the former category belongs Iphidamas, who was brought up in the house of his maternal grandfather Kisseus (*Il.* 11.221–6). We do not hear of any sons of Kisseus, only of two daughters, of whom one is Iphidamas' mother and the other is offered in marriage to her nephew Iphidamas: with this offer Kisseus sought to keep Iphidamas in his household. The very same phrase, 'he tried to detain him there', is used elsewhere in the *Iliad* (6.192) of the King of Lycia detaining the valiant exile Bellerophon with an offer of his daughter and land. Bellerophon falls into our second category, the man isolated from his own *oikos*, like, for example, Odysseus in Phaeacia offered the hand of Nausikaa by her father King Alkinoos.[8] An isolated man can be made part of the girl's natal family. He is in effect adopted. And if he is valiant, like Bellerophon or Odysseus, this will have the advantage of increasing the household's strength. Indeed, the practice of bringing husbands into the bride's natal family for military reasons is found even where the bride undoubtedly has brothers. The best example is the house of Priam, which contains both sons and sons-in-law (*Il.* 6.245ff.). Othryoneus was promised Kassandra by Priam in return for military service (*Il* 13.364ff.). And Hektor even boasts that he will hold the city merely with the aid of his brothers and his sisters' husbands (*Il.* 5.473ff.).

By the time of Euripides, however, the military self-sufficiency of the family was a thing of the past. The military function of the kinship group, together with, for example, its role in vengeance for murder, had passed to the *polis*, the city-state. The consolidation of the city-state also produces a change in the function of marriage. 'One can speak', according to Vernant,[9] of a break between archaic marriage and marriage as it became established within the framework of a democratic city in Athens, at the end of the sixth century. In the Athens of the period after Cleisthenes matrimonial unions no longer have as their object the establishment of relationships of power or of mutual service between great autonomous families; rather their purpose is to perpetuate the households, that is to say the domestic hearths which constitute the city, in other words to ensure, through strict rules governing marriage, the permanence of the city itself through constant reproduction. It is agreed that the measures which established the supremacy of the type of 'legitimate' marriage should be dated to the period of Solon or just after.

The *polis* limits the autonomy of the household in respect of its sexual relations in various ways, and does so in the interests of *defining* the body of citizens (by the legitimacy of their parents' marriage) and of *maintaining* the citizen body (by legislation to ensure the legitimate continuity of the citizen households). The opposition between the legitimate wife and the concubine becomes more marked than it is in Homer. It was not a simple matter for a citizen without a son and heir from his wife to produce one, as Menelaos did, from a slave-girl, for such a son would be a full member neither of the *oikos* nor of the *polis*.[10] But the other two solutions we found in Homer were also available in the city-state. Citizens might be adopted from one family into another. But then the law required that 'the separation of an adopted son from his original family was total'.[11] And presumably males already isolated from their kin were less numerous, and less attractive as adoptees, in the city-state than in the world imagined or described by Homer. The exiled Perseus, who would to a military autonomous family be welcome as a heroic son-in-law, was in the *Andromeda* apparently rejected by Andromeda's father (anachronistically) as a pauper and a bastard (frr. 141, 142). As for the third of the solutions we described, marriage within the kinship group, this was very common in the Athenian *polis*;[12] and the brotherless girl, on whom her father's *oikos* would devolve, could by law be claimed in marriage by her next of kin on the male side, the so-called law of the *epikleros*.

On the whole, as suggested in the previous section, we will find that the selection and treatment of myth by Euripides reflects to some extent these social changes. Let us start, though, with a theme that seems anachronistic in the *polis*. The *Temenos* may have concerned the murder of Temenos by his sons as a result of their fear that Temenos would make his son-in-law Deiphontes his successor, a fear based perhaps on Temenos' choice of Deiphontes as his chief military officer.[13] And in the *Archelaos* the Thracian King Kisseus promises the exiled Archelaos his daughter and his kingdom in return for military service, but is then persuaded by his friends to go back on his promise. ('Friends' in Hyginus is *amici*, deriving probably from the Greek *philoi*, which could include his kin.) Eventually Archelaos kills Kisseus. These plays[14] are about the disaster to the girl's natal family that results from the claim established by her husband's military service. In Homer we found the practice of military service by the son-in-law, but not any resulting conflict. This distinction is in keeping with the general tendency of the *Iliad* and the *Odyssey* to avoid conflict within the *oikos* and the contrasting tendency of tragedy to focus on it. But the danger to the *oikos* dramatized in *Temenos* and *Archelaos* was unlikely to arise in Athens of the fifth century BC, where the *oikos* had, of course, no need of military aid, and so a father with existing sons was presumably unlikely to adopt his son-in-law. We do not, so far as I know, find the problem anywhere else in Euripides. The closest case is from the *Suppliants* (132ff., 219ff.): the Argive Adrastos, having married his daughters to aliens (*xenoi*), the Aetolian Tydeus and the Theban Polyneikes, feels obliged to lend *them* military service in what turns out to be a disaster, the famous attack on Thebes. More successful was the Argive military support of Peisistratus, led by his son by his Argive wife, which helped him to the tyranny of Athens ([Aristotle], *Ath. Pol.* 17.4).

Although the military dimension of the problem was an anachronism in the time of Euripides, this does not mean that the relation with the son-in-law was necessarily felt to be without its dangers. The audience of the *Suppliants* may well have felt the force of the general terms in which Adrastos is censured by Theseus:

you gave your daughters to *xenoi* ..., and mixing your bright house with a muddy one you have wounded your house. No wise man should mix unjust bodies with just ones, but should obtain as *philoi* for his house people of good fortune.

(220–5)

And Adrastos himself seems to regret that he did not marry his daughters to kin (*ouk engenēs kēdeia*). In the *Phoenician Women* the attack on Thebes is imagined, from the perspective of the Thebans, with the metaphor of Polyneikes bringing in a *foreign* bride (343 *gamon epakton atan*, cf. 349).

The importance of marriage within the kinship group is central to Herodotus' (5.92) account of the Bacchiadai, the endogamous ruling clan of Corinth. It is through a girl of the family, Labda, who because lame is married outside the clan, the *genos*, that it is overthrown – by her son Kypselos. This story illustrates the importance of endogamy to the well-being of a *genos*, but also, because it is still an autonomous *genos* within a state, the *ruling genos*, the potential importance of endogamy to political power. So too Adrastos should have married his daughters within the *genos*, i.e. to an Argive: the Argives are, it seems, envisaged as kin, a *genos*, just as the citizens of Athens suppose themselves to be Erechtheidai, the descendants of Erechtheus. The exclusivity of endogamy has a role even in the democratic state. The developing city-state of Athens tends to marginalize marriages and sexual unions with non-Athenians, a tendency which culminates[15] in the Attic citizenship law of 451 BC which required that both a man's parents be citizens for him to be a citizen, and which, whatever its motives, struck a blow at the interstate marriages that we find not only in myth but also among the tyrants and such families as the Athenian Alcmaionidai.[16] This point brings us to the *Ion*.

Erechtheus, although given sons in the later tradition, is in Euripides imagined as without a son and heir. His daughter Kreousa has been given as wife to a *xenos*, Xouthos from Achaia, in return for military service. Xouthos has inherited the house of Erechtheus, but the marriage has produced no children. Xouthos is led by the oracle at Delphi to believe that Ion, a temple servant there, is his son, and supposes him to be the result of a drunken sexual encounter. Xouthos' desire to make Ion his successor is desperately resisted by Kreousa. But in the end Ion turns out to be the offspring of a premarital sexual encounter not of Xouthos but of Kreousa – with Apollo in Athens. Ion can then take his place as the rightful successor to the house of Erechtheus.

The alien origins of Xouthos are constantly stressed. He is *ouk engenēs* (63) – not of the kin, the *genos*; he is *epaktos ex allēs chthonos* (290), brought in from another land. 'How', it is asked, 'could a *xenos* marry a woman who was *engenēs*?' (293): i.e. why did she not marry someone of her own *genos*? (The answer is that the Athenians needed military help.) And so on (813ff., 1070, 1296ff.). The marriage is tolerable for the house of Erechtheus (the adoption of a valiant outsider as son-in-law was after all one of the solutions we found in Homer to the lack of a male heir), provided that it produces a successor. But it has not done so. And then events at Delphi threaten to produce the worst possible outcome. The old servant of the royal household complains that Xouthos (813–16) 'has as a *xenos* married you and come to Athens and taken over your house and inheritance, and has now proved to have produced children secretly from another woman'. The house of Erechtheus is, it seems, about to disappear entirely, its inheritance to pass to a man of alien blood. But finally, although Ion will indeed be Xouthos' heir, the situation turns, in a manner that prefigures Menander (*Epitrepontes* etc.), into its opposite. Ion turns out to be the son of Kreousa by Apollo, and the anxious desire of the chorus, 'may nobody rule the city other than the well born offspring of Erechtheus' (1058–60), is in the end fulfilled. For Ion is, as Athena says, 'the offspring of Erechtheus, and so entitled to rule my land' (1573–4). And Kreousa can proclaim, 'No longer are we childless. The house has a hearth, the land has a ruler. Erechtheus is young again, and the earth-born house no longer looks at night' (1463–6). The continuity of the house of Erechtheus triumphs in the end over the spectre of its annihilation.

More than once in the play the house of Erechtheus is described as 'earth-born' (*gēgenetas*) or 'sprung from the land itself' (*autochthōn*). This cannot fail to be associated with the 'autochthonous' nature of the Athenians as a whole, which is also stressed in the play. 'They say', declares Ion, 'that Athens is autochthonous, not a race brought in from outside [*ouk epeisakton genos*]' (590, cf. 29). In the *Erechtheus* (fr. 360.7–8) the Athenian people are called 'not brought in [*epaktos*] from elsewhere, but autochthonous'. But in the *Ion*, Xouthos is twice called *epaktos*, brought in from outside (290, 592). The conclusion to the play represents, therefore, a vindication of the Athenians' proud claim to autochthony against the danger that seemed about to annihilate it. The four Attic tribes, Athena announces at the end (1575ff.), will be named after Ion's sons, and the Ionians after Ion himself.[17] In earlier versions ('Hes.' *Cat.*, Hdt.) Ion was the natural son of Xouthos. Whether or not Euripides was the first to make him the son of Apollo,[18] the play seems to express the incompatibility between marriage with foreigners and the identity of the Athenians as *Erechtheidai*, 'offspring of Erechtheus'. The same incompatibility is expressed in the Athenian citizenship law of 451 BC. The aristocratic, interstate marriage of Xouthos and Kreousa, based on military service, has in the city-state become not only anachronistic but even undesirable.

The advantage of having a god (Apollo) as Ion's father is not only in his superior status. It is also that he does not belong to another human household, and in this respect resembles the noble exile adopted as son-in-law, who, we saw, represented one solution in Homer to the problem of the brotherless daughter. Homer also provides cases of the union of a god with a mortal girl producing offspring. Hermes, for example, falls in love with Polymele, daughter of Phylas. The result is Eudoros. Polymele then marries a mortal, but Eudoros stays in the home of his mother's father: 'old Phylas brought up Eudoros, loving him as if he had been his own son' (*Il.* 16.191–2). This seems a highly satisfactory arrangement, and the other Homeric examples [19] are no more problematic. In a number of Euripidean plays, on the other hand, *Alope, Antiope, Auge, Danae*, and *Melanippe Sophe*, a girl having offspring by a god creates conflict within her natal family.[20] It is, for example, presumably Kerkyon, after discovering his daughter's unmarried motherhood, who says (*Alope* fr.111; cf. fr.320), 'What is the point of guarding women? The best brought up ones destroy households more than those whom nobody bothers about.'

This distinction between Homer and tragedy is in keeping with the tendency of tragedy to focus on family conflict, which Homer tends to avoid. It may also reflect the changed nature of marriage in the city-state. The military advantages of marriage in the Homeric world (alliance and offspring) are replaced in the city-state by new ones: the dowry (the bride's share of the inheritance), and the legitimacy required to produce children who will be full members of *oikos* and *polis*.[21] In contrast to the more autonomous family of the Homeric texts, the continuity of the later family is limited by the *polis* to the offspring of a legitimated, monogamous union. This is one reason perhaps for the preoccupation of the Attic *polis* with the chastity of its women.[22] In a well-known passage of Lysias (I.33) it is claimed that the adulterer is punished by death because, getting what he wants by persuasion, he corrupts the woman's mind as well as her body, and casts doubt on her children's parentage. Certainly the all-important matter of the legitimate continuity of the *oikos* can be attained only by ruling out the mere possibility of adultery. The wife is a means not so much of an alliance between households as of this continuity. It is an imperative which would no doubt have affected the choice as well as the treatment of a wife. There is evidence to suppose that an Athenian girl who had been seduced would not find a husband, and might even by a law of Solon be sold into slavery. Sanctions or restrictions on non-marital coitus are in general more severe in 'inchoate incorporative states', a category to which the Attic *polis* in the classical period certainly belongs, than in other forms of society.[23]

A fragment of the *Melanippe Sophe*[24] (497) appears to be spoken by someone urging punishment of Melanippe for her unmarried motherhood: 'Punish her. For this is why women go wrong. Men who have taken a bad wife do not destroy her, either in hope of children or because of her kin. And then this vice affects many women and spreads.' If Melanippe is not put to death, she may be married off, and the vice will spread. In the *Cretan Women* Aerope, seduced by a servant, was handed over by her father to Nauplios with instructions to throw her into the sea, but he instead engaged her to Pleisthenes. She was then inherited by Atreus and seduced by his brother Thyestes. A *male*'s promiscuity, on the other hand, does not endanger the continuity of his *oikos*; and this distinction would undermine, at least from the male perspective, the kind of argument used by Phaidra (in the first *Hippolytos*) when she defends her extra-marital passion by reference to the transgressions of Theseus (Plutarch *Moralia* 28a).

Along with the disgrace of the girl there is the problem of the destiny of the child. In *Alope, Antiope, Auge, Danae, Ion*, and *Melanippe Sophe* the god's male offspring is rejected and exposed either by its mother in fear of disgrace (e.g. *Ion* 898, 1497), or as punishment by her father, or, in at least one case (*Danae*), by her father in fear of his new grandson. It may have been characteristic of this kind of play that the girl's claim that her lover was a god is disbelieved (*Ba.* 27–31; *Ion* 1523–7; *Danae* frr. 322, 324–8; cf. Pherekydes 3 *FGH* F 10), so that the truth may have to be revealed or confirmed by a deity. Certainly it does seem that all these plays (except *Auge*) ended with a divine demand or prophecy that the exposed offspring will succeed to the kingdom of his maternal grandfather.[25] (Similarly, in Herodotus' account of the endogamous Bacchiads, oracles predict that Kypselos, son of the lame Labda by an outsider, will replace his mother's family as rulers of Corinth. And one of the oracles compares Kypselos to a lion conceived *in the wild*.) This succession from the outside to the kingdom may resolve a conflict within the family (*Ion, Melanippe Sophe*), or it may on the other hand involve violence within the family (*Antiope, Danae, Alope*?). With the first type we should compare Menander's *Epitrepontes*, in which, in the relatively realistic world of New Comedy, an unambiguously happy ending is created by the revelation of the father of the exposed child not as a god, but as the girl's husband, who had without realizing her identity raped her before marrying her. With the second type we should compare the *Bacchae*, in which the son of Semele and Zeus is rejected by his kin (26–31), returns to Thebes, destroys his kin, and installs his cult.

The theme of exposure in the wild and return is not of course confined to the myths we have been considering. The theme seems to derive from the initiatory practice of departure to the margins of civilization as a preparation for return to a new status as adult.[26] In the wild the young person is outside the household, but will return, the male to his own household (Jason, Paris, etc.), the female to a new one (her husband's: e.g. the Proitids). The ambiguity of this location in the wild, in which the young person is outside the household but will succeed to it, is the necessary element of 'liminality' in the transition from childhood to adulthood. But in the myths we have been considering it has been deployed to express another kind of ambiguity, the ambiguous position of the daughter and her son, who on the one hand should move out of her natal household but on the other hand may exercise a claim to it (particularly if she has no brothers). An ambiguity of ritual origin has been deployed to express an ambiguity in the social structure. The deployment is facilitated by the presence of conflict even in those myths in which a son returns to his own household (Oedipus, Paris, Theseus, etc.).

As an example of the type we have been discussing, let us look more closely at the *Antiope*. The myth of Antiope of Thebes was as follows. Made pregnant by Zeus in a cave, she escapes from the wrath of her father Nykteus to the mountainside, from where she is taken as wife by an outsider, Epaphos of Sikyon. After the consequent suicide of her father, she is recaptured and imprisoned by her uncle Lykos. But on the way back to Thebes she gives birth to the twin sons of Zeus, Zethos and Amphion, who are brought up by a shepherd. Antiope eventually escapes again to the mountainside, and with the help of the young men, revealed as her sons, turns the tables on Lykos' wife Dirke, who had come to kill her. Zethos and Amphion are then prevented from killing Lykos himself by Hermes, who tells Lykos to yield the kingdom to Amphion.[27]

We do not know all the details of Euripides' lost play.[28] Zethos and Amphion are already grown up, and the earlier part of the story was presumably narrated. The play is set on the mountainside, where Antiope had been sexually united with Zeus and then later abducted by Epaphos. The story centres on the polarity between seclusion of the girl in the home by her natal family and their dangerous loss of control of the girl on the mountainside. It is a polarity which seems to express, in the extremist logic of myth, the dilemma of the family with a daughter (particularly a brotherless one, as Antiope seems to be) between the two undesirable alternatives, on the one hand of retaining her within the household[29] by refusing to release her for marriage, and on the other hand of releasing her, the heiress of the household, into the control of an outsider.

The polarity between the woman confined and the woman or her offspring in the wild recurs in Euripides. Pasiphae, in the *Cretans*, is imprisoned after being sexually united, presumably in the pastures, with a bull. In both *Alope* and *Melanippe Sophe*, apparently, it is proposed that the unmarried mother be confined and left to die (like Antigone in Sophokles), her offspring exposed in the limitless wild, to be brought up as it turns out by shepherds (like Zethos and Amphion in *Antiope*). In the *Melanippe Desmotis* Melanippe is a prisoner, but the action turns on the victory in the wild of her sons over their enemies. In *Danae* the daughter is first imprisoned, to preserve her virginity, and then, when this fails, she is enclosed in a chest with her baby son and sent out into the limitless sea.[30] In *Auge* too the girl is submerged by her father with her son in a chest in the sea.[31]

One way in which women, married or unmarried, may pass from the male-dominated enclosure of the home to the danger-ous freedom of the mountainside is in the worship of Dionysos. Maenadism represents in an extreme form the loss of control by the male of the female, and was indeed imagined as involving the danger of illicit sex.[32] In *Ino*, when Ino goes to the mountain as a maenad her husband Athamas thinks she is dead and marries again. Discovering the truth, he has her brought back, and conceals her; and his second wife, on discovering her, takes her to be a captive. The story of *Antiope* is closely associated with Dionysos. Zeus takes the form of a satyr, one of Dionysos' mythical followers, to make love to her. According to Pausanias (9.17.6) she roamed all over Greece in a frenzy inflicted by Dionysos. Her miraculous escape from imprisonment to the mountainside is described by Apollodorus (*Bibl.* 3.5.5) in a manner strongly reminiscent of the miraculous escape to the mountainside of the maenads imprisoned by Pentheus in the *Bacchae* (446). From the fragments of Euripides we can detect that the play was set before a cave sacred to Dionysos and that Dirke arrives there with a chorus of maenads.[33]

Another girl associated in tragedy with maenadism is Antigone. In Sophokles her burial of her brother represents loyalty to her natal family at the expense of her marriage to Haimon. About to be confined in a ghastly 'bridal chamber', she looks forward to her welcome from her natal family in Hades, and even says, in words wrongly deleted by some editors, that she would not have done what she did for a husband or children (i.e. for a family by marriage). The chorus compare her fate with Danae's and then, after Kreon's panicked order for Antigone's release, sing a prayer for Dionysos to come down from the mountain to purify the city (1155ff., 1144). In the *Phoinissai*, as in Sophokles' *Antigone* (73), Antigone expresses her devotion to her dead brother in almost erotic terms, simultaneously rejecting marriage with Haimon.[34] And she is in this play closely associated with her father. They are both confined within the house, Antigone as a maiden (194), her incestuous father enclosed by his sons in the 'dark inner chamber' (64, 1542). Antigone emerges as a 'maenad of the dead' (1489–90), and is at the end of the play told by Oedipus to go to the mountain shrine of Dionysos, where she has in the past been a maenad (1751–70). In Euripides' lost *Antigone* the external, Dionysiac pole of the confinement/ independence polarity is of still more importance. Antigone escapes the death penalty (presumably death by seclusion, as in Sophokles), and goes to the mountainside. It seems that she was recaptured, and appeared on stage as a maenad, and that Dionysos himself appeared *ex machina*.[35] The assimilation of the story to the type represented by Antiope seems to have extended still further: Antigone is married to Haimon and has a son, whose eventual entry into Thebes may have been predicted by Dionysos.[36]

One of the solutions we noted to the dilemma of keeping a daughter unmarried at home or losing her to an outsider is endogamy. Accordingly, we find that in some versions of the myth Antiope is sexually united with her uncle (and captor) Lykos, and that in some versions Danae, while in confinement, is sexually united with her uncle Proitos.[37] Whether these events formed part of the Euripidean versions we do not know. We have already emphasized the quasi-erotic passion of Antigone for her brother in the *Phoinissai*. A Euripidean play which may well have concerned the erotic love of father for daughter is the *Oinomaos*: almost all we know about this play is that it was presumably about the famous chariot race in which Pelops won Hippodameia from her father Oinomaos, who was unwilling to give her in marriage – either because of an oracle that he would be killed by her husband, or (and this is what the scholiast on Euripides' *Orestes* 990 affirms) because of his incestuous passion for her. Certainly Euripides dealt directly with the theme of marriage within the family in the *Aiolos*. Makareus and his sister Kanake have secretly produced a child. Makareus persuades his father Aiolos to marry off his daughters to their brothers, using the argument that this will retain the wealth within the family.[38] But a happy outcome is prevented, apparently by the drawing of lots, which fail to assign Makareus to Kanake, and by Aiolos' discovery of Kanake's child, which causes him to send her a sword with which to kill herself. Makareus then succeeds in reconciling Aiolos, but too late to prevent Kanake's suicide, and he too probably kills himself. A favourable outcome would have been the one that occurs in *Ion, Melanippe Sophe*, and Menander's *Epitrepontes*: the family conflict created by an illegitimate child is eliminated by recognition of the child as the successor to the household; and indeed Kanake's son Triopas had a glorious future.[39] But in fact, as in the myths of Oedipus and Jocasta, and of Lykourgos, incest ends in self-destruction.

III

In some plays a woman puts loyalty to her husband above loyalty to her natal kin. The *Temenidai* may have continued the story of the *Temenos* (described in Section II).[40] Temenos has been murdered by his sons because they feared he might make his son-in-law Deiphontes his successor. They then try to persuade their sister Hyrnetho to leave her husband Deiphontes and return to Argos. Failing in this, they take her by force, and in the ensuing battle with Deiphontes Hyrnetho and her brothers are killed. The unsuccessful attempt by a father to detach his daughter from her husband is a theme of New Comedy.[41] In other plays the loyalty of the wife is the more remarkable for being to a *lost* husband. In *Suppliants* Evadne defies her natal family (her father) by throwing herself onto the funeral pyre of her husband. In the *Protesilaos* Laodameia comes into conflict with her father Akastos as a result of her devotion to a statue of her dead husband. Akastos orders the statue to be burned, and so Laodameia throws herself onto the blaze.[42] The story of *Alkmaion in Psophis* is told in Apollodorus (3.7.5–6): Alkmaion, as an exile, first marries Arsinoe, and then, exiled again by famine, he marries Kallirhoe. When he regains by trickery the wedding present he had given to Arsinoe, so as to give it to Kallirhoe, and the trickery is discovered, Arsinoe's brothers kill him. When Arsinoe complains at this, her brothers enclose her in a chest and send her off to Tegea to be a slave.[43] Most remarkable of all perhaps is Euripides' version of the Oedipus myth, in which it appears that after the discovery of Oedipus' killing of Laios, Iokaste expressed a loyalty to Oedipus which brought her into conflict with her brother Kreon. Mention might also be made here of *Alkestis* and *Antigone*, in which the husband is alienated from his natal family, in the *Alkestis* with the irony that the continuity of the *oikos* for which Alkestis dies is combined with total estrangement within the male line of descent.

IV

We turn now to those plays in which a wife's residual loyalty to her natal family damages her family by marriage (the reverse of section III). Despite Hippolytos' regret that children have to be engendered rather than bought (*Hipp.* 616ff.), and despite Apollo's argument in Aeschylus' *Eumenides* that the parent of the child is the male, a woman – generally from another household, an outsider [44] – is required for the continuity of a man's household. The child, as we have already seen (section I), is attached to its father's hearth in the ritual called Amphidromia. This association between child and hearth is expressed in the story of Meleager. Seven days after his birth (i.e. at the time the Amphidromia was normally celebrated) the Fates declared that he would die when a brand burning on the hearth burnt out. His mother Althaia took the brand and kept it safe in a chest. After the hunt of the Calydonian boar, Althaia's brothers, in dispute with Atalanta for the skin, were killed by Meleager, who was in love with Atalanta. As a result, Althaia killed her own son by returning the brand to the fire. There is here a poignant combination of opposites: the symbol of Meleager's belonging to the hearth and the household of his father, the brand, is used by his mother in such a way as to put her loyalty to her natal family, her brothers, above her loyalty to her family by marriage, her son. Meleager, on the other hand, rates the sexual tie above kinship. In *Iliad* book 9 mention is made of Meleager killing his mother's brother and of her consequent prayers for his death: this is one of the rare exceptions to the rule that Homer excludes conflict within the *oikos*, though even here the death of Meleager was not described. But the death was certainly important in Euripides' version (*Meleager*), and so was Althaia's consequent suicide.

Meleager hunts with his maternal uncles. We are reminded of Odysseus, 'as soon as he reaches manhood' (*Od.* 19.410), visiting his maternal grandfather Autolykos and joining his maternal uncles in the hunt in which he received his famous scar. The importance of hunting in initiation into adulthood is well known.[45] In order to return to his household and community as an adult, the young man must leave it to spend some time in the wild (section II). The temporary reversal of norms characteristic of initiation may include a spell of association with his maternal kin. Fosterage by maternal kin is a theme of Indo-European myth.[46] Greek examples include Hippolytos, Theseus, Pyrrhos, and the sons of Periander.[47] In the case of Meleager the temporary association, in the wild, with his mother's natal family serves to realize the potential contradiction with her family by marriage, and the consequent catastrophe is irreversible.

In the *Melanippe Desmotis* the situation is comparable.[48] Two young men, Aiolos and Boiotos, are believed to be the children of Metapontos and Siris, but are in fact the children of Melanippe by Poseidon. It seems that they had been exposed, and then introduced by Siris secretly into the household as her own. But then Siris gave birth to children of her own. While out hunting Aiolos and Boiotos are attacked by Siris' brothers, i.e. by the men they take to be their maternal uncles, whom they kill. What has happened, it appears, is that Siris has conspired with her brothers to kill them so as to ensure the succession for her own children. Again the hunt, in which a woman's family by marriage (her sons) should be associated with her family of origin (her brothers), is in fact the scene of their conflict, except that here Aiolos and Boiotos (unlike Meleager) turn out not to be her own sons. The theme is combined with the theme of the wicked stepmother (section V) and with the type represented by *Antiope* (section II): once again, the ambiguity of the location of the young outside the household in the wild (and, in this case, the association there with maternal kin) has been deployed to express ambiguity and conflict over the succession to the household. Another example of the association with maternal kin occasioning family conflict is the story told in Herodotus (3.50–3) of the sons of Periander: they were taken in by their maternal grandfather, who, by hinting at the truth that their father had murdered their mother, succeeded in alienating one of them from his father.

In *Andromache* the Spartan Hermione is married to Neoptolemos, the son of Achilles, but is barren. He has off-spring only by his Trojan concubine Andromache. In the consequent attack on Andromache and her son which forms the theme of the play Hermione is assisted by her father Menelaos.

We will return to this play in section V. Suffice it here to note
Hermione's stunning first entry, dressed in Spartan style: 'this
golden headdress', she begins, 'and this lavish robe do not
belong to the house of Achilles or Peleus. They are from Sparta.
My father Menelaos gave them to me along with many gifts, so
that I have freedom of speech.' A divorced woman would take
her dowry with her back to her kin.[49] Plato wanted to abolish the
dowry, so that wives would be less insolent and men less
servile.[50] And the undesirability for a man to marry above
himself is a recurrent piece of wisdom in Euripides (*El.* 936–7,
frr.214, 502, 775, *Rhes.* 168).

In *Medea*, Medea destroys her family by marriage and then
escapes in a chariot which, she says (1321–2), has been given her
for the purpose by her grandfather, the Sun. It is also worth
mentioning the prologue of *Alkmene*, in which it seems that
Alkmene is described as saying that she will marry nobody other
than the avenger of her brothers.[51] Plays by other authors in
this category include several about Meleager (e.g. Sophokles'
Meleager and perhaps Phrynichos' *Pleuroniai*), perhaps also
Xenokles' *Likymnios*, in which it appears that Alkmene lamented
her brother Likymnios killed by her grandson Tlepolemos, and
Moschion's *Pheraioi*, which probably concerned the murder of
Alexander of Pherai by his wife assisted by her brothers.[52] The
theme occurs also in New Comedy: in Menander's *Misoumenos*
Krateia rejects Thrasonides as a husband because she believes
him to have killed her brother, and when the belief is found to
be mistaken they marry.

V

This section and the next concern plays in which the mutual
loyalty of monogamy and the unequivocality of succession to the
household are threatened not by the contradiction between
households connected by marriage but by a second sexual
union, whether the man's with another woman (section V) or the
woman's with another man (section VI). This theme is sometimes combined with the earlier one, as in *Andromache*.

We noted (section II) that one of the solutions to the problem
of a barren wife was to produce offspring by another woman.
There are two Homeric passages known to me which imply a
wife's resentment at the infidelity of her husband.[53] But I know

of no examples in Homer of a triangular situation producing conflict over the *offspring* – indeed children produced outside the marriage may live without disadvantage in the parental home. I gave earlier (section II) the example of Megapenthes, son of Menelaos. Another is Pedaios, son of Antenor, a bastard 'brought up by Theano equally with her own children, to gratify her husband' (*Il.* 5.70). And there are others.[54] However, again in keeping with our distinction between the genres and with the development of the *polis* (section II), Euripides focuses on conflict over the succession. I cannot resist inserting here the (unreliable, of course) tradition recorded by Aulus Gellius (*Noctes Atticae* 15.20) that Euripides himself once had two wives simultaneously.

In *Andromache* Neoptolemos lives with two women, his barren wife Hermione and his concubine Andromache, who has produced for him a son. Hermione believes that Andromache has made her barren by sorcery and that she wishes to replace her as Neoptolemos' wife (32–5, 156–8). Neoptolemos' paternal grandfather Peleus defends Andromache against the aggression of Hermione and Menelaos, arguing that if Hermione 'has the misfortune to produce no children, does that mean that *we* must remain without children?' (712–13). But of course at the time the play was produced Attic law did not allow legitimacy to children produced by a concubine. Hence perhaps Hermione's fear of being replaced as *wife* by Andromache, despite the power of her Spartan natal family and the powerlessness of Andromache (155–6, 196–7), whereas in Homer there is no suggestion that, for example, Helen feared replacement by the mother of Menelaos' only son (section II), for in Homer such replacement would be unnecessary. But there is an extra complication. The Attic law of 451 BC (section II) required that for a man to be a citizen both his parents must be citizens. Transposed intact to heroic Phthia, such a law would marginalize even the marriage of Neoptolemos with the Spartan Hermione. But much more obviously against the spirit of the legislation would be marriage with Andromache, who is not even Greek. 'Will Phthia endure my offspring, if you are barren?' she asks (201–2), trying to persuade Hermione that she is no threat. And later in the play Hermione herself, with good reason now to regret her plot against Andromache, recognizes that Andromache's children would have been, as 'half slave and illegitimate' (942),

no threat. The inconsistency of this with her earlier position has
its dramatic advantages, but may also to some extent reflect the
historical shifts in attitudes to marriage during the transmission
of the myth, in the period in which the city-state was formed.

Alkmaion in Corinth also concerned a wife's fear of being
replaced. According to Apollodorus (3.7.7), Alkmaion left his
two children, Amphilochos and Tisiphone, in Corinth in the
care of Kreon. But Kreon's wife sold Tisiphone into slavery, in
fear that Kreon would marry her. Alkmaion then happened to
buy Tisiphone without recognizing her as his daughter, and
finally returned to Corinth, where he also recovered his son.
The play seems to have contained a struggle between Alkmaion
and Kreon for the children. The role of Kreon's wife would
presumably have been to make the identities of Alkmaion and
his two children known to each other, so as to be rid of them and
thereby of the threat to her position. If Webster is right to
suppose that fragment 76 – 'See the tyrant. He goes into exile,
a childless old man' – refers to Kreon, then his wife was
barren, and this perhaps explains her fear of being replaced by
Tisiphone. In *Medea*, on the other hand, the replaced wife,
Medea, does indeed have children by her husband. But she is
foreign, abandoned by Jason for a local princess. The pathos of
this should be seen in the context of the citizenship law of
451 BC, which, twenty years before the play was first produced,
marginalized marriages with non-Athenians.

It cannot have been uncommon in the city-state for one
of the marriage partners to have offspring from a previous
marriage.[55] The potential conflict in such a situation is obvious,
and we hear of protective and preventive legislation.[56] In
Homer no man remarries. But in *Aigeus* and in his second
Phrixos[57] Euripides dramatized the scheming of the stepmother
against her husband's children. In a fragment (338) of *Diktys*
somebody, presumably urging Polydektes not to marry Danae,
says 'you already have offspring, but want to beget new children
in the house and thereby create very great hostility to your
children'. Alcestis' last request to Admetus is that he should not
inflict a stepmother on their children (*Alc.* 303–10; cf. *Hipp.*
858–9). In *Ino* the situation is complicated by the reappearance
of Athamas' first wife, Ino, who had been presumed dead. His
second wife, Themisto, plans to kill Ino's children, but is tricked
by Ino into killing her own children by mistake instead. The

Melanippe Desmotis (section IV) also contains the wicked step-mother motif (Siris), and so does the *Ion* (section II) – although here Kreousa's murder plot against Ion turns out to be based on an error and the step-parent turns out to be Xouthos.[58] This brings us to our final category.

VI

Given the frequency of death in battle, and the fact that women married much younger than men, it was perhaps more often women than men who brought to a new marriage the offspring of a previous one.[59] Young widows, even with children, were expected to remarry.[60] W. E. Thompson[61] finds fifty-three people in Athens of the fifth and fourth centuries BC who remarried, of whom thirty are women and twenty-three men.

In *Phaethon*, Phaethon is believed to be the son of Merops and Klymene. But Klymene has revealed to him that in fact his father is Helios. Phaethon resists the marriage arranged for him by Merops, but we do not know whether this conflict also set Klymene against her husband. In *Kresphontes*, Polyphontes has killed his own brother Kresphontes and married his widow Merope. He has also killed two of Kresphontes' sons; the third, also called Kresphontes, escaped, but has returned unrecognized to the palace and eventually, with the help of Merope, kills Polyphontes during a sacrifice to mark Merope's feigned reconciliation with Polyphontes. If this reconciliation contained any reference to Polyphontes' desire to have children by Merope,[62] that would be an extra element of irony in the brutal assertion, by the son of her earlier marriage, of his right of succession.

As the extruded child who eventually returns and inherits the kingdom, Kresphontes resembles Perseus, Ion, Hippothoon (in *Alope*), Aiolos and Boiotos, Zethos and Amphion. But the closest parallel is with Orestes, whose return, like Kresphontes', ends with the killing of the usurping king, his mother's new husband, at a sacrifice. But between Kresphontes and Elektra there is also a crucial difference. Klytaimnestra, unlike Merope, supports her living husband rather than her dead one. This means that the close link between mother and son that we have seen in so many plays is broken. The matricide is the more horrible for reversing the typology. And one reversal gives rise to another. Orestes, like Oedipus, fails to remain as king in succession to his father.

As a matricide (1251–2) he has to leave Argos, never to return. And so does Elektra. In the type to which *Elektra* half belongs, and which is represented by *Aigeus*, *Alope*, *Antiope*, *Danae*, *Ion*, *Kresphontes*, *Melanippe Sophe*, *Melanippe Desmotis*, and other plays, the family conflict surrounding an extruded male child (or children) is ended, with or without violence, by the prophesied or actual inheritance of the household by the child. Internal contradiction is resolved in the final continuity of the household. But to *Elektra* there is no such positive conclusion. It is the contradiction that prevails. The type is reversed. The house of Atreus is destroyed utterly, not, like the house of Hektor, by its external enemies, but by its own internal contradictions.[63]

NOTES

1 W. K. Lacey, *The Family in Classical Greece* (London, 1968), pp. 147–9. By a man's *oikos* (household) I mean his property and his offspring as inheritors of his property (excluding his married daughters and their offspring).

2 Lacey (n. 1), pp. 22–3, 73, 77, 89–90, 92–3, 141, 146; Dem. 43.57.

3 *Mor.* 271d; Pausan. (3.20.10–11) tells a story that suggests that the bridal veil may have had a similar significance. Penelope has to choose between her father and her bridegroom and veils herself to indicate preference for her bridegroom.

4 John Gould in *JHS* 93 (1973), pp. 97–8.

5 Including perhaps the cult of the dead, as is maintained by Fustel de Coulanges, *The Ancient City* 47; presumably he is thinking of Rome (I know of no such evidence for Greece).

6 Noticed, but not explained, by K. J. Dover, *Greek Popular Morality*, p. 98.

7 See J. P. Vernant, *Myth and Society in Ancient Greece*, trans. Janet Lloyd (Brighton, 1980), pp. 45–70. It should be added that the former practice does not *ipso facto* preserve the household of the girl's father. For that the bridegroom must be adopted by the bride's father, or the children of the marriage must remain in the household of their maternal grandfather (see D. M. Schaps, *Economic Rights of Women in Ancient Greece* (Edinburgh, 1979), p. 32); but these arrangements may have been facilitated by a pre-existing kinship bond between father and bridegroom (as seems to have been the case with Kisseus and Iphidamas); and failing that, a man's daughter's children would at least, if their parents were, say, cousins, preserve (entire) the *oikos* of his *father* (rather than contributing their maternal inheritance to the *oikos* of a complete outsider).

8 *Od.* 7.313ff.; see also *Il.* 14.119ff. (cf. 5.410–15); *Od.* 7.65–6. Cf. the story of Penelope's father wanting Odysseus to remain with him in Lacedaemon (n.3 above).

9 Vernant (n. 7), p. 50.

10 It has been suggested that bastards (*nothoi*), though disadvantaged in inheritance and excluded from the phratries, may nevertheless after the reforms of Kleisthenes be eligible for citizenship: see, for example, most recently D. M. Macdowell in *CQ* 26 (1976), pp. 88–91. But cf. P. J. Rhodes in *CQ* 58 (1978), pp. 89–91, and in his *Commentary on the Aristotelian Athenaion Politeia* (Oxford, 1981), p. 496; S. C. Humphreys in *JHS* 94 (1974), pp. 88–94; M. H. Hansen, *Demography and Democracy* (Herning, 1986), pp. 73–6; see also W. Erdmann, *Die Ehe im alten Griechenland* (1934; repr. New York, 1979), pp. 369, 375ff. Vernant (n. 7), p. 50.

11 Lacey (n. 1), p. 147.

12 Lacey (n. 1), p. 106; Erdmann (n. 10), p. 185; W. E. Thompson, 'The marriage of first cousins in Athenian society', *Phoenix* 21 (1967), pp. 273–82.

13 Or this may have been the theme of the *Temenidai*: see Annette Harder, 'Euripides' *Temenos* and *Temenidai*', forthcoming in the proceedings of 'Fragmenta Dramatica Symposium in honour of Professor Dr. Stefan L. Radt' (held at Groningen in September 1987).

14 In the *Erechtheus*, Xouthos may have appeared as an adopted son of Erechtheus, who dies in battle: T. B. L. Webster, *The Tragedies of Euripides* (London, 1967), pp. 128–9; H. van Looy in *Hommages à M. Delcourt* (Coll. Latomus 114, Brussels, 1970), p. 112. Cf. also Pacuvius *Hermione* (esp. frr.184–6 Warmington); Hygin. *Fab.* 100 (from Soph. *Mysoi*?).

15 Vernant (n. 7), p. 57.

16 Lacey (n. 1), pp. 67–8; Erdmann (n. 10), pp. 168f.

17 So too Hdt. 5.66; see Robert Parker in *Interpretations of Greek Mythology*, ed. Jan Bremmer (London, 1987), pp. 206–7. For autochthony in the play, see Arlene W. Saxonhouse, in *Greek Tragedy and Political Theory*, ed J. Peter Euben (California, 1986) pp. 252–73.

18 See Parker (n. 17), p. 207.

19 *Il.* 2.514–15, 6.198, 16.174ff. See further Erdmann (n. 10), pp. 373ff.

20 Other tragedians: S. *Akrisios, Danae, Tyro*; Astydamas *Tyro*; Carcinus II *Alope*; Aphareus *Auge*.

21 This is not to say that there was no interest in the quality of in-laws in the *polis* (see, for example, Erdmann (n. 10), pp. 147ff.), although marriage does not seem to have been a widespread way of creating political alliances: see S. C. Humphreys, *The Family, Women and Death* (London, 1983), pp. 24–6.

22 Lacey (n. 1), p. 113; one might add perhaps the greater opportunities for adultery provided by urban life.

23 Athenian girl: Lacey (n. 1), p. 115. Comparative anthropology: Y. A. Cohen in *American Anthropologist* 71 (1969), pp. 658–87, who argues *inter alia* that the marital tie when strengthened contributes to the weakening of local and kin groups, but does not constitute a

challenge to state authority. An 'inchoate incorporative state' is the centrally ruling body of a society that has 'been united by groups who are geographically contiguous and who are at approximately the same level of cultural development', but that 'has not yet completely subverted local sources of solidarity, allegiance, and authority'.

24 It has also been attributed to the *Melanippe Desmotis*: see Webster (n. 14), pp. 147–9.

25 *Danae*: cf. Apollod. 2.4.4; *Antiope*: Hygin. *Fab.* 7; *Mel. Soph.*: Ennius fr. CXIX, H. D. Jocelyn, *The Tragedies of Ennius* (Cambridge, 1967) (and Webster (n. 14), p. 149); *Alope*: Hygin. *Fab.* 187.7 (Poseidon appeared at the end, it seems); *Ion* 1571ff.; even Telephos, the son of Auge, was said in one version of the myth (Alcidamas *Odysseus* 14–16) to have returned to his birthplace: Hygin. *Fab.* 100 (from Soph. *Mysoi?*); Anth. Pal. 3.2. See in general Webster (n. 14).

26 On the theme generally see G. Binder, *Die Aussetzung des Königskindes Kyros und Romulus* (Meisenheim am Glan, 1964). For a recent treatment of our theme ('the girl's tragedy') see J. N. Bremmer and N. M. Horsfall, *Roman Myth and Mythography* (*BICS Suppl.* 52, 1987), pp. 27–30.

27 See esp. Hygin. *Fab.* 7 and 8; Apollod. *Bibl.* 3.5.5; schol. A.R. 4.1090; Anth. Pal. 3.7; Propert. 3.15.11–42.

28 See J. Kambitsis, *L'Antiope d'Euripide* (Athens, 1972).

29 With the mythical theme of imprisonment one might compare the small and probably dark interior of urban houses, and Klytaimnestra's reference to her daughters (*IA* 738) as 'guarded well in the secure maiden quarters'.

30 Danae was imprisoned, according to E.'s contemporary Pherekydes (3 *FGH* F 10), in a bronze underground chamber (*thalamos*) in the courtyard of the house, according to E. himself in a bronze bridal chamber (*Archelaos* fr. 2 Austin 8), and according to Hygin. (*Fab.* 63) within a stone wall. She is *enclosed* in the chest in Pherekydes, and in E.: Johannes Malalas, p. 34, 19.

31 Strabo 13.1.69 (615).

32 Aesch. frr.382, 448; E. *Ba.* 223, 237, 260, 354, 487, 958; M. Daraki, *Dionysus* (Paris, 1985), pp. 101–3.

33 Webster (n. 14), pp. 205–11; Kambitsis (n. 28).

34 1659 (cf. A. *Ag.* 1446, *Cho.* 906, 894f., and Garvie ad loc.), 1671–5.

35 Hygin. *Fab.* 72; *P. Oxy.* 3317; R. Scodel in *ZPE* 46 (1982), pp. 37–42.

36 Hygin. *Fab.* 72; cf. Hypoth. 'Aristophanis' S. *Ant.*; cf. n. 35.

37 Antiope: Apollod. 3.5.5; Schol. A.R. 4.1090; Hygin. *Fab.* 7; Propert. 3.15.12. Danae: Pi. fr.284, Snell; Apollod. 2.4.1.

38 Frr.20 and 22; cf. D. H. *Rhet.* 9. 11; S. Jäkel in *Grazer Beiträge* 8 (1979), pp. 101–18. On this theme in Aeschylus' *Suppliants* see Seaford in *JHS* 107 (1987), pp. 117–18; for the phenomenon generally see, for example, Henry Rosenfeld in *International*

Archives of Ethnography 48 (1957), pp. 23–62; cf. F. Barth in *South Western Journal of Anthropology* 10 (1954), pp. 164–71.

39   Webster (n. 14), p. 159.

40   Though not according to Harder (n. 13).

41   Menander *Adelphoi* A (or *Philadelphoi*), *Epitrepontes*, *Daktylios* (?). Cf. Aeschylus' *Niobe*. For real life see Dem. 41.4.

42   It seems that Akastos wanted her to remarry: see H. Oranje in *ZPE* 37 (1980), pp. 169–72 (on *P. Oxy.* 3214. 10–14). Cf. *Od.* 15.518–22 (Penelope's natal family pressing her to remarry).

43   We do not, of course, know all the details of E.'s play. Other tragedies on this story may have been Soph. *Alkmaion*, and plays called *Alphesiboia* (cf. Pausan. 8.24.8) by Achaios, Chairemon, and Timotheos.

44   Cf. *Alc.* 532–3, 778 with schol., 805, 810–14, 828, 1117; Margaret Visser in *Greek Tragedy and its Legacy*, ed. M. J. Cropp, E. Fantham, and S. E. Scully (Calgary, 1986), p. 161 n. 14.

45   See, for example, R. Lonis, *Guerre et religion en Grèce à l'époque classique* (Paris, 1979), p. 202.

46   Jan Bremmer in *Journal of Indo-European Studies* 4 (1976), pp. 65–78, and in *ZPE* 50 (1983), pp. 173–86; Bremmer and Horsfall (n. 26), pp. 53–6; cf., for example, J. R. Goody, 'The mother's brother and sister's son in West Africa', *Journal of the Royal Anthropological Institute* 89, 1 (1959), pp. 61–88; R. M. Keesing, *Kin Groups and Social Structure* (New York, 1975), pp. 46–7.

47   Apollodorus *Bibl.* 3.13.8, *Epit.* 5.11; Plut. *Thes.* 4; Pausan. 1.22.2; Hdt. 3.50–3.

48   For this play see H. van Looy, *Zes verloren Tragedies van Euripides* (Brussels, 1964); Webster (n. 14), pp. 150ff.

49   Lacey (n. 1), pp. 108f.; cf. n. 41 above.

50   *Leg.* 774c; cf. M. Gluckman, 'Bridewealth and the stability of marriage', *Man* 53 (1953), pp. 141–2 (and E. R. Leach at pp. 179–80); J. R. Goody and S. N. Tambiah, *Bridewealth and Dowry* (Cambridge, 1973).

51   Fr. 151, col. III Austin (*Nova Fragmenta Euripidea*) = *Pap. Hamb.* ed. E. Siegmann (Hamburg, 1954), 119.

52   For Moschion, and the minor tragedians generally, see B. Snell, *Tragicorum Graecorum Fragmenta* (Göttingen, 1971), vol. 1.

53   *Od.* 1.432 (Laertes and Eurykleia), *Il.* 9.451 (the parents of Phoinix); cf. also *Od.* 11.421ff. (Agamemnon and Klytaimnestra).

54   *Il.* 8.283, 14.204ff.

55   Lacey (n. 1), p. 108; Erdmann (n. 10), pp. 403–8; W. E. Thompson in *Californian Studies in Classical Antiquity* 5 (1972), pp. 211–25.

56   Erdmann (n. 10), pp. 404–5.

57   For Ino as Athamas' second wife in this play (in the papyrus hypothesis in *P. Oxy.* 2455) see W. Luppe in *Archiv für Papyrusforschung* 30 (1984), pp. 31–7.

58   Other plays in this category include *Tennes* (probably Euripidean), S. *Euryalos, Tyro, Phineus*, and perhaps also the plays (by various authors) called *Athamas* and *Phrixos*.

59   On the other hand it appears from skeletal remains that women
     tended to die younger than men (see, for example, S. B. Pomeroy,
     Goddesses, Whores, Wives, and Slaves (New York, 1975), p. 68).
60   Lacey (n. 1), p. 108; Thompson (n. 55), pp. 222–3.
61   Thompson (n. 55).
62   This is apparently the theme of a fragment of Ennius' *Kresphontes*
     (LIV Jocelyn (n. 25) – see his discussion). For a full recent
     discussion of *Kresphontes* see Annette Harder, *Euripides' Kresphontes
     and Archelaos* (Leiden, 1985).
63   I am grateful to the editor of this volume, and to Jan Bremmer,
     Helene Foley, and David Harvey, for their improvement of an
     earlier draft of this chapter.

7

THE STATE AND THE INDIVIDUAL: EURIPIDES' PLAYS OF VOLUNTARY SELF-SACRIFICE

John Wilkins

During the period of the Peloponnesian War, Euripides wrote at least six plays of voluntary self-sacrifice, plays portraying a young person who chooses to die for a large group, a city, or an army, of which he or she may or may not be a member. The necessity to die arises from a critical situation, of divine origin. Of these plays, one is almost entirely lost (*Phrixus B*); one exists in some substantial fragments (*Erechtheus*); two are virtually complete (*Hecuba* and *Phoenissae*); one, produced posthumously, has suffered later modification (*Iphigenia at Aulis*); and the sixth (*Heraclidae*) has been suspected of mutilation and refurbishment.[1] None of these plays is among the best-known of Euripides' works now, though two of them were selected for preservation in antiquity (*Hecuba* and *Phoenissae*).

It is the purpose of this study to investigate Euripides' treatment of war, religion, and society in these plays, and in particular to examine the role of the victims, four young women and two young men, within their social context. Discussions of the conflicting demands of the state and the private individual, both ancient and modern, generally refer to men: in these plays it is predominantly a woman who sacrifices herself for the community.

No other author as far as we know wrote self-sacrifice plays of this kind, though there are germs of the self-sacrifice theme in *Seven against Thebes*, *Antigone*, and Euripides' own *Alcestis*. *Protesilaus* and *Supplices* introduce brave deaths of women with strong pathos.

I shall draw together the argument towards the end of this chapter with a study of *Heraclidae*, for two reasons. (i) It is probably the earliest of the plays, and sets the pattern.[2] (ii) It is set in Athens and appears to draw on a complex of Athenian rituals. This is probably important. Critics have often divorced the self-sacrifice scene from the other ritual aspects of the play, wrongly I believe.

HUMAN SACRIFICE

In the plays of voluntary self-sacrifice Euripides is portraying an action both familiar and novel, but above all disturbing. The Greeks expressed strong views on human sacrifice in general: the practice was alien to them and, they thought, to their gods.[3] In a sophisticated passage in *Iphigenia in Tauris*, for example, Iphigenia, priestess in the human-sacrifice cult of Artemis Tauropolos, believes such sacrifice to be the invention of the barbarian mind, falsely attributed to the goddess.[4] On the other hand, there is some evidence that the Greeks did perform human sacrifices. There is no support for the claim of Phylarchus[5] that 'all the Greeks performed a communal human sacrifice before setting out to war'. But there is scattered evidence of human sacrifice from Bronze Age Crete[6] and from the Linear B tablets.[7] There is the doubtful evidence of *pharmakos* rituals scattered over the Greek world;[8] and there are the celebrated cases of Themistocles sacrificing the Persian prisoners before the battle of Salamis[9] and Pelopidas considering human sacrifice before the battle of Leuctra.[10]

Whether or not the Greeks ever did perform human sacrifices before major enterprises such as battles, the possibility of such a sacrifice was familiar from mythical versions, whence it came to tragedy. On stage the most famous human sacrifice was that of Iphigenia, whose ritual death mirrored the ritual slaying of an animal in blood-sacrifice. Other deaths on stage are presented in sacrificial language – Aeschylus' *Agamemnon* and Euripides' *Electra* and *Heracles* provide obvious examples. I do not wish here to rehearse the reasons for presentation of murder as perverted sacrifice, an area in which there have been numerous studies.[11]

In the plays of voluntary self-sacrifice it is important to note that the context and ritual detail are similar to those of the enforced sacrifices in Plutarch's narratives of Themistocles and Pelopidas.[12] Even if, as is likely, the sacrifices mentioned by Plutarch are not historical, they were described to be believed. For Plutarch at least, human sacrifice at a time of crisis in the fifth and fourth centuries BC was credible. Circumstances could arise in which sacrifice in some form might become necessary, almost acceptable.[13]

DYING FOR THE CITY

A form of sacrifice to meet a crisis in the fifth and fourth centuries BC that is well attested is the non-literal self-sacrifice of the hoplite soldier in battle. In the narrative of the Leuctra incident in his *Life of Pelopidas* (ch. 21) Plutarch leads into a non-literal idea of self-sacrifice via examples of literal self-sacrifice in tragedy: Menoeceus (E. *Phoen.*), Macaria[14] (E. *Hcld.*), Pherecydes in Sparta, and Leonidas, the man 'who put himself forward as a sacrifice in a sense for Greece'. A man can give his life for his country without the ritual cutting of the throat over an altar. A stand to the last man is sacrifice 'in a sense'.

I want to put aside for the moment literal sacrifice and consider a man giving his life for his country, a notion familiar in patriotic speeches, and particularly in funeral speeches.[15] In Thucydides 2.43, for example, we find 'in terms of the community they gave their lives but in personal terms they gained ageless praise'; in Lysias 2.25 (of Marathon) 'they were fine men, unsparing of their lives, and when it came to valour willing to give all'.[16] According to the funeral speeches, Athenians were prompted to give their lives because of the example set by their ancestors, the standard examples being, Aristotle tells us,[17] the Heraclidae, and the battles of Marathon and Salamis. These examples, together with the defending of the suppliant women at Thebes and the battle of Erechtheus against Eumolpus, are found in most of the funeral speeches. The thought behind the speeches is exemplified by Demosthenes 60.28, 'they chose to die rather than live a safe life with the system of Theseus destroyed among the Greeks', or Lysias 2.69, 'these men both in life and death are to be envied. They were brought up in the fine deeds of their ancestors, and when they reached manhood they preserved the fame of those ancestors and displayed their own fine qualities'.[18] Some of the speeches may have been influenced by Euripides' plays *Heraclidae*, *Supplices*, and *Erechtheus*; to a greater extent the plays in their own time drew on the ethos of the funeral speeches and took their basic story-line from these patriotic myths.[19]

WOMEN DYING FOR THE CITY

A forensic speech, Lycurgus *Against Leocrates*, picks up Euripides most closely with a long quotation from *Erechtheus* (fr.50A), introduced as follows: Euripides should be praised for his play 'in that he considered their actions would be the finest example to the citizens, and that by looking at them and admiring them they would become used in their souls to loving their fatherland'. The example Lycurgus is referring to is not of the citizen hoplites sacrificing their lives in battle, but of the daughter of Erechtheus who, with her sisters, sacrificed herself for the state.[20] Instead of the soldier sacrificing his life for his ancestors, his old relatives, his wife and children, here a female child is sacrificed. There follows the mother's (Praxithea's) speech from the play, in which we find the following lines: 'we have children for this purpose, to protect the altars of the gods and the fatherland', and 'all of the city is comprised in a single name, and many people dwell in it. How can I bring destruction on them when one can put herself forward to die for all?'[21] Praxithea goes on to argue for the sex of the victim: 'if I had sons I would send them out to fight; my daughter equally can face death and be sacrificed'. The contribution of each sex is clear: sacrifice is required of all children of suitable age (and a corresponding sacrifice from parents): eligible boys must stand in the battle-line; eligible girls may be called upon for human sacrifice to promote victory.

THE CITY AND THE INDIVIDUAL

Here we are given an extreme version of the sacrifice of the individual for the community, of the conflict in general between private and communal interests which is a feature of the Peloponnesian War years. Thucydides 2.60.2–3 expresses this well:

> I consider the city is more use to the individual citizens if the whole is on a sound footing than if the city is fine for

individuals but as a whole is stumbling. For the man who is getting along fine in private comes to grief no less if the city is destroyed, whereas if the city's fortunes are good he has a better chance of escaping any misfortune.

Jacqueline de Romilly[22] has collected numerous passages from Thucydides and Aristophanes, and has compared them with Euripides' plays. The tension between κοινός (communal) and ἴδιος (private), she finds, becomes ever more prominent in the plays, culminating in *Phoenissae* and *Iphigenia at Aulis*. She is right, on a formal basis, in terms of quantity, but similar expressions are found in *Heraclidae* (e.g. 223), *Hecuba* (860), and *Erechtheus* (fr.50A). And the whole notion of voluntary self-sacrifice in these earlier plays works on a similar tension. The city must come before the individuals in it; but the individuals have their lives at stake, a concern not only for the individuals but also for their dependent families and kinsmen.[23]

HUMAN SACRIFICE FOR THE STATE

When the sacrifice is transferred from the soldiers in the army to the literal but equally voluntary sacrifice of the individual – where the individual is usually a young woman – are we to view this as in any way a perverted sacrifice, an act of barbarity, or as a city-saving patriotic act? Many critics have looked at the sacrifices of women in Euripides in adverse terms, exemplified by T. B. L. Webster who writes, 'Praxithea's speech is to the modern ear unforgivable.'[24] But comparison between Lycurgus' introduction to Praxithea's speech and the quotations from funeral speeches above suggests that the sacrifice of a young woman and the sacrifice of the soldier in battle could be seen in a similar, positive, light. Before addressing this question I consider Euripides' six plays in some detail, or at least the five we may reasonably consider (*Hcld., Hec., Erechth., Phoen., IA*).

Some preliminary points:

1   Those plays with an Athenian setting share with funeral speeches stress on εὐγένεια (courage worthy of ancestors), ἐλευθερία (individual and state liberty), and other claims to distinction such as autochthony (where applicable).[25]

2   The self-sacrifice elements vary in length from a single scene

(in *Hcld.* and *Phoen.*) to virtually a whole play (*IA*). In the case of the single scenes, no preparation or warning is allowed the audience in the prologue, as might be expected: the emotive scene comes, then, as a surprise.

3 Some plays are conversions of famous myths, from enforced sacrifice to voluntary sacrifice (Iphigenia, Phrixus, Polyxena); others are much less familiar in myth, and may have been invented for the occasion (Macaria and Menoeceus).

4 With a certain amount of variation, Euripides adheres to a ritual and rhetorical pattern in all five cases. The plays illustrate his use of set scenes with a series of common elements. Compare suppliant scenes, where in each case an extra dimension is added: in *Heracles* the suppliants give in; in *Andromache* mother and child are separated; in *Heraclidae* the suppliants must make a contribution themselves. Composition in such units by no means implies a uniformity of meaning or significance from case to case.

I will now survey the ritual and rhetorical elements of voluntary self-sacrifice, for the present without moral evaluation.[26]

RITUAL

1 There is a crisis. *Heraclidae*: battle against the Argives; *Hecuba*: a wind is needed; *Erechtheus*: battle against Eumolpus; *Phoenissae*: safety of Thebes at stake; *Iphigenia at Aulis*: a wind is needed; *Phrixus*: plague and famine.

2 An oracle or seer passes on a demand from a god or hero for a human victim (in *Hec.* there is the ghost of Achilles; about *Erechth.* we cannot be certain).

3 A perfect victim is needed (i.e. εὐγενής, of high status). In *Heraclidae*, the victim is not specified; elsewhere a particular victim is named (*Erechth.* is uncertain on this point). The victim must be like an unblemished animal. There are reminders of the analogous animal sacrifice at *Heraclidae* 490 οὐ ταῦρον οὐδὲ μόσχον ('not a bull or a calf'), *Hecuba* 206 ὥστε μόσχον ('like a calf'), *Phoenissae* 947 πῶλος ('colt'), *Iphigenia at Aulis* 1083 μόσχον ἀκήρατον ('a calf undefiled').[27]
As part of his or her perfection the victim must not be married: *Heraclidae* 408 παρθένον ('virgin'), and *Phoenissae* 947f.

4 In the case of a famous story, a god or hero demands the

sacrifice (Artemis in *IA*, Achilles in *Hec.*). Otherwise the demand comes vaguely from a god who might be important if more were said, or may be equivalent to Death (Kore in *Hcld.* and *Erechth.*, Ares in *Phoen.*).

5　The victim must consent (see below for the rhetoric of the volunteer, equivalent perhaps to the sprinkling of water on the animal's head to gain a nod of agreement). The slayer is then freed from guilt (cf. *Hcld.* 558f.).

6　Garlanding of the victim: *Heraclidae* 529, *Iphigenia at Aulis* 1477.

7　Other preliminary rites (κατάρχεσθαι): *Heraclidae* 529, *Iphigenia at Aulis* 1470f., *Hecuba* 535f.

8　The sacrificing priest is Achilles' son in *Hecuba*, Agamemnon in *Iphigenia at Aulis*. Who sacrifices in *Heraclidae* and *Erechtheus*?

9　The sacrifice is a σφαγή ('cutting of the throat') (though sometimes a θυσία ('offering'), in *Erechtheus*, and in *Iphigenia at Aulis* where Artemis is the receiving goddess).[28]

RHETORICAL ELEMENTS[29]

	Hcld.	Hec.	Erechth.	Phoen.	IA
Not want to die	—	commos	?	—	1211f.
Parent/guardian not want X to die	539f.	417f.	Erechtheus	962	1146f.
Parent/guardian volunteers instead	453f.	385f.	—	962	—
Victim volunteers[30]	500f.	342f.	?	991f.	1368f.
Death equivalent to battle	503f.	—	fr.50	999f.	—
Rejects φιλοψυχία ('love of life')[31]	518, 533	348	—	—	1385
One for many	580–1	—	fr.50	—	1386f.
Life not worth living	515	349f.	—	1003f.	—
(Women worth less)	—	—	—	—	1394
All I am losing (marriage etc.)	579f. 591f.	418f.	—	—	1399
Remember[32]	588	—	fr.65.65f.	—	1398

The principal rhetorical force of the scene is the great desire of the victim to die, against the wishes of the *philoi*, relatives or friends.[33]

After these scenes of affecting pathos and patriotism a death scene may or may not be reported. Later reference may be made in various formal parts of the play.[34] In *Hecuba* Polyxena dies bravely and decorously, and is ritually honoured with flowers thrown upon her body – elements confined to the messenger speech. However they died, the Erechtheids in *Erechtheus* are honoured in a speech *ex machina* by Athena. Menoeceus' death in *Phoenissae* is briefly reported, and he is honoured by the chorus. The daughter of Heracles in *Heraclidae* is honoured by the chorus, having taken precautions for a decorous death in the self-sacrifice scene.

The moral excellence shown by these victims may be referred to in any of these forms: the daughter of Heracles has εὐγένεια ('noble birth') in the choral ode at 626; Polyxena is εὐκάρδιος ('stout-hearted') in the messenger speech at *Hecuba* 579; Menoeceus is a credit to his family in the choral ode at *Phoenissae* 1060–1; the γενναιότης ('nobility') of the Erechtheids is mentioned in the *ex machina* speech at *Erechtheus* fr.65.69.

In their various elements, then, these scenes show us the individuals giving their lives for the community (or at least putting the community first), the city, or the army, as enjoined by Pericles at Thucydides 2.60. The individual is universally admired, though the community may not be (see below, p. 189). But why must the victim be nubile and why must she or he go through the full ritual of self-sacrifice?[35] If Athenians in the fifth century all agreed that human sacrifice was not practised by them, that it was a foreign practice, and that they only had mythical memories of sacrifice, voluntary or involuntary, why did Euripides have frequent recourse to this subject? The answer in the first instance is that tragedy in general is created around areas of moral complexity: treatment of such complexities does not necessarily imply adverse criticism of society. The introduction of choice for the victim is difficult to assess for dramatic effect.[36] Does that make the sacrifice any more palatable than the enforced sacrifice of Iphigenia in *Agamemnon*, for example? There is also the excitement in wondering whether the gods will intervene in the crisis and provide an alternative resolution. In fact this occurs in only two of our six plays, in *Phrixus* and *Iphigenia at Aulis*.

HERACLIDAE

For more concrete considerations we must now examine Euripides' earliest play of voluntary self-sacrifice, *Heraclidae*. I shall consider three aspects, the scene of voluntary self-sacrifice, the balancing of that scene against the later scenes with Alcmene, and a political interpretation of the play. The third part will consider the relevance of the pre-battle human sacrifice to an *Athenian* setting and will suggest that in this first presentation of a voluntary self-sacrifice at least the sacrifice is not to be interpreted in adverse terms.

At the beginning of the play the Heraclidae are suppliants, quickly accepted by Athens, to be defended against the Argives. The Argives consider the Heraclidae slaves (δραπέτας (140), runaway slaves), the property of Eurystheus (68, 267), and wish them to be returned for stoning (60, 141–2). The Heraclidae have saved their lives but lost their city (14–15) – conduct, we might note, that is the reverse of that enjoined in funeral speeches.[37] They are helpless, stateless, the object of pursuit and claims of ownership.[38] Once successful as suppliants, however, and under the protection of a temporarily adoptive city which will defend them with war, they are confronted with another demand, this time for the sacrifice of a virgin if Athens' victory over the Argives is to be assured.[39] Such is the extra dimension of the suppliant scene in this play (see above, p. 182). Euripides has an anonymous daughter of Heracles meet this obscure requirement from a virtually anonymous goddess in almost spontaneous acceptance of sacrifice. She displays nearly all the rhetorical features set out above (except for the initial reluctance to die, a significant omission); she is accorded high praise;[40] but she has no messenger speech for further display of her greatness. Perhaps this is in line with her sudden and anonymous appearance on stage.[41]

The daughter of Heracles dies, then, with appeals to her father's reputation (to be compared with appeals to the ancestors of the Athenians and their reputation in funeral speeches); she dies πρό τ' ἀδελφῶν καὶ γᾶς (622) 'for her siblings and her country' (by which we must understand Athens). She in effect reverses the conduct of the Heraclidae when they fled from Argos, saving their lives but not their city (14). This time she has saved a city, the foreign city of Athens. All this takes place in the wider context of choral odes loudly praising Athens (348ff., 748ff., 892ff.).

The anonymous girl can hardly be said to have been given detailed characterization in her brief scene, even within the limitations of tragic characterization. She is heard no more. But her action has a great impact and the scene has great rhetorical character, and sets a strong contrast with the following scenes. In contrast with the daughter of Heracles, Alcmene, the mother of Heracles, sacrifices nothing. Rather she pursues her own revenge, contrary to the wishes of the Athenians, against Eurystheus. The king, once a persecutor, is now transformed into a prisoner, into a victim. The play, resolutely Athens-centred, transfers sympathy from Alcmene to Eurystheus in personal terms; in social terms his status is lost, as was that of the Heraclidae in the first part of the play. In religious terms he is, he announces, to become a hero at death, a protection for Athens against the return of the Heraclidae as Spartans. Like the daughter of Heracles, he is ritually devoted, by oracular decree, to Athens.

The rhetorical contrast between the two women, the daughter of Heracles and the mother of Heracles, is stark. There is a strong division in the play between lines 1–629 and 630 to the end. The play in effect starts again at 646.[42] The daughter is a standard-bearer for those Heraclidae who recognize their role and obligations, that is, the Heraclidae who stay in Athens;[43] the mother represents those Heraclidae who will be the ancestors of the Spartans, the future aggressors against Athens.[44] This contrast sets the pattern for the following self-sacrifice plays, where political orientation no longer applies. In *Hecuba* the play also divides in the middle, offering the contrast between Hecuba the sorrowing mother and Hecuba the woman of vengeance. In *Phoenissae*, as Foley has set out,[45] Menoeceus' patriotic death contrasts with the conduct of his cousins, Eteocles and Polynices, which threatens the city. And in *Iphigenia at Aulis* Iphigenia's sacrifice offsets the indecisive and perhaps unsavoury world of the army at Aulis.

SELF-SACRIFICE IN ATHENIAN MYTH AND RITUAL

I return to *Heraclidae* in order to give at least one reason why literal self-sacrifice is portrayed in these plays rather than non-literal sacrifice of the self in the city's interests. This reason is political in a wide sense. The play is intensely Athenian, or rather Attic, for it is set in Marathon with an Athenian chorus. The daughter of Heracles, later called Macaria, is modelled upon a number of young Athenian women who died for the city and became 'saviours' of the city and protectors of the young men and women in the city. In other words, Praxithea's statement about young women dying for the state in *Erechtheus* fr. 50 is not unusual or bizarre.

Other virgins sacrificed themselves in Athens: Aglauros and the daughters of Cecrops in one version of their myth died for Athens;[46] the daughters of Erechtheus sacrificed themselves for Athens, identified with the daughters of Hyacinthos in Euripides' *Erechtheus*;[47] the daughters of Leos died to avert plague.[48] Aglauros and the others are almost certainly courotrophic figures, protectors of the youth of the city, 'female saviours' of Athens.[49] In mythical and ritual terms they, as courotrophic figures, are sometimes nurses of the gods,[50] sometimes with rites for children, both boys and girls.[51] In the fourth century, Aglauros and the Hyacinthides were overseers of the ephebes, young men preparing to train for military service, as they left the city: the ephebes took their oath in the sanctuary of Aglauros, and set out from the temenos of the Hyacinthides.[52] It seems to me likely that the daughter of Heracles in *Heraclidae* is based on these courotrophic goddesses.[53] There is no cult of Macaria parthenos in Attica, nor of the hero Eurystheus; nor does Euripides mention any cult in the play.[54] But the pattern of thought is clear: the daughter of Heracles offers herself for sacrifice in a pattern akin to the self-sacrifices of the city's guardian goddesses. She dies 'for her siblings and the country'.[55] The ritual in the play is not gratuitous, nor is it limited to literary considerations. On the contrary, it locks into a familiar religious pattern.

HERACLES AND THE EPHEBES

The daughter of Heracles is not the only protector of youth in the play. The play is set at Marathon because of Heracles' presence there. In addition to being the site of an important temple and precinct, and the Heracles games, it was at Marathon that Heracles was said to have first been recognized as a god.[56]

In the version adopted in the play, Heracles confirms his divinity by miraculously intervening with his new wife, Hebe or the personification of Youth,[57] with whom in Athenian cult he protects the young and the armies of Athens.[58] He is a further example of Athens' assimilation of foreigners into her religious life, in this case widely recognized in cult, unlike his daughter and Eurystheus who are saviours of Athens only within the play. In the play Theseus and Heracles are held up as parents whose virtues are to be emulated by their children, Demophon, the nameless daughter of Heracles, and the other Heraclidae. In Athens, Theseus and Heracles are both divine protectors of the ephebes.[59] The play then focuses on the young, on their obligations and on the paradigms they should look to, namely Theseus and Heracles. The rejuvenation of Iolaos at the temenos of Athena Pallenis by Heracles and Hebe is a miraculous reinforcement of these cults of patriotic youth. The young, sustained by, and sustaining, the city's gods are at the heart of the play.

The play after all is called the *children* of Heracles; it is the child of Theseus who protects them; Athena as protectress of the city, and a courotrophic figure herself, is addressed in the ode at 748–88;[60] Heracles, the consort of Youth and protector of young soldiers, is affirmed as a god at 910ff. (Note that Heracles' divinity is expressed in terms of his *marriage* to Youth, the state which was denied his nubile daughter.) Ritual and divine elements sustaining the youth of Athens thus extend far beyond the self-sacrifice scene. In its ethos, therefore, and in its ritual background, *Heraclidae* is a strong patriotic play, a play about the young person, with the young woman in the foreground rather than the young man, a play about the sacrifices given and demanded.[61]

THE PLAYS OF VOLUNTARY SELF-SACRIFICE

This is the form in which the feature of voluntary self-sacrifice was first used by Euripides. In dramatic and literary terms some critics have interpreted the play ironically: Demophon is seen by Nancy and Vellacott[62] as a cowardly or ironic figure, unable himself to deal with the mysterious demand for self-sacrifice, unwilling to offer an Athenian virgin for sacrifice.[63] And the oracular decree itself, in its vagueness, is presented as of doubtful authenticity by the poet.[64] I would interpret Demophon rather differently. He is given the quasi-parental role, showing horror at the proposed sacrifice,[65] and refuses to sacrifice an Athenian, not least because the play is about a reciprocal process. Athens gives strong support to justice and the protection of foreigners; and receives in return strong ritual support from those grateful foreigners. Like Oedipus at Colonus, Eurystheus becomes an Attic rather than an Argive or Theban hero, and the daughter of Heracles dies as a protection for Athenian youth.

While I would interpret *Heraclidae*, the prototype, in this way, I do not resist 'ironic' interpretations of other plays, such as those of *Phoenissae* and *Iphigenia at Aulis* by Vellacott and Foley. In those plays there clearly is an antithesis between the selfless action of the victim and the corrupt world which in Foley's terms 'threatens the myth'. Euripides' adaptations of his self-sacrifice theme in his later plays are fascinating and many-layered. In *Heraclidae* itself there is, to be sure, the adverse force of Alcmene and the Spartans. Do these prevail in the end, ironically? If we accept the final lines of the play as they stand,[66] perhaps Athens does appear to acquiesce in a barbarous act. But such an interpretation demands a radical reversal in the presentation of Athens, more abrupt and curtly treated than anywhere else in Euripides. I do not believe Athens is undermined in *Heraclidae* or in *Erechtheus* (as far as we can tell about that play). Where we do find a different treatment of the self-sacrifice theme is in plays with other locations, Thebes in *Phoenissae*, Aulis in *Iphigenia at Aulis* (with Argive kings), and Thrace in *Hecuba* (with Argive kings). In these plays, with the sacrifice far removed from Athens and her cults, the context makes for a very different presentation, as Helene Foley and others have shown. In *Iphigenia at Aulis*, Iphigenia's marriage is simply a screen for Agamemnon's true ritual intentions: contrast *Heraclidae*, where the daughter of Heracles denies herself marriage but divine marriage is accorded to Heracles himself. In *Phoenissae*, Menoeceus gives his life for the state, but it is a state whose gods and myths are undermined by her present rulers: contrast *Heraclidae*, where the sacrifice of Heracles' daughter complements the city's nurture of young people in ritual.

Why does Iphigenia die? To resolve the problems of an indecisive father? For his vainglory? Why does the daughter of Heracles die? In Athens the young men, on reaching manhood (ἄνδρες ἀγαθοί γενόμενοι, 'proving themselves like men', in the language of the messenger speeches),[67] face death on the battle-field; a young woman, nearing marriage, faces death as part of the same crisis.

In those three later plays, the appeals to the liberty of Greece in *Iphigenia at Aulis* or the city of Thebes in *Phoenissae* are disturbing in their context. In the case of Iphigenia, her volun-teering to die with all the rhetoric of the self-sacrifice scene makes for a very different scenario from the sacrifice in Aeschylus' *Agamemnon*; however, the sacrifice remains disturb-ing. But even in that play is the amazing transformation of the sacrifice of Iphigenia, from the brutality of *Agamemnon* to the voluntary act of a virgin who speaks of defending the glories of Greece, of no account?

However we interpret the plays, and however resistant critics may be to direct correlation with city rituals, the plays are 'political' in the sense that they show sacrifices being made for divine support before battles or equivalent critical moments, just as all Athenian armies made (animal) sacrifices before battle. A political commentary is being made, and interpretation will depend on what we mean by 'a just battle', 'a sacrifice for the state', 'the common good', and so on. Euripides' inventiveness, and his rhetorical variation upon a theme, make it inevitable that our interpretation will be similarly inventive and varied. I stress ritual aspects in part because 'ironic' interpretations are some-what subjective, and because the self-sacrifice scenes are closely linked with other rituals and customs at the heart of the Greek city. In *Hecuba*, Polyxena's fate is linked to the fall of Troy and proper burial for Polydorus the outraged ξένος ('guest-friend'). *Erechtheus*, like *Heraclidae*, concerns self-sacrifice and a hero; *Phoenissae* (as Foley shows) links self-sacrifice with the foundation myths of Thebes; *Iphigenia at Aulis* links sacrifice and marriage. These plays are pre-eminently 'social' and 'political'.

NOTES

1 Wilamowitz put the case most powerfully in his 'Exkurse zu Euripides Herakliden', *Hermes* 17 (1882), pp. 337–64 = *Kl. Schr.* 1.82–109. *Hcld.* is much censured in the fine analysis of the rhetoric of the self-sacrifice plays by Joanna Schmitt, *Freiwilliger Opfertod bei Euripides* (Giessen, 1921).

2 Probable dates for these plays are: *Hcld.* 430?, *Hec.* 424?, *Erechth.* 422–420, *Phoen.* 411–409, *IA* 407–6, *Phrixus?*

3 οὐδενὶ τῶν κρειττόνων καὶ ὑπὲρ ἡμᾶς ἀρεστὴν οὖσαν οὕτω βάρβαρον καὶ παράνομον θυσίαν [Plut. *Pelop.* 21]; ἡμῖν...οὐ νόμος ἐστιν ἀνθρώπους θύειν, ἀλλ᾽ ἀνόσιον. Καρχηδόνιοι δὲ θύουσιν ὡς ὅσιον καὶ νόμιμον αὐτοῖς [Plato *Minos* 315].

4 *IT* 380–91, and esp. 386–91: ἐγὼ μὲν οὖν / τὰ Ταντάλου θεοῖσιν ἐστιάματα / ἄπιστα κρίνω, παιδὸς ἡσθῆναι βορᾶι, / τοὺς δ᾽ ἐνθάδ᾽, αὐτοὺς ὄντας ἀνθρωποκτόνους, / ἐς τὴν θεὸν τὸ φαῦλον ἀναφέρειν δοκῶ· / οὐδένα γὰρ οἶμαι δαιμόνων εἶναι κακόν.

5 ap. Porphyry *de abstinentia* II 56.

6 Collected in E. A. M. E. O'Connor–Visser, *Aspects of Human Sacrifice in the Tragedies of Euripides* (Amsterdam, 1987), pp. 212–14. Add P. Warren, *Archaeological Reports* (1980–1), pp. 89–92.

7 See O'Connor–Visser (n. 6), pp. 214–16.

8 See O'Connor–Visser (n. 6), pp. 216–22.

9 Plut. *Them.* 13.

10 Plut. *Pelop.* 20–2.

11 See, for example, W. Burkert, 'Greek tragedy and sacrificial ritual' *GRBS* 7 (1966), pp. 87–121; J.–P. Guepin, *The Tragic Paradox* (Amsterdam, 1968).

12 On the ritual authenticity of the Themistocles incident, see A. Heinrichs, *Le Sacrifice dans l'Antiquité*, Fondation Hardt, Entretiens 27 (Geneva, 1981), pp. 195–235. Heinrichs believes the incident to be fictional, but for our purposes the details are instructive. A seer conveys a sudden demand (cf. *Hcld.* 403f.) while the usual pre-battle sacrifices are being conducted (cf. *Hcld.* 399f.); the victims are pre–eminent; the general is horrified; *soteria* is certain if the human sacrifice is made. The Pelopidas case is perhaps based on Euripides' pattern of voluntary self-sacrifice, for the filly, which at the vital moment replaces a human victim, comes forward boldly and spontaneously.

13 See E. *El.* 1023f.: Clytemnestra says, à propos of Iphigenia (and sincerity is irrelevant for our purposes) λευκὴν διήμησ᾽ Ἰφιγόνης παρηίδα. / κεἰ μὲν πόλεως ἅλωσιν ἐξιώμενος / ἢ δῶμ᾽ ὀνήσων τἄλλα τ᾽ ἐκσώιζων τέκνα, / ἔκτεινε πολλῶν μίαν ὕπερ, συγγνώστ᾽ ἂν ἦν.

14 The daughter of Heracles is not named in the text of *Hcld.* She acquired the name Macaria not later than the date of the hypothesis. In this chapter I refer to her simply as the daughter of Heracles.

15 For a stimulating investigation of the Athenian funeral speech, see N. Loraux, *The Invention of Athens* (Cambridge, Mass., 1986), English version of *L'Invention d'Athènes* (Paris, 1981).

16 See also Dem. 60.28, Loraux (n. 15), pp. 105 n. 167.

17 *Rhetoric* 1396a. Ross's change of τὰ ὑπὲρ τῶν Ἡρακλειδῶν πραχθέντα to τ. ὑπὸ τ. Η. π. in the Oxford text seems to me arbitrary and undesirable.

18 See also Plat. *Menex.* 246, Dem. 60.27–8, Loraux (n. 15), pp. 101f.

JOHN WILKINS

19 For the relation between the genres see the discussion in Loraux
   (n. 15), pp. 64–9.
20 See also Dem. 60.27.
21 For the one (woman) dying for many, cf. *IA* 1384–90, *El.* 1026.
22 Jacqueline de Romilly, in *Revue de Philologie*, 39 (1965), pp. 28f.
23 See Loraux (n. 15), pp. 104f.
24 T. B. L. Webster, *The Tragedies of Euripides* (London, 1967), p. 130.
25 For εὐγένεια see, for example, *Hcld.* 409, 513. Critics have
   generally dwelt on the secondary aspect, moral nobility. For the
   importance of ancestors see my 'The young of Athens: religion
   and society in the *Heraclidae* of Euripides' (forthcoming). For
   ἐλευθερία, see, for example, *Hcld.* 62, 287, for Ἀθηναῖοι
   αὐτόχθονες *Erechth.* fr. 50.7–13A. For the funeral speeches see
   Loraux (n. 15), Index s.vv.
26 Excessive moral evaluation has spoilt many good studies, e.g.
   G. Zuntz, *The Political Plays of Euripides* (Manchester, 1955 and
   1963).
27 Cf. H. S. Versnel, 'Self-sacrifice, compensation, anonymous gods',
   in *Le Sacrifice dans l'Antiquité* (n. 12), p. 154 for horses.
28 For σφαγαί and θυσίαι see O'Connor–Visser (n. 6), pp.
   190–5.
29 See further Schmitt (n. 1).
30 The use of the imperative is significant. A hitherto silent person
   (particularly the daughter of Heracles and Iphigenia) takes the
   initiative in a crisis that adults are unable to resolve. The victims
   are of an age when they may take initiatives: they are not children
   (for whom in tragedy others speak) though they are not fully adult
   (women unmarried, men not in the fighting line).
31 φιλοψυχεῖν and cognates first appear in Tyrtaeus. Thereafter
   nearly all occurrences are in Euripides' self-sacrifice plays and in
   funeral speeches. For the shared vocabulary cf. n. 25.
32 Just as the funeral speech is in memory of the dead, so do the
   victims of sacrifice wish to be remembered. Cf. Loraux (n. 15), pp.
   104f.
33 On the wish to die in funeral speeches, and the *philoi*, see Loraux
   (n. 15), pp. 98f., 45f.
34 In this matter we should not, as did Wilamowitz, take *Hec.* as the
   model.
35 On the cultural tensions aroused when war replaces normal sexual
   organization, see W. Burkert, *Homo Necans* (Berkeley, Calif., 1983),
   pp. 63–4.
36 See p. 190.
37 Contrast the ethos of the funeral speeches, Loraux (n. 15),
   pp. 98f.
38 The position of the suppliants is similar to that of, for example, the
   Danaids in A. *Supp.* and is not peculiar to this play.
39 For the sudden demand by Kore, who is virtually equivalent to
   Death, see H. S. Versnel (n. 27), pp. 135–94. Versnel shows that
   this demand fits perfectly the Greek notion that the gods or fate

192

simply require a life. There appears to be nothing irreligious or deviant in Euripides' treatment of the goddess here.

40 Her motivation, avoidance of τὸ αἰσχρόν ('shame'), is similar to the motivation of Athens in accepting the Heraclidae as suppliants. Her choosing to die places her close to the dead of the funeral speeches who are said to have faced death in their desire for a good name. For the funeral speeches, see Loraux (n. 15); for the daughter of Heracles see *Hcld.* 507, 510, 516, 533, 597, 598, 621, 623.

41 Contrast *Hec.* where Polyxena is mentioned in the prologue, sings in a commos, and is given a long narrative in the messenger speech.

42 Alcmene re-enacts in her imagination the opening scene of the Argive herald attacking the suppliants.

43 Cults of the Heraclidae in Attica: at Aixone (*IG* II² 1199), Erchia (*SEG* XXI 541 B 42), Porto-Rafti (*IG* II² 4977), Thoricos? (R. Parker, 'The Herakleidai at Thorikos', *ZPE* 57 (1984), p. 59). At the Pyanopsia? (Plut. *Thes.* 22–3).

44 For a different interpretation of the role of the Heraclidae, in terms of tribe, see A. P. Burnett, 'Tribe and city, custom and decree in 'Children of Heracles'', *CP* 71 (1976), pp. 4–26.

45 Helene Foley, *Ritual Irony* (Ithaca, NY, 1985), pp. 106–46.

46 Philochorus *FGH* 328 F 105. See also W. Burkert, 'Kekropidensage und Arrhephoria', *Hermes* 94 (1966), pp. 1–25.

47 E. *Erechth.* fr. 65.73f.A.

48 Paus. 1.5.2, Diod. Sic. 17.15.2, Eitrem in *RE* 12.2 (1925), 2058–9.

49 See E. Kearns, *The Heroes of Athens* (forthcoming), ch. 3.

50 See Kearns (n. 49).

51 See Kearns (n. 49).

52 Philochorus (n. 46), with Jacoby's note, Plut. *Alcib.* 15.4, E. *Erechth.* 65.73f.A.

53 I have argued the case in more detail in the article cited in n. 25.

54 There is a possibility that an *aition* of some kind has been lost at the end of the play, in the lacuna of uncertain length after line 1052.

55 *Hcld.* 622.

56 For Heracles at Marathon see Paus. 1.15; S. Woodford, 'Cults of Heracles in Attica', *Studies Presented to G. M. A. Hanfmann* (Harvard, Mass., 1971), pp. 211–25.

57 *Hcld.* 851f.

58 My article cited in n. 25.

59 My article cited in n. 25.

60 For Athena *meter* (771–2) see N. Loraux, *Les Enfants d'Athèna* (Paris, 1981), pp. 59–60; my article cited in n. 25.

61 It is interesting that there are no *aitia* at the end of the play (though see n. 54). In view of her anonymity perhaps the daughter of Heracles could not be subject of such an *aition*. Eurystheus gives a kind of negative *aition*: no libations must be made at his grave (1040–41). But it is perhaps strange to have no formal mention of Heracles' presence at Marathon or in Attica. If the play is indeed as

Euripides wrote it, then we could say that the ideology of the civic voluntary sacrifice was of paramount importance and that that ideology had perhaps been sufficiently enforced by the action of the play. (We may note in contrast that *Erechtheus* with similar Attic orientation furnishes *aitia* for the Hyacinthides, the Erechtheum, and Praxithea as priestess of Athena.)

62 C. Nancy, φάρμακον σωτηρίας in *Théâtre et spectacle dans l'Antiquité* (Strasbourg, 1983); P. Vellacott, *Ironic Drama* (Cambridge, 1975), pp. 178f.

63 At *Hcld.* 411–13 he refuses to sacrifice his own, or Athenian, children.

64 See n. 39.

65 Compare Creon at *Phoen.* 963f.

66 I consider the lacuna proposed by Hermann after 1052 certain.

67 On the ἄνδρες ἀγαϑοί of the funeral speeches, see Loraux (n. 15), pp. 99f.

INDEX

Greek names have been hellenized wherever possible; thus, Akhilleus, Alkinoos, Lykourgos, but Ajax, Andromeda.